Bring Up BOYS Who Like Themselves

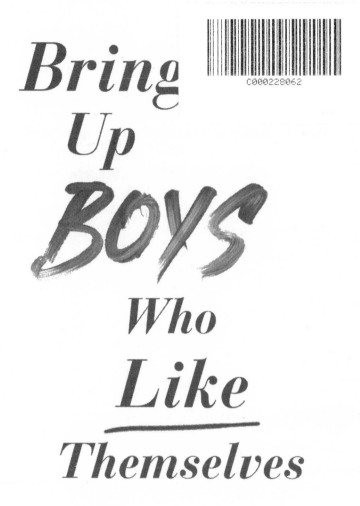

Kasey Edwards is a researcher, columnist and bestselling author of nine books, including *Thirty Something and Over It*.

Christopher Scanlon is a researcher, writer, and academic at Deakin University.

Kasey and Christopher are the authors of *Raising Girls Who Like Themselves*. They live in Melbourne with their two daughters.

Also by Kasey Edwards and Christopher Scanlon

Raising Girls Who Like Themselves

Bringing Up *BOYS* Who <u>Like</u> Themselves

KASEY EDWARDS

DR CHRISTOPHER SCANLON

PENGUIN LIFE

UK | USA | Canada | Ireland | Australia
India | New Zealand | South Africa | China

Penguin Life is part of the Penguin Random House group of companies
whose addresses can be found at global.penguinrandomhouse.com

Penguin
Random House
Australia

First published by Penguin Life in 2023

Cover design and illustration by Louisa Maggio
Typeset in 12/16 pt ITC Berkeley Oldstyle by Midland Typesetters, Australia

Printed and bound in Australia by Griffin Press, an accredited
ISO AS/NZS 14001 Environmental Management Systems printer

A catalogue record for this
book is available from the
National Library of Australia

ISBN 978 0 14377 873 8

penguin.com.au

MIX
Paper | Supporting
responsible forestry
FSC® C018684

We at Penguin Random House Australia acknowledge that Aboriginal and Torres
Strait Islander peoples are the Traditional Custodians and the first storytellers
of the lands on which we live and work. We honour Aboriginal and Torres
Strait Islander peoples' continuous connection to Country, waters, skies and
communities. We celebrate Aboriginal and Torres Strait Islander stories, traditions
and living cultures; and we pay our respects to Elders past and present.

We dedicate this book to Kate Hall, who has devoted her life to supporting children to grow into the best version of themselves, and to Meagan Sweeney, our friend, our sounding board and our voice of reason.

Contents

Disclaimer

Families come in all different forms: heterosexual parents, sole parents, same-sex parents, separated and blended families, legal guardians and multi-generational families, all of which are capable of bringing up a boy who likes himself. Throughout this book we have referred to the carers of children as 'parents', 'mothers' and 'fathers' for simplicity, but we believe these roles can be fulfilled by any number of people in a boy's life, regardless of biology, gender or family structure. We have chosen to focus specifically on boys aged toddler to tween; however, our parenting strategies and much of the research we discuss also apply to bringing up non-binary children and girls of all ages. Our parenting framework and strategies are primarily for neurotypical children, but we warmly welcome parents and carers of neurodiverse children to read our book – though we encourage you to seek out resources that are more specific to your child's needs.

This book draws on and expands upon many of the ideas developed in our previous book, *Raising Girls Who Like Themselves*. While boys and girls differ in many ways, and our society expects them to behave differently, there are many, many commonalities between them. Many of the strategies we outline in *Raising Girls Who Like Themselves* work just as effectively for boys. However, we have adapted the language and delivery of these messages and strategies for this book, and have also written brand new sections that are more relevant to boys.

Out of respect for the privacy of the children and parents who have shared their stories with us, some names and identifying details have been changed and some anecdotes have been merged.

There is more than one way to bring up a boy who likes himself. Every child is different, every parent is different and every family is different. We invite you to read, ponder, take what works for you and your family, and discard what doesn't. While our recommendations are backed by evidence and expert opinion, this book is not a substitute for medical advice. If you have serious concerns about your boy's physical or mental health please consider talking to your doctor.

Introduction

We were sitting in a cafe with three friends and excitedly telling them about our book *Raising Girls Who Like Themselves*, when, to our surprise, tears started to well in the eyes of one of our friends. 'My son doesn't like himself,' she said, reaching for a tissue. The second friend sat back in her chair, ran a hand over her face and whispered, 'Mine doesn't either.' All eyes turned to our third friend, also a mother of a boy. She paused for a moment before speaking. 'I don't want to say this out loud,' she said, her voice cracking. 'But if I'm being really honest, I have to say my boy hasn't liked himself for a while.'

We soon noticed our friends weren't the only ones with this concern. The questions started coming in on social media, in our webinars and in emails, and they haven't stopped: 'What can I do so that my boy will like himself too?'

All these people are right to ask this question. Because, as with girls, absolutely everything that we hope and dream of for our boys starts with bringing them up to like themselves. A boy who likes himself will be successful, striving for his goals because he has faith in his ability to achieve them. When he stumbles he will have the inner strength and resources to pick himself up, learn from his mistakes and move on. A boy who likes himself will have the courage to apologise and make amends rather than leaving a trail of resentment and unresolved conflict. He will be respectful and kind because he will not have to denigrate others or exploit their weaknesses to feel okay about himself. He will have the self-belief to stand up to his critics – and his friends – when it's the right thing to do. He will have the strength to face and deal with his own pain rather than trying to repress it or offload it onto someone else. A boy who likes himself will prioritise his physical and mental health because it is natural to care for what you love.

We spent ten years researching how to raise a girl who genuinely likes herself, believes in herself, and will go into the world ready for anything. We didn't deliberately exclude boys from our research and writing; since we are the parents of girls they naturally became our focus. As it turned out, we realised many of the strategies we covered in *Raising Girls* could help anyone – boys, non-binary children and adults. We have heard from many parents who have applied our strategies to their boys and who have seen profound and life-changing improvements in their boys' self-belief and wellbeing. We share some of these stories in the following chapters. We have also heard from many women who have said that our strategies allowed them to re-parent themselves and to understand why they grew up feeling like they were never good enough. And, most importantly, that it wasn't their fault.

But no matter how much we may wish it were otherwise, there are significant differences in how the world treats girls and boys; differences that affect how they experience the world. Research shows that from the moment a baby boy takes his first breath the world will treat him differently to how it treats girls. This will happen even if his parents are aware of gender stereotypes and try to parent neutrally.[1]

For decades people have been debating, campaigning and legislating to dismantle the social and cultural conditions that limit and restrict our girls. And rightly so. But many of our 'social rules' are also restrictive and damaging to boys. Our society still often expects boys and men to be tough, to not cry, to suppress their emotions, to like sport and hate dancing, to assert their dominance and always be in control, and to never show weakness or ask for help. As Rachel Giese writes in *Boys*, 'We believe that girls can and should play sports, that they're capable of excelling at science and math, that they can be both vulnerable and strong, that they may grow up to be soldiers, presidents, teachers, doctors, and engineers . . . [b]ut when it comes to challenging gender stereotypes and their effects on boys, we haven't been nearly as thorough or thoughtful.'[2] There is still a 'right' way to be a boy and man. And, as we'll see in the next section, this 'right' way is suffocating them, stunting their growth, sucking the joy out of their lives and in some cases literally killing them.

Boys' report card

The following report card shows that many of our boys are struggling academically, emotionally and socially. Fortunately, there are answers to these problems, and we have every reason to be optimistic for our boys and their future prospects. But if we want to get to the solutions, we need to know what we're up against.

Mental health

Seventeen per cent of boys aged 4–11 experience a mental health disorder.[3]

Suicide

Suicide is the leading cause of death for Australians aged 15–44. Seventy-five per cent of those who die by suicide are male.[4]

Academic performance

Boys' academic performance is lagging behind that of girls. According to the Australian Curriculum, Assessment and Reporting Authority (ACARA), girls outperform boys in writing and reading in all tested year levels, with the disparity growing as they get older. In 2022, only 79.2 per cent of boys in Year 9 reached the national minimum level of writing, compared to 89.3 per cent of girls, and only 86.5 per cent of boys reached the national minimum standard for reading, compared to 92.9 per cent of girls.[5]

Reading

Fifty-three per cent of boys of reading age do not read for pleasure. That's a decline of 13 per cent since 2000.[6] Non-readers perform worse academically,[7] even in maths.[8] They also have poorer mental health, poorer relationships[9] and less empathy.[10]

University entrance

Boys are 16.3 per cent less likely to obtain a HSC qualification than girls. Their academic performance has fallen so far behind girls' that when it comes to getting into university, being male is now a greater disadvantage than any other recognised disadvantage.[11]

Behaviour

Boys account for 70 per cent of school suspensions,[12] with suspensions and expulsions starting as early as the first year of school, when boys can be as young as 4 years old.[13]

Body image

Eating disorders have traditionally been viewed as a 'girl problem', but it is estimated that males account for 20 per cent of people experiencing anorexia nervosa, and 30 per cent of people experiencing bulimia nervosa.[14] Almost half of those who experience a binge eating disorder are men.[15] Body dysmorphic disorder, which is 'a mental illness characterised by constant worrying over a perceived or slight defect in appearance',[16] also affects men and appears to be on the rise,[17] as boys are increasingly presented with unrealistic and mostly unachievable male bodies as the ideal.

Nine big worries

Going beyond the official statistics and reports, we asked around 15,000 parents to share with us their biggest questions and concerns about raising their boys. There were striking similarities between the responses, so we have distilled the concerns into 'nine big worries'. We have addressed and suggested evidence-based solutions for all nine of these worries in this book.

1. How to get your son to tell you about his day and maintain a close and loving bond as he gets older (p. 195)
2. How to give your boy the skills and confidence to resist peer pressure and unhealthy influences (p. 171)
3. How to teach him the most effective way to stand up for himself without resorting to violence or losing his sweet nature (p. 176)
4. How to encourage your boy to try new and hard things (p. 137)
5. What to do about screens and porn (pp. 112, 190)
6. How to motivate and encourage achievement without the nagging (p. 93)
7. How to teach your boy to be respectful and to take responsibility for his actions without making him feel ashamed (p. 41)
8. How to give your boy the gift of rock-solid confidence and self-belief (pp. 133, 222)
9. How to give him a positive and healthy body image (p. 73).

Girls can do anything and boys are hardwired

If we're going to address these issues so our boys can grow up liking themselves, we need to clear away some of the myths that surround boys and the men they become. One of the big ones is that boys' brains are wired differently to girls' brains from birth and that this difference is fixed for life. For example, a 2013 study reported in *Scientific American* claimed that adolescent boys are 'optimized for motor skills', whereas girls are 'optimized for combining analytical and intuitive thinking'.[18] Filtered through the media, this led to claims that boys and men are better at reading maps than girls and women, whereas women are better at 'remembering a conversation'.[19] One of the study's authors was quoted as saying that women's intuition – their 'thinking without thinking' – tends to make them 'better than men at these kinds of skill which are linked with being good mothers'.[20] The problem with these kinds of claims is that they are, politely, rubbish.

Another study even claimed that boys' and men's brains are hardwired to prefer the colour blue, whereas girls' and women's brains are hardwired to prefer pink. In 2007, visual neuroscientists Anya Hurlbert and Yazhu Ling speculated that boys and men 'are more attuned to the blue end of the [light] spectrum' because, as hunters, they needed to scan the horizon, whereas girls and women prefer pink because they needed to be able to spot ripe fruit and berries.[21]

If this were true, then it should follow that these colour preferences would be more or less uniform through time. But they're not. In 1918, for example, a column published in *Earnshaw's*, a children's fashion publication aimed at retailers, advised readers that 'the generally accepted rule is pink for the boy and blue for the girl'.[22] Pink was still a 'boy colour' in the 1950s. Just look at the 1953 version of Walt Disney's *Peter Pan*, in which Michael, the youngest boy, wears a pink onesie throughout the film. So much for hardwiring.

Researchers have been trying for decades to find differences between boys' and girls' brains, and men's and women's brains. And guess what? There's no evidence to suggest that boys' brains are 'hardwired' differently to girls'. For example, in the 2013 study we mentioned earlier, the differences in behaviour were so small in many instances that if you took a boy or girl at random and asked them to perform a skill, 'the "right" sex would be superior less than 53 per cent of the time'.[23] People who spend their days studying the brain for a living describe popular claims about the 'hardwiring' as 'neuromyths', 'neurofoolishness' or, less kindly, 'neurobollocks'.[24]

Nevertheless, some parents with children of both sexes insist that their boys and girls behave so differently from one another that it must have something to do with their brain. We are not disputing this common experience. But this isn't 'hardwiring'. It simply reflects the fact that boys and girls are treated differently from day one.

Neurobiologist Gina Rippon writes in her book *The Gendered Brain* that what we think of as 'hardwiring' in the brain is, in fact, the result of environmental factors.[25] Our brains respond and change according to the environment around us. 'If we could follow the brain journey of a baby girl or a baby boy', writes Rippon, 'we could see that right from the moment of birth, or even before, these brains may be set on different roads. Toys, clothes, books, parents, families, teachers, schools, universities, employers, social and cultural norms – and, of course, gender stereotypes – all can signpost different directions for different brains.'

This is called neuroplasticity. Our brains mould like plastic in response to what we do – and don't do. As Rippon puts it, 'Brains reflect the lives they have lived, not just the sex of their owners.'[26] And our brain structure can change remarkably fast. One study that Rippon mentions showed observable changes in brain structure over as little as three months.[27] This is great news for boys (and everyone). Rather than limiting boys' horizons, lowering our expectations of them, and pushing them into particular activities because we think they are 'hardwired' to behave in a certain way, we can support them to grow and flourish into the unique and wonderful person they choose to be.

The bottom line here is that boys (and girls) are not 'hardwired' to behave in any particular way. Their brains are shaped by the external environment and what they do on a day-to-day basis. And, crucially, what *we* say and do to them.

But I don't treat my boy any differently to my girl

At this point, if you have a girl and a boy, you may be saying to yourself that you parent your children exactly the same. Or, if you only have a boy, you may believe that you parent him in a way that is gender neutral.

While you may sincerely believe this and may have gone to some effort to parent neutrally, studies consistently show that parents treat boys and girls very differently. And when people know the sex of their baby in the womb, these differences start even before the baby is born, and continue to be amplified after that. For example, mothers are likely to talk more to daughters compared to sons and to use more emotional language.[28] This becomes significant when we consider that talking to babies improves language skills.[29] Fathers are more likely to engage in rough-and-tumble play with sons and to use more achievement-focused language – such as 'top', 'win' and 'proud' – with their boys than with their girls.[30] Fathers are also more likely to sing and whistle with their daughters, and tend to be more engaged with and responsive to daughters compared to sons, which 'may facilitate the development of increased empathy in girls'.[31] Boys are also less likely to be discouraged from engaging in risky activities.[32] A study of conversations about safety between parents and children who presented to a hospital emergency room after an injury found that parents were four times more likely to tell daughters to be more careful in the future.[33] [34]

The fact that we unknowingly interact with boys and girls differently was clearly shown in the BBC documentary *No More Boys and Girls: Can our kids go gender free?*[35] In an experiment both male and female carers were asked to play with two toddlers who were given names and dressed in clothes associated with the opposite sex. Marnie became 'Oliver' and Edward became 'Sophie'. The different styles of play were striking. 'Oliver' (Marnie) was given robots and shape games whereas 'Sophie' (Edward) was offered a doll and soft puppets to interact with. Boys were presented with toys that taught and encouraged spatial awareness, whereas girls were encouraged to play with toys that were more about interaction. The carers were genuinely surprised by the different ways they had interacted with the children, as they'd considered themselves to be neutral when it came to gender. But these differences in play have an impact on the brains of children. And as mentioned earlier, it's estimated that if these behaviours are repeated, they can change the brain in as little as three months.[36] [37]

If you're still not convinced, listen out for the pet names we routinely give boys and girls. Parents and carers of boys often refer to them as 'buddy', 'mate' or 'little man'. How many times have you heard a girl called 'buddy', 'mate' or 'little woman'? On the flip side, girls are often referred to as 'sweetheart', 'honey' or 'princess'. These terms (or the male equivalent, 'prince') are used far less frequently for boys.

As Professor Rippon writes, 'a gendered world will produce a gendered brain.'[38] It's not so much hardwiring that shapes boys' brains and girls' brains, but the way we treat boys and girls. The good news is that since the external environment plays such a key role, you have an enormous capacity to influence the development of your boy. This is not about 'turning boys into girls', or, conversely, 'turning girls into boys'. It is about creating environments that give your boy opportunities to discover his authentic self, rather than deciding in advance that he is 'hardwired' to behave in a particular way. So, let's free our boys from outdated ideas about brain development and empower ourselves to provide the right environments for our boys to flourish and grow up liking themselves.

The seven pillars of a boy who likes himself

The good news is that there is every reason to think a boy can grow up liking himself if we can help him develop the skills and inner strength he needs to thrive. Think of bringing up your boy (or boys) as a bit like building a house. If you want him to be able to withstand the cyclones of life – many of which we cannot imagine, let alone anticipate – and if you want him to soar high and meet his potential, then he needs a strong foundation.

There are seven pillars that every boy needs if he is going to grow up ready for anything. But the thing about these foundational pillars is that they don't often develop naturally. In fact, there are many forces in today's society that will chip away at these pillars so they won't be sturdy enough to support your boy when the storms hit.

With small everyday parenting tweaks you can build and strengthen these pillars within your boy. It doesn't matter what the structure of your family is, or how complicated or busy your life is – you can still build these pillars.

Many of the challenges your boy is likely to face will be caused or made more complex by his foundational pillars not being strong enough. Instead of just addressing the symptoms – which is a long and frustrating process – you'll have more success addressing the root cause by working out which foundational pillar needs to be strengthened. We will explain each of the following seven pillars in the coming chapters and show you how to build and strengthen them in your boy.

1. A boy who likes himself has a power perspective.
2. A boy who likes himself has strength of character.
3. A boy who likes himself has body confidence.
4. A boy who likes himself has balance.
5. A boy who likes himself has mastery and independence.
6. A boy who likes himself has strong relationships.
7. A boy who likes himself is himself.

Building these pillars does not require upending every aspect of masculinity as it is traditionally conceived. It's not about reinventing or redefining boyhood (and manhood) from the ground up. Not only is such a wholesale recasting of masculinity unlikely to succeed, it's also both undesirable and unnecessary. Rather, this is about retrieving and celebrating all that's good about masculinity for our boys. And it's about making sure that masculinity is enabling for our boys, rather than trapping them in a dead end that will eventually undermine them.

Check your baggage

We all carry baggage from our childhood and the experiences we have gathered along the path to parenthood. Some of it you'll want to hold on to, particularly if you had a great childhood and know things will be rosy if your boy turns out half as well as you! But some baggage is probably not going to aid you in your quest to bring up your boy to like himself. Some of our unhelpful baggage can be dropped easily, but some can't – no matter how much therapy we have! The important thing when it comes to being the parent your boy needs you to be is to know that you're carrying it, because once you're aware that it's there, you can make a conscious choice not to unpack it in front of your boy.

The following list of questions is to prompt you to think about your own parenting baggage. Don't worry, this is not a test! It's just a quick little exercise to build awareness. If you've got a parenting partner then maybe you'd like to go through this list together. The results might surprise you.

Think specifically about how the following questions relate to *your* boy. This is not about boys in general or a theoretical issue, but rather about what *you* think about *your* boy in real life.

What is your baggage as a parent?

- Does your boy *need* to be good at sport?
- Will you feel okay if your son wears a tutu to kinder, childcare or school?
- Is it okay for your boy to cry and express emotions?
- Do you want your boy to be like his other parent, or not like his other parent?
- Will you be disappointed if your boy has different interests and values from your own?
- Do you sometimes make parenting decisions based on not wanting to feel embarrassed or judged by other parents, your partner, your own parents or in-laws, parenting 'experts' or even complete strangers?
- Do you think that gender stereotypes are 'natural' and therefore cannot be changed?
- Do you really 'just want your boy to be happy'?
- Do you find yourself rewarding your boy with more love and attention when he makes you proud?
- Is your boy already good enough just the way he is or does he have to meet certain conditions?
- Do you care if your son is popular or not?
- Do you wish your son was a daughter?

1

A boy who likes himself has a power perspective

Audrey's ten-year-old son, Spencer, was in a world of hurt. It was a fight every morning to get him to school. He said school was pointless because he was dumb and that everybody hated him because he was a loser. When Spencer did achieve something worth celebrating he would dismiss it as a fluke. When a friend reached out to him he rejected the invitation, claiming it was out of pity. The problem wasn't just with academics and friendships. Spencer flat-out refused to participate in the school cross-country and had already told Audrey he would rather die than go on school camp, which was six months away! And to put the icing on this cake of woe, he was miserable and grumpy at home as well.

Initially Audrey thought this was just a phase and that if she was loving and patient Spencer would snap out of it. But then she got a call from the school after Spencer would not attempt his benchmarking test. He sat at his desk for the entire test with his arms crossed, refusing to even pick up his pencil.

Audrey realised that things with Spencer were not resolving on their own as she had hoped. In fact, they were getting worse. She started to look for what might have changed in Spencer's life to make him feel so hopeless and to give up trying. But she came up blank. Sure, there had been the usual dramas that come with raising kids, but she couldn't account for his dramatic decline. In fact, through talking with Spencer, Audrey realised that pretty much the only thing that had changed was Spencer's attitude. Judged in objective terms, Spencer's life wasn't terrible. It was just that Spencer *thought* it was. The only thing that had changed was Spencer's *perspective* on his life.

And that's when it clicked – for Audrey, at least. Spencer would need a bit more convincing.

Spencer was so focused on the things in his life that he didn't like that he couldn't see the richness beyond. Even when good things happened, Spencer either didn't notice them or would dismiss or diminish them. He was so invested in finding evidence to support his perspective that his life sucked and that he was powerless to change it, that he was oblivious to all the evidence that there were some really good things in his life and he had the power and capability to seek out even more good things.

So Audrey set out to change her boy's perspective. Just two weeks later her intervention started to pay off. Not only did Spencer run the cross-country, he received an award for sportsmanship. Soon afterwards Audrey overheard Spencer playing Xbox with three boys from school. She had to fight back tears when she heard her boy chatting away and laughing with his friends. By the end of the term Spencer was not only doing the benchmarking tests without a fuss, he was also choosing to tackle some of the extension work. And he went off to camp without too much complaint. While he didn't exactly love it, he was proud of himself for going.

To be clear, nothing external actually changed in Spencer's life. He didn't all of a sudden become a genius or a star athlete, or meet more nurturing friends. Although his schoolwork and his friendships likely improved as a consequence of his changed perspective, they did not spark the change in him. The extraordinary transformation in Spencer was a direct result of the shift in his perspective. All he did – with his mother's help – was choose to think in a way that worked for him rather than against him.

What produced this remarkable change in such a short time? How did Spencer shift his perspective? That's the focus of this chapter. We're going to show you how to build what we call your boy's power perspective. Doing this will help to solve or at least minimise any problem your boy (or you!) will ever face. That's a big claim, we know. But we feel confident making it because, well, it's true.

What exactly is a power perspective?

Have you ever done one of those 3D Magic Eye pictures? They were big in the mid to late 1990s. If you haven't, or haven't looked at one in a while, do a Google image search and you'll find a stack of examples online. Don't worry – we'll be here when you get back.

When you first look at the image, it's just a blur of patterned colours and shapes. But stick with it, keep looking at it, cross your eyes ever so slightly while softening your focus and a fish, or a car, or a face will appear in 3D. And if you keep looking, the 3D effect will deepen, allowing you to change your angle and 'look into' the picture. It really does seem like magic, but the important point about Magic Eye pictures is that nothing about the picture actually changes. It's just the same blurry mass of colours it was before. What changes is you: you make a conscious effort to alter your perspective and, in doing so, you have a different experience. And you can choose to make that change any time you like.

Magic Eye pictures are a practical lesson in the power of perception. They teach us that you see what you focus on. And that what you focus on, you see. Two people can look at exactly the same picture and yet one will see the wonder of a 3D image while another will see a disappointing blur. It all depends on their perspective.

In the same way, two boys with similar capabilities can be faced with exactly the same situation, and one boy will thrive while the other can be crushed. The difference? Their perspective.

3

We'd like to introduce you to two boys who are going to pop up a few times in this book – Sam and Liam. These two boys are very similar in a lot of ways. They both come from loving families, they have similar hobbies, and they have very similar strengths and weaknesses. The biggest difference between them is that Sam is growing up with the seven essential pillars he needs to like himself. Liam, on the other hand, has not developed these pillars yet.

The boys walk out of school having just received their marks for their maths test, which was scored out of twenty. Sam is beaming as he bounces over to his mother. 'I got fifteen sums right,' he says. 'I'm great at maths.'

Liam walks over to his mother with his shoulders slumped, staring at his shoes. His mum can tell just by looking at him that he's about to cry, so she hurries him into the car. On the drive home Liam's tears flow as he says, 'I got five sums wrong. I'm terrible at maths.'

Both boys' test results are exactly the same. They both scored fifteen out of twenty. But their perspectives are totally different. Sam has a power perspective and Liam does not.

Some might think that Liam's negative response is a good thing; that if he feels bad about his test result he might be motivated to work harder and do better next time. This is a myth of 'old-school' parenting, particularly when it comes to boys. It's also ineffective. Kids who feel negatively about their performance are more likely to avoid practising because it will make them feel bad.[1] It's likely that the last thing Liam wants to do is practise his maths, because this will just remind him of his disappointment and sense of failure. Without a power perspective Liam might explain his test result by thinking that he's dumb and a hopeless case. This is likely to demotivate him from trying harder next time and crush his self-belief.

Sam, on the other hand, is probably even more motivated to work hard so he can do well again next time and feel this good again. Renowned parenting and education expert Alfie Kohn writes in *The Myth of the Spoiled Child* that 'As a rule, it's hard to *stop* happy, satisfied people from trying to learn or from trying to do a job of which they can be proud.'[2]

It's okay if Liam is genuinely disappointed with his test results. We are not suggesting he should lie to himself and tell himself he's satisfied when he's not. We all fall short of our own expectations from time to time. What's important is the way we explain our 'failure' to ourselves and what we choose to do about it.

A more productive way of explaining Liam's result could be: 'I didn't do as well as I'd like on my test so next time I'm going to practise more so I will.' Rather than passively accepting a situation that he's not happy with and feeling powerless to change anything, Liam could use a power perspective to take responsibility for the result that didn't meet his expectations, and empower himself with a plan for next time.

The author of mega-successful book *Atomic Habits*, James Clear, says that some people approach situations with the empowered perspective of 'How can I make this work?', while others approach the same situation by devising a list of all the reasons why it couldn't possibly work.[3] 'Both people will be forced to deal with reality,' says Clear. 'But the first person will only have to solve problems that actually occur, while the second person will often avoid taking action entirely because of the potential problems they have dreamt up before starting.'

The crucial point here is that we *always* have the power to choose our perspective. We can't always control the events in our lives. In fact, *often* we can't control the events in our lives. We can't control how people respond to us. People are going to hurt our feelings. We're going to miss out on that spot on the football team and not get invited to that birthday party. We're going to have days where, despite our best intentions and preparation, things are not going to go as we hoped. But we do have the power to control the way we interpret and perceive these events – and then how we respond to them.

The power perspective as we define it is simply this: the certain belief that you have the capacity to choose how you respond to external events. It's the opposite of seeing yourself as the victim of fate or tossed and turned on waves of seemingly uncontrollable emotion. It's the certainty that you have the capacity to weather storms that life throws at you and that you have the strength to live by your own standards.

Boys who have a power perspective believe that they have the power to influence what happens in their lives. This is called agency. It's acting like you're an active player in your own life rather than a passive spectator. Boys who have agency, for example, will attempt to climb a tree even if it's a challenge. And even if they don't succeed at first, they'll keep at it until they eventually do, even if it takes a while. If they want to do well on a test they will believe that they have the power to make that possible by working hard. If they have a bust-up with a school friend, they believe that they can sort it out tomorrow. If their friend is unwilling to repair the relationship, a child with a power perspective will still be okay, because while they may be upset and disappointed, it will not affect their self-worth, so they will be able to bounce back and know that they can make a new friend.

Boys who don't have a power perspective are more likely to suffer from helplessness, believing their life is controlled by luck, fate or chance events, or powerful others such as parents, teachers, coaches and dominant peers. Boys who believe they are helpless and powerless are more likely to suffer from depression and anxiety.[4] They may also appear to be lazy because they don't see the point in trying if they can't influence the outcome.

A power perspective is not woo-woo thinking

A power perspective is not woo-woo New Age thinking. It is not about denying reality. Nor is it about putting your intentions out into the universe in the hope that it will magically provide you with whatever you dream of without you having to work for it. And it's not just repeating positive mantras and anticipating that this – and this alone – will change your life.

Having a power perspective is the opposite of magical thinking. That kind of thinking is passive: it's waiting for an external force, whether the universe or some other omnipotent power, to bestow gifts on you. A power perspective, by contrast, comes from within. It's the internal belief that you are enough to face the challenges life throws at you and to achieve your goals.

Psychologists call this your 'locus of control': where you think control is located. People with an internal locus of control tend to believe that control over their own life is internal to them.[5] Those with an external locus of control believe – you guessed it – that control over their lives comes from external sources. That might be other people, powerful institutions and organisations, an all-powerful god or luck, fate or chance. This belief can make the world a really scary place for children (and adults) because their life may seem unpredictable and out of their control.

People with a power perspective have an internal locus of control. They believe that they have the capacity to control their own lives. And just so we're perfectly clear on this point, having a power perspective doesn't mean you live a charmed existence and you somehow get to sail through life avoiding the pain of disappointment, loss or injustice. And it certainly doesn't remove systemic injustices such as racism or sexism. Rather, people with a power perspective tend to do better at overcoming life's challenges and making the most of life's opportunities because they *choose* to approach life in a positive and empowered way, no matter what cards life deals them.

To go back to the Magic Eye example, it's like willing yourself to see the 3D image rather than just a blur of colours and shapes. The thing about perspective is that it's just that: a perspective. Whatever perspective we choose, we will be able to find 'evidence' to 'confirm' that it's true.

For example, one day our daughter Violet bounded home after playing interschool netball.

'How did you go?' we asked.

'Great!' Violet said. 'I scored two goals!'

The two goals were Violet's evidence that she'd had a great day.

'Well done,' we said. 'What was the score?'

'We lost 68 to 4.'

This is a perfect example of a power perspective. Violet could have taken those exact same facts and used them as evidence that she'd had a terrible day. She could have said, 'Today sucked. We got completely thrashed. They beat us 68 to 4.' This is also evidence, but it supports a completely different – and far less helpful – perspective. The thing about choosing a power perspective is that you focus on what you can control – or at least influence – in life. If nothing else, people who have a power perspective believe that they can control how they respond to outcomes.[6]

Research shows that children who think in this empowered way are more likely to exhibit higher self-esteem as adults.[7] They are more resilient and tend to be healthier,[8] and enjoy more success and stronger relationships[9] than people who feel powerless in their lives. They tend to work harder because they believe their hard work will pay off and that they will eventually achieve their goals, even though they will deal with setbacks along the way.[10] Children who have a power perspective approach life with an 'I've got this' mentality, so they keep trying despite challenges and are therefore more likely to overcome adversity.[11]

When we said that a power perspective can help to solve or minimise absolutely any problem, we meant that literally. Any situation or setback can be overcome or made more manageable if you think in an empowered way. A power perspective not only helps kids to deal with life's challenges, but also sets them up to make the most of life's opportunities. A power perspective is a crucial pillar in your boy reaching his potential.

What's your perspective?

Quiz time! One of the first steps to bringing up a boy with a power perspective is to discover how *you* see the world. Respond to the following statements as honestly as you can. If your boy is old enough, you can ask him to do the same to find out how he views the world.

When you do well on a test, do you:

A. Attribute your success to your own abilities and hard work?
B. Put it down to luck, an easy test or that the teacher liked you?

If someone criticises your work, do you:

A. Decide for yourself the quality of your work?
B. Figure that they must know more than you, and conclude your work is substandard?

In a new and unknown situation, do you:

A. Feel excited stepping into the unknown, confident that whatever happens you'll be okay?
B. Worry about everything that could go wrong and stress about how you are going to cope?

When you make a mistake, do you:

A. Learn from it so you can do better next time, and then move on?
B. Take it as proof that you're a bit hopeless and feel bad about yourself?

Do you believe:

A. That in the long run people get the respect they deserve in this world?
B. That an individual's worth is often unrecognised no matter how hard they try?

Thinking about the world at large, do you believe:

A. That by taking an active part in political and social affairs people can control world events?

B. That as far as the world is concerned, most of us are the victims of forces we can neither understand nor control?[12]

If you answered A to all or most of the above, it's likely you have a power perspective. You believe you have the power to influence what happens in your life.

If you answered B to some or most of the above, it's likely you feel helpless and powerless in some aspects of your life. It doesn't mean that you are less capable or skilled than those who answered A – you may just think you are.

Keep in mind also that it is unlikely for someone to have a consistent locus of control in every part of their lives. Most of us fall somewhere in the middle. We may feel that we have control in some areas of our lives, and less control in others.

Born this way?

You may be thinking that a power perspective is just a matter of winning the genetic lottery or being lucky enough to have your brain wired for success. Or maybe you think such people just live a charmed life. Consider Audrey and her son Spencer at the beginning of this chapter. Spencer's new perspective (which then went on to improve pretty much every aspect of his life) wasn't some freakish and unexplainable accident. It was a direct result of his mother's efforts to build his power perspective. Audrey taught Spencer that he had a choice in how he approached life. Before Audrey's intervention, when Spencer was invited to play Xbox, he *chose* to see it as an act of pity from the kid at school, because he'd decided he was a loser, so he said no. But he could have *chosen* to see the invitation as someone wanting to hang out with him because he's fun, and then he would have said yes. When it came

10

to going to camp, Spencer could have *chosen* to spend six months worrying about it and refusing to go and making himself stressed and angry; or he could have *chosen* to think about some of the fun things that he would do there and perhaps even have felt a little excited. Sure, he might not love every aspect of the camp, but that would be okay. There would surely be some things there that he'd like. For school benchmarking tests he could have continued to have *chosen* to give up without even trying and to feel hopeless. Or he could have *chosen* to use them as an opportunity to learn and practise and to show his teacher where he's at so she could tailor her teaching to best help him. When he stopped saying no to everything – no to going to school, no to friends, no to camp, no to cross-country, no to doing tests, no to any prospect of joy – and *chose* to say yes, his life became filled with more opportunities for fun and learning. Audrey taught her boy that he could change his situation by *choosing* to interpret events differently and to act in ways that work for him rather than against him.

And this isn't just a sample of one. Dr Michele Borba, author of *Thrivers*, investigated why some kids find it easier to overcome life's challenges and reach their potential, and concluded that it wasn't due to genetics, IQ, the type of school they attended, their sporting ability or even whether they had experienced trauma such as homelessness, abuse or family breakdown.[13] The kids who thrived had the kinds of traits and beliefs that fall within what we call a power perspective.

Building your boy's power perspective

While a power perspective is created rather than inherited, some research suggests that people are becoming more externally oriented when it comes to their locus of control. One US study found that between 1971 and 1998, the average child aged between nine and fourteen became substantially more externally controlled. 'Children, even those as young as age nine,' wrote the researchers, 'increasingly feel that their lives are controlled by outside forces rather than their own efforts.'[14]

If your son (or you) currently see the world as a scary place, like a little boat being tossed around on an unforgiving sea, totally at the mercy of external events, don't despair. Most likely nobody has ever you taught you how to take charge of your thoughts and perspective, rather than helplessly letting the waves of life crash over you. The good news is that this is something you can change – for yourself and for your boy. There is a growing body of evidence that shows it is possible for a person to change their perspective. Adults can do it and it's even easier for kids.[15] A power perspective is a skill and, just like any skill, we get better at it with practice. The attitudes and predispositions that create a power perspective can be taught and learned. Some people will learn this skill easily while others will take more time. For example, twelve months on from Spencer's transformation, Audrey still has to remind him about his power to choose when she notices him slipping back into his old negative and passive habits. But a simple reminder is all it takes for Spencer to choose to adjust his perspective and improve every aspect of his life. Either way, it doesn't take enormous, time-consuming and expensive interventions to build a power perspective. You can build your son's power perspective with small, consistent everyday parenting tweaks.

'What will other people think?'

The trouble is, we can undermine a boy's growing sense of himself in all kinds of ways – some big and some small. For example, when we were growing up, 'What will other people think?' was a constant refrain. If a child cut their own hair, what would other people think? If we went to school with jam on our jumper, what would other people think? If we were bickering in the supermarket, what would other people think?

While these phrases are well-intentioned, their constant repetition means that children come to believe that what other people think and expect *really* matters. And, more worryingly, that this is more important than what they themselves think.

To be clear, we are not advocating that boys should be raised without boundaries or without high expectations. Our point is that this can – and should – be done without constantly teaching them to defer to the judgement of other people – even random strangers – and letting it decide their worth.

For example, imagine a boy losing his temper in a cafe. His parents might try to manage his behaviour by saying something like, 'What will people think?' or 'You're embarrassing yourself' or 'People are looking at you' or 'You look silly'. All these statements are no doubt said with the best of intentions: the parents are considerate of the people around them and they want to teach their boy to be the same. But you can teach your boy to be considerate without effectively teaching him that other people are – and should be – judging him.

Instead, the parents could say something like, 'You need to quieten down because it's good to be considerate of other people.' This is an empowering statement because it's telling the boy that he has the power to choose to behave in accordance with his own good values. That is, after all, one of our most important jobs as parents. We don't want to teach our kids to behave well when other people are looking so they don't feel judged; we want them to behave well all the time because they are doing what they know to be right.

Of course, this strategy may do nothing to stop the boy's outburst in the moment. Shaming your boy with other people's judgements is hardly a winning strategy either. As any person who has ever met a child knows, these lessons are learned through years of repetition. But we get to choose whether we are going to spend all these hundreds of moments making our boy insecure or building his power perspective.

Protecting your boy's superpower

Each morning at the gate of the school our youngest daughter, Ivy, attends, a little girl lunges at her big brother to give him a hug, before he disappears inside. One particular day the sister wasn't there so the boy walked into school without his hug. We remarked to him that he didn't get his hug from his little sister this morning.

'Sometimes it's embarrassing,' the boy replied.

When we asked him what he meant, he said, 'Well, some people don't say anything, other people think it's cute, and then there's the kids who say it's embarrassing and tease me about it.'

We asked, 'What about you? What do you think?'

He looked up at us with a sweet little smile and said, 'I like it.'

We told him, 'Well, that's what matters. Don't let other kids decide what you should or shouldn't do. That's your superpower, don't give it away to anyone else.'

In an instant his little smile grew, lighting up his whole face. That's empowerment. And relief. In a world that surrounds our boys with unhealthy messages (such as 'Don't hug your sister'), it is a gift to remind our boys that they have the power to decide who they are, what they do, and whether they are good enough.

If boys become fearful of criticism from others, they end up living half-lives, avoiding situations where they might be criticised, or being inauthentic because they fear that showing their true self will lead to teasing. But the good news is that, if we are intentional, we can teach our boys that the person who has the biggest say over who they are and whether they are enough, is them. It is their superpower and they should not give it away to someone else.

The Giraffe

If your boy is young then you can subtly teach him not to give away his superpower by using what we call The Giraffe.

When your boy comes to you to report that someone has said something mean about him, such as 'Joe said I was stupid' or 'Katie said I'm a big baby', ask him: 'If Joe/Katie said you were a giraffe, would that make you a giraffe?'

This question usually provokes a laugh, or at the very least a smile, so it's great for defusing the emotion. But it's also something that even young children can understand. They are not a giraffe no matter who says that they are.

When your boy has composed himself after your hilarious giraffe gag, explain that it doesn't matter what Joe or Katie says, it doesn't make it true. Tell your boy that his opinion of himself is what matters most.

As your boy outgrows The Giraffe you can move on to the phrase 'Don't accept criticism from someone you wouldn't take advice from.' If your boy tells you about kids who are teasing him or if he is reluctant to do something out of fear of criticism, help him to understand that he gets to decide whose opinion of him he will listen to.

When it comes to criticism, tell your boy that somebody has to *earn* the right to be listened to. There are four reasons why someone criticises you: to hurt you, to make fun of you, to silence you, or to help you. Only the last one is valid. Ask your boy to think about why the person said what they said to him. If they are genuinely trying to help him then he can consider their feedback and decide for himself what he'll do with it. If they are not trying to help him, then they can talk to the hand. Tell him: Don't let someone who is being mean or someone you don't respect ruin your day. Don't give them that power.

What went well?

Another effective – and very simple – way to build your boy's power perspective is the 'What Went Well' exercise. This was developed by world-renowned authority on positive psychology

Martin Seligman, who is a former president of the American Psychological Association. He says that if you do this exercise for a week, 'the odds are that you will be less depressed, happier, and addicted to this exercise six months from now'.[16]

In the 'What Went Well' exercise, encourage your boy to focus on what went well in his day, his weekend, his school camp or his holiday. And get him to think about what he did to make it go well. This is the most important part of this exercise: the action or actions that your boy took to make things go well.

This is different from gratitude. Being grateful for good deeds that other people do or for chance events is lovely, but it doesn't build a power perspective. A power perspective comes from within – what matters is the actions your boy took to make sure he and others had a great day, rather than waiting around passively and hoping that something good would happen.

If you or your boy are having trouble thinking of something that went well, keep in mind that these don't have to be earth-shattering or award-winning accomplishments. Here are some everyday examples to get you thinking:

I went down the big slide at the pool.
I crossed the monkey bars.
I saw a kid being left out at playtime so I asked him if he wanted to play with us.
I carried my own schoolbag all the way to school.
I cracked the eggs for dinner.
I shot a goal at the park.
I practised my handwriting.

If you are able to sit down for a family dinner some evenings, you might want to incorporate this into the family ritual. Your kids will love it. We have heard from many parents that their children now initiate this conversation at dinnertime. We also do it at the end of each school term. We ask our kids what the best thing they did this term at school was.

You can also do this exercise at bath time, right before bed, or, if you've got a chatty child, when you pick them up after school. One mother told us that her boy would clam up when she would ask him how his day was. Now that she asks him each day what he's done that he's proud of, he yabbers all the way home.

Flipping praise

Tweaking the way we praise our boys is another easy, everyday strategy we can use to strengthen their power perspective. Just think for a moment how many times in a week your boy comes to you seeking praise. Ten times? Twenty?

It's normal for boys to seek out praise from their parents and other adults. They'll show us their paintings, their karate kicks, their school projects, and ask, 'Do you like it?'

Our inclination as parents is to tell our children that they, and everything they produce, are wonderful. But enthusiastically approving your boy's every achievement isn't necessarily doing him any favours when it comes to building a power perspective. We are effectively reinforcing the idea that our opinion or judgement about his drawing, kick, Lego creation, whatever it is, matters more than his. It's not him who is deciding if he is good enough – it's us. He is essentially giving his power to us rather than claiming that power for himself.

But there is a simple way to handle praise that builds your boy's power perspective rather than corroding it. Here's how: rather than simply praising his work, take the opportunity to turn his question around and direct it back at him. When he asks you, 'Do you like my X?', flip the question around and ask him, 'Do *you* like your X?'

If your boy says 'yes' then tell him that it's his work, so his opinion matters most and he should be proud of himself. If he says 'no', then you can talk about what he'd like to do differently next time and the importance of practising.

In the larger scheme of things, this strategy might not seem that significant. But think back to how many times each week your boy comes to you seeking praise. Times that number by fifty-two for each week in a year. Then times it by his age minus two years. If your arithmetic is as rusty as ours, here's one we prepared earlier. If from the age of two your son seeks your praise twice a day, then, by the time he is ten, you will have had almost 6000 opportunities to teach a power perspective and subtly tell your boy that his opinions about his achievements, behaviour and appearance matter more than anybody else's – even yours.

That's a lot of powerful reinforcement for very limited effort on our part.

What if my boy interprets my flipping praise as lack of interest?

You may be worried that flipping praise in this way could send the message that you are not interested in your boy's work. We have had parents try this strategy only to find their child getting frustrated or even dejected because they felt their parents weren't really interested in their achievement.

To avoid this, make sure that whenever you flip praise, you give your boy your undivided attention so he doesn't think you are fobbing him off. When your boy seeks praise he is also seeking a connection with you, so make sure he is getting that connection.

If he is still looking for praise, get him to say one thing he likes about his creation or performance, and then say one thing you like about it. Be specific here. Pick out something that you genuinely like or find impressive about his efforts. And take the opportunity to remind him that when it's his work, it's his opinion that matters most, so that's why you genuinely want to know what he thinks. This whole process is about us showing our boys that we are interested in their opinions, not just what they produced.

Keep in mind that our primary job as parents is not to make sure our kids never get annoyed or frustrated. It is to prepare them to be well-functioning adults who, ultimately, don't need us. One of the most important parts of this mission is teaching them to live by their own standards and not to give their power to other people by letting them decide if they are good enough.

Worst-case thinking

All of these strategies are well and good if your boy is going along smoothly most of the time. But what about when your boy seems to have crawled into a dark pit of negativity? He may think that nothing is going his way and be overwhelmed by big, scary negative feelings. If boys get into the habit of worst-case thinking they make problems, both large and small, into huge, insurmountable obstacles. For many kids, the worst case isn't just a possible outcome. It's the *only* outcome. Some examples of worst-case thinking are:

I'm the *worst* on the team.
I'm *never* going to pass this test.
Everyone can do it better than me.
I'm *always* in trouble.
Everything about camp is going to be awful.

An easy way to tell if your boy is engaging in worst-case thinking is to keep an ear out for 'absolute' words. Absolute words are words that block out alternative ways of seeing a situation or interpreting an event. Examples of these words include 'can't', 'worst', 'never', 'always', 'devastated', 'impossible' and 'everyone'.
While these are 'just' words, words matter. They matter a lot.

Words matter

To understand just how much words matter, let's look at what's become known as Coué's Law. Coué's Law is named after Émile Coué, who is considered the grandfather of psychotherapy and self-improvement based on optimistic autosuggestion. Coué is probably best known for coming up with the mantra 'Every day, in every way, I am getting better and better.'[17] Coué's Law states that 'When the will and the imagination are opposed to each other, it is always the imagination which wins, without any exception whatever.'[18]

The word 'imagination' here refers to that little voice inside our head; the inner critic that amplifies our every fear. The one that says 'You're not good enough' when you're about to walk into a job interview, or the one that says 'You're going to drop it' when you go to catch a ball.

A great example of Coué's Law in action is an experiment conducted by UK hypnotist Derren Brown.[19] To show how our imagination (our inner voice) often wins against conscious will (what we want to happen), Brown teamed up with tightrope walker Henry Ayala. Henry Ayala isn't just any old tightrope walker – he holds the world record for the highest number of skips with a rope on a highwire in one minute.[20]

At the time of filming in 2012 Ayala had never fallen.

Not once.

Unbeknown to Ayala, Derren Brown had set out to break Ayala's unbroken streak using Coué's Law. Brown arrives at the circus tent to film Ayala on the tightrope. But before Ayala goes up to the tightrope, Brown tells him, 'Make sure you don't wobble and fall off.' And he doesn't just say 'Don't fall' once. Brown repeats it a few times to really penetrate this poor tightrope walker's thoughts and imagination. To psych Ayala out even more, the production team launch a safety airbag underneath the rope.

You know how this ends, don't you?

Having been reminded not to fall, the best tightrope walker in the world is thinking to himself, 'Jeez, I'd better not fall. I can't fall. Don't fall. Fall, fall, fall . . .' And sure enough, Ayala's imagination wins out and he falls.

Think about that. With just a few words, this world-famous tightrope walker, who'd never fallen while performing his trick, overbalances on the highwire and tumbles onto the safety airbag.

When your boy makes statements about the worst possible outcome, he's not simply expressing how he feels. He's also telling himself that this is his reality, regardless of whether it's true or not. This applies to flippant and self-deprecating statements too. Even if your boy is making a dramatic statement that he doesn't actually believe or knows to be an exaggeration, on some level his brain believes it. And by saying these words, he is choosing to make himself unhappy and turn his fears into a reality.

Worst-case thinking also makes your boy helpless, because absolute words remove the possibility of seeing things differently now or in the future. And because absolute words rule out other possibilities, they have the effect of magnifying problems and making boys feel alone and powerless to change the situation that they find themselves in.

Your boy might want to do well on his maths test, but if he says 'I'm terrible at maths', it's likely that that little voice inside his head will be telling him the same thing. And if 'You suck at maths; you're stupid; you're going to fail this test' is what he hears in his head, then that is probably what is going to happen.

Why?

Because if he believes he's no good at maths, he's less likely to be motivated to pay attention in class or practise effectively. After all, what's the point of working if you're convinced that it won't make any difference to the outcome? Even if he does put effort in, there's a good chance he will feel stressed and anxious before and during the test. His heart is likely to beat faster, his palms might be sweaty, meaning he'll probably be less able to think straight. Even the sums he does know may seem a mystery to him because he's psyched himself out.

The lesson here is that when our kids are worried or anxious they are thinking about and visualising their fears. These could include anything from going to the dentist or going on camp to getting dropped off at school, doing a presentation in front of the class, or sitting a test. They are thinking about all the things that could go wrong, and visualising all the ways they believe they are not going to cope. They are essentially living Coué's Law.

Hacking Coué's Law

But here's the good news: you can help your boy to hack Coué's Law so that it works for him, rather than against him.

How? By aligning his imagination (that little voice inside his head) with his conscious will (what he wants to happen). Coué also said when the will and the imagination are in agreement they multiply each other.[21] The exciting part of this is that your boy can learn to direct his imagination so he envisions what he *wants* to happen, and his thoughts empower him rather than disempower him.

Elite athletes have been using this technique to improve performance for years.[22] Before an Olympic swimming race, do you think the swimmers are sitting in the change room imagining all the things that could go wrong and telling their coaches that they are going to get thrashed and it's going to be the worst day of their life? Hardly. They are visualising the perfect race, stroke by stroke. The real-life applications of Coué's Law extend far beyond athletics and sport. The Institute of Public Speaking in the US recommends visualisation to its students to reduce nerves and improve performance.[23] Researchers have also found that stroke patients who use mental imagery have greater success in learning to use their limbs than those who don't.[24]

What went right?

When your boy is worrying about something, help him to use his power perspective by imagining things going right, rather than wrong. Ask him: 'What would it be like if everything went right?'

For example, if he's worried about speaking at assembly, talk through what is going to happen and get him to imagine what it would be like if everything went right. Chances are he's never even thought about what this could be like.

Getting specific

One practical strategy to teach your boy to hack his thoughts is to help him choose more accurate descriptions for the situations he finds himself in. For example, when he comes home and tells you he had the 'worst' day of his life, the objective is not to try to convince him his day was in fact wonderful. Rather, it's to encourage him to be specific and accurate and frame the disappointment or unpleasant situation in an empowering way.

Ask him: 'Was it really the *worst*?' Ask what specifically made it the worst.

He may say something like: 'Because my teacher *hates* me.'

This is, once again, worst-case language. 'Hate' is a really strong word.

Challenge him on that statement. Is he really talking about hate? Ask him to break that down for you and be more specific. Why does he think his teacher hates him? What did the teacher do or say to make him think they hate him?

Worst-case thinking such as this also becomes a self-fulfilling prophecy. For example, if your boy believes his teacher hates him, he might spend the whole year with a negative and powerless perspective, so that even when the teacher is neutral towards him he perceives it as dislike and takes it as further proof of his teacher's attitude. If he believes his teacher hates him he's unlikely to behave to the best of his ability, which will likely mean he gets in trouble from the teacher and receives less positive reinforcement for good behaviour, thereby creating a vicious cycle that results in a really bad year.

Help him come up with a more accurate and empowering statement about his day at school. He might say, 'My teacher yelled at me when I was talking during reading.'

Now we're making progress. By getting to the specifics of the situation, your boy is not just getting a more accurate and objective view of his reality, he is also reframing that reality in a more empowering way. A specific statement like this opens the door to other possibilities and solutions. If the teacher simply called out his behaviour on this particular day, then he can always try harder to behave tomorrow. You could chat about what he could do so he doesn't talk in reading. Does he need to try harder to pay more attention to the teacher? Does he need to sit next to a different person so he's not distracted?

By encouraging your boy to be more specific about the situation, you have not denied his version of events. Nor have you pretended that there is no problem at all. You are validating his feelings, while also empowering him to find solutions to improve his situation.

A moment in time

When boys get into the habit of worst-case thinking they tend to talk about their struggles as if they are permanent conditions that can never be changed. For example, your boy might say, 'I'm *terrible* at drawing.' This statement implies that he will *always* struggle with drawing, as if it's an unchangeable part of his DNA. Thinking like this will likely make him feel miserable, helpless and demotivated.

Encourage your boy to reframe his thought or statement as something more helpful. For example, 'I struggle with drawing at the moment, but I'm practising.' Not only is this a more empowering way of seeing his skills, it's also a more accurate statement. Almost anything in life can be improved upon if we practise at it. That improvement might be small and take time, but it's still improvement. Talking in this way helps your boy realise that whatever his current challenges are, they are temporary and, crucially, they can be changed if he chooses to work at them.

If he's not convinced, give him examples of other activities that he found challenging to begin with but improved at with practice. These could be anything from skateboarding to multiplication to playing computer games. Giving him examples of his own achievements is powerful because they are difficult for him to deny or dispute.

The objective here is not to try to convince boys that their lives are perfect and that they don't face any challenges or difficulties at all. This is unlikely to work, and, taken to the extreme, just leads to delusional thinking. Rather, building a power perspective is coaching your boy to develop an accurate and objective view of reality, and the confidence and skills to act in ways that make his life better.

Help him to understand the connection between thoughts and feelings

Another way you might help your boy to shortcut worst-case thinking is to help him to understand the connection between thoughts and feelings. People sometimes think that stuff just happens in life that will make us feel bad, and that there is nothing we can do about it. This looks something like this:

Something happens → Feelings are triggered

This is a common misconception. But the truth is that feelings don't just happen to us. Feelings are triggered by our thoughts.[25] Something happens, you have a thought about it (assuming the worst, for example), and then the thought you have triggers the feeling.

Something happens → Thought(s) about it → Feelings are triggered

Let's go back to Sam and Liam's reaction to their maths test to see how this works. Something happens (they get the same test result – 15 out of 20). They then have a thought about it. Sam thinks, 'I got fifteen right. Awesome!' Liam thinks, 'I got five wrong. I suck.' And then those thoughts trigger their feelings. Sam is on top of the world, while Liam is in tears.

Usually this happens in the blink of an eye, so we often miss the middle part – namely that we have a thought about it. But if you're conscious of this, you can help your boy hack this process to make himself feel better by choosing more accurate and empowering thoughts.

Help your boy to understand that he has a choice in how he thinks about something, and that this will change how he feels about it. If he has more positive and empowering thoughts he will have more positive and empowering feelings. This is something that we adults can do too!

Self check-in: Listen to yourself

If you are unsure how to help your boy break his habit of worst-case thinking, first focus on what he hears coming out of *your* mouth. Do you run yourself down as a joke or default to self-deprecating humour because someone decades ago told you not to get 'too big for your boots'? If you do, don't feel bad. It's likely you were never taught how we can empower or disempower ourselves with our words. The two of us certainly didn't learn this when we were growing up. Either way, it's not too late to change your way of thinking.

When you catch yourself using worst-case thinking, stop yourself and choose more helpful language – make sure what you say is accurate, specific and empowering. And let your son hear it. For example, if you forget your friend's birthday, instead of saying that you're the worst friend in the world and a hopeless case, say out loud that you forgot your friend's birthday but it was the first time you've done this in twenty years and you're going to set an alert on your phone so you remember next year. Not only will this make you feel better, it will also allow you to model a power perspective to your boy.

Who has the time for this?

One piece of feedback we often hear from parents is that they don't have time to teach their child a power perspective. But our response is that you don't have time *not* to. Audrey could have spent countless hours trying to diagnose and address all the problems that Spencer appeared to have – not wanting to go to school, friendship problems, an aversion to exams, not wanting to participate in cross-country or go on camp.

That's a lot of individual problems to try to take on and solve!

So rather than setting out to tackle all the external problems, Audrey decided to work on changing one thing: Spencer's perspective. As we said at the beginning of this chapter, every single problem your boy is ever going to face can be improved or minimised by a power perspective.

Final thoughts

Bad things are going to happen in life and we as parents will be powerless to protect our children from them. They are going to be disappointed, rejected and heartbroken. They are going to stuff up and make a mess of things. Helping your son develop a power perspective will give him a solid foundation so that he can withstand the hardship of life. It will also help him find contentment in his life and within himself by focusing on what he does have rather than on what he doesn't. It will give him a can-do approach to life, which will help him pursue his dreams and reach his potential, and guard against depression, underachievement and helplessness.[26]

Just tell me what to do!

Boys who have a power perspective do better at school, have better relationships, have better physical and mental health and are more likely to be successful in life and work. Build your boy's power perspective by:

- Teaching him that while he cannot control everything that happens in his life, he can choose how he perceives it and responds to it. In any situation he can focus on what he doesn't like, or he can focus on what he does, or what he can do to improve the situation. That's his choice, and no one can take it away from him.

- Using an exercise we call The Giraffe. Help your boy understand that something isn't true just because someone says it is, by asking him, 'If Joe/Katie said you were a giraffe, would that make you a giraffe?' He gets to decide who he is and if he is good enough. That is his superpower and he should not give it away to anyone.

- Flipping praise. When your boy comes to you looking for praise, flip his question to 'What do you think?' This teaches him to care about and value his own opinions and judgements about his work and achievements more than anybody else's opinions.

- Hacking Coué's Law, which states that 'When the will and the imagination are opposed to each other, it is always the imagination which wins.' Teach your boy to imagine and visualise things going right, instead of imagining and worrying about all the things that could go wrong in a particular situation.

- Watching his words. Chances are you don't let your boy say mean or cruel things about other people. This rule should also apply to what he says about himself, because what he says, his brain likely believes. Pull him up on comments that will damage his power perspective, such as 'I'm the worst' or 'I suck at X', and help him choose words that are more empowering, such as 'I currently struggle with X but I'm working on it.'

2

A boy who likes himself has strength of character

At a school family picnic in the park, kids were playing a game of 'keep it off' with a basketball. Some were tweens and some were much younger. The little kids were being roundly defeated by the older kids.

One older boy realised this and decided to level the playing field. Clearly a highly confident athlete, he started passing the ball to the little kids. But he didn't just throw it their way. He used his skill to take the basketball from the older children – his peers – and then sneakily passed it to the smaller children behind his back or by faking a pass and then planting it in their hands.

It was the sneaky passes that did it. He didn't just throw the ball to the younger kids; it was as if he'd picked them out specially and made the play all about them. Suddenly the little ones were in the game, their faces lighting up with delight as the ball landed in their hands as if by magic. They now had the feeling that they were part of the play; that they had levelled up and were able to compete with the bigger kids at their own game.

The older boy seemed to delight in including the little kids. He did not need to win or dominate to feel okay about himself. He did not need to prove his basketball skills to his peers or anyone else. He also didn't need public recognition or praise for the good deeds he was doing for the little kids – most people would have been oblivious to his actions. He did the right thing simply because it was the right thing.

This boy was giving a masterclass in strength of character, one that can be applied to any sphere of life, whether sport, music, academic pursuits, friendships or just hanging out.

So what exactly is strength of character? It's about using your skills and abilities generously to include others rather than being solely focused on yourself. It's about having the courage to live with integrity and stand apart, rather than going with the flow. Strength of character is taking responsibility for your actions. It's winning with humility and losing with grace. The US sociologist Richard Sennett writes that character 'focuses upon the long-term aspect of our emotional experience. Character is expressed by loyalty and mutual commitment, or through the pursuit of long-term goals, or by the practice of delayed gratification for the sake of a future end.'[1] He continues: 'Character concerns the personal traits which we value in ourselves and for which we seek to be valued by others.' You might say that strength of character is doing the right thing when everyone is watching – and when nobody is watching. In this chapter we are going to debunk some myths about strength of character and show you why real strength of character is an essential pillar for your boy's current and future wellbeing.

Traditional masculinity builds boys and men from the outside in. Boys are taught to seek external signs of power and dominance in the hope that this will make them feel good enough on the inside. This belief can be summed up as: 'If I look good and have lots of stuff that everyone else wants, then I will feel good about myself.' This is an endless struggle and an impossible task because boys are constantly relying on external things they cannot control for validation and self-worth.

On the other hand, boys who have strength of character have learned to build themselves from the inside out. They don't seek external validation in order to feel good about themselves. Their strong and robust sense of self means they already feel good about themselves, and it is this internal resource that leads to external success.

At its core, strength of character comes from the certainty that self-worth comes from within. Once developed, it is endless and self-generating. You can use your strength to benefit someone else, knowing that it will never deplete you because it is an infinite resource. And because self-worth is internal and unending, it gives you the foundation to try new things even when you are unsure of the outcome. Because of that bedrock of certainty, you have the courage to fail, knowing that you can always try again. And again. A boy who is raised with strength of character will not shatter in the face of challenges or adversity; he will have the internal resources to withstand it and flourish.

Building character versus toughening him up

If strength of character sounds like a traditional 'masculine' trait, well, that's because it is. As we said in the introduction, bringing up boys who like themselves doesn't mean rejecting everything about masculinity. It's not about spending weekends out in the bush beating drums and trying to recover some lost (and largely mythical) masculine essence. It's not about turning your life and your family members' lives upside down. It's about retrieving the best of what we've taken to be traditional masculinity and building on it. As well as protecting our boys from the unhealthy parts of traditional masculinity.

But there's a twist. Historically, it was thought the best way to develop strength of character in boys was to follow pretty much the same process used to turn carbon into diamonds: boys would be thrown into high-pressure, stressful and often traumatic situations where, if everything went to plan, their character would magically reveal itself in all its sparkly glory; and this process, it was believed, would set up boys, and the men they would become, for life.

These were typically physically demanding feats of endurance on the sporting field, and demeaning (and often dangerous) hazing rituals to gain acceptance into peer groups or associations. Further back in time, these situations took place on the battlefield or in brutal boarding schools where harsh teachers would sooner beat a boy than hug him.

The goal, in short, was to break a boy down in order to transform him into something so tough as to be impenetrable. It might sound like a good plan but it's actually complete BS. Why? Because toughening boys up does not make them strong. Sure, intense pressure on carbon means that some rare diamonds will emerge, but carbon's extreme stiffness makes it brittle and it is therefore far more likely to crack under pressure.

Here's the thing: toughness and strength are not the same. Let us explain. Think of it this way: toughness is like tempered glass. You know the kind of glass most smartphone screen protectors are made of? That's tempered glass. As many of us know, the screen protectors on our phones can usually withstand a lot. Scratches from the keys in our bag or pocket, or a full-frontal hit with a ball, don't seem to have much effect on it.

Tempered glass is tough because it's put under tension when it's being made. Once it's formed into the shape of a phone screen, that tension is locked in. But that tension is also the Achilles heel of tempered glass. If you've ever dropped your phone and it's fallen at precisely the wrong angle, you'll know it takes just the tiniest of nicks in the wrong place and suddenly all that tension is released and starts to work against the glass. The tension that made it tough in the first place is released and the whole façade cracks, often making the phone unusable and even dangerous.

By now, you've probably guessed where we're going with this. Something similar happens when we try to instil toughness in our boys by putting them into tense, stressful situations. Under ideal conditions, when everything is going to plan, they're tough as anything. But, just like the tempered glass in a screen protector, toughness can work against them. It just takes something out of left field, even something tiny, and the tension maintaining that façade of toughness is released almost instantly, exposing the inner brittleness.

The false choice between tough and weak

When we asked parents about their biggest concerns about boys, they were worried that if they didn't raise their boys to be tough, their boys would be weak. And if these responses from parents are anything to go by, while parents may not love the idea of their boys being 'tough', they are equally concerned, if not more so, about them being 'weak'. Presented with a choice between the two, in a moment of total honestly, it is likely that many parents would prefer tough to weak.

This is understandable. Nobody wants their child to be a doormat or a victim, and when it comes to bringing up boys, today's society seems to believe that parents are caught between two extremes: 'tough thug' at one end of the continuum and 'weak wimp' at the other.

The good news is that the choice between weak and tough is a false choice – and one you do not have to make. Contrary to popular belief, weak is not the opposite of tough. As we've just explained, weakness is *caused* by toughness. What we should be aiming for instead is *strong*. To instil strength of character in our boys we need to get clear on the difference between tough and strong.

Toughness comes from a place of deficit. It's about making up for feeling that you are never enough and that you can never be enough. As such, it is jealously guarded. It is fragile and insecure because it is always relative to the weakness or inferiority of other people. Tough is also a mask that can be torn from you at any moment, shattered by a single word. A tough boy can only like himself when he believes he is superior to, or dominating, someone else. A boy with a strong character, on the other hand, can like himself all the time.

If we are to bring up boys who like themselves, then our boys need us to be brave enough to reject the stereotype of stoicism and emotional repression that's been associated with masculinity for . . . well, seemingly forever. What we are striving for is to build within our boys the solid foundation of strength of character, not the brittleness of toughness.

But wait, don't nice guys finish last?

If 'nice guys' are the ones who do the right thing, when nobody or everybody is watching, then it really depends on the race being run. If the race is to poor mental health, then yes, nice guys are more likely to still be at the starting blocks while those without strength of character win gold for anxiety and depression. If the race is to status anxiety and discontentment with who you are and what you have, then yes, nice guys are more likely to finish last. Nice guys are more likely to have real friends and soul-enriching bonds and to be too busy enjoying meaningful relationships to even care about the race.

From Batman to Wolverine, there is a mythology that tough and successful men are self-absorbed individualists, devoid of humanity or compassion, who will trample over anyone in the pursuit of power, riches or babes. It's 'winner takes all' or 'kill or be killed'. This is the model of masculinity that is presented over and over to boys. The message is as simple as it is clear: you cannot rely on anyone else, so you have to go it alone. But let's not forget that Batman ends up a lonely, angry man with nothing but expensive toys for comfort. (And no, his butler Alfred and sidekick Robin don't count; they're both on his payroll.)

If you're still not convinced that Batman and the Lone Ranger are damaging templates for bringing up boys, then flick back to the Boys' Report Card in the introduction (p. xiii) and take another look at the rates of suicide, mental health disorders and poor academic outcomes. This is what we are risking if we continue to raise our boys to be tough rather than strong.

Punishment does not build strong character

Away from the sporting field (or the battlefield), one of the ways we have historically tried to build strength of character in boys has been discipline. And what's often meant by discipline is punishment. While we might have stopped beating our boys for talking at the dinner table or caning them for failing tests, the idea that punishment builds character is still very much alive. Strengthening character through punishment may fit with old-school parenting approaches and values, but there's just one hitch. It does not work.[2]

Let's repeat that: punishment does not build character.

Remember, strength of character is built from the inside out, so a boy will have the values, self-regulation, empathy and good judgement to do the right thing even when nobody is looking. The end goal is not to get immediate cooperation or control over your boy by whatever means necessary. It is to build the right foundation in your boy so he is capable of being self-motivated and having meaningful relationships and a good life when you are not there, so he can go into the world with the prerequisites he needs to like himself.

Punishment or arbitrary consequences are external. They build a boy from the outside in. They may stop his poor behaviour in the moment but the overall lesson is more likely to be 'What can I do to make sure I don't get caught next time?', rather than 'What can I do to become a better person?'. As clinical psychologist Dr Shefali Tsabary puts it, 'punishment perpetuates the problem, instead of resolving it.'³ She writes, 'Ironically, the most heavily disciplined children are often those least able to control themselves.'⁴

And we're not just talking about corporal punishment such as smacking, slapping or that old favourite, 'a good clip around the ears'. Forms of punishment that are regularly pulled from the modern parenting toolkit include yelling, grounding, banning screens, cancelling birthday parties, sending a child to the corner and even washing mouths out with soap.

If you have used any of these tactics, you're not alone. In fact, many of these strategies are presented to parents wrapped up in a shiny bow emblazoned with the words 'Good Parenting'. When our daughter Violet was very young we considered ourselves enlightened parents. We didn't smack her, but we did give her timeouts and withdrew all sorts of privileges from her. Timeouts even come with a semi-scientific formula, such as the length of a timeout corresponding with a child's age. A three-year-old gets a three-minute timeout, for example, while a four-year-old gets four minutes, and so on.

It all sounds quite reasonable – until you look at the research.

Research shows that boys who have the poorest behaviour are those who receive the harshest punishments. It is impossible to know for sure if the poor behaviour leads to harsher punishments, or if the harsher punishments lead to poor behaviour. The most likely answer is that it's a bit of both.⁵

But what is clear is that in the long run, harsh punishment does not inspire the kinds of behaviour we associate with strength of character. If a boy does the right thing simply because he wants to avoid punishment, once the threat of punishment is removed, or he thinks he can get away with something, all bets will naturally be off.

If you want your boy to develop a strong character, or just behave in a decent way when you're not around, then you are unlikely to achieve your goal by using punishments. This might be difficult for you to read, and even more difficult to believe if you've always subscribed to the idea of 'spare the rod, spoil the child'. What we are suggesting is the opposite of conventional parenting wisdom. But think about it: if punishment actually led to a desired change in behaviour then we wouldn't need to keep punishing children, would we? About the only thing that punishment produces is . . . wait for it . . . more punishment. That's right: the more you punish, the more you punish.[6]

Executive director of The Men's Project at Jesuit Social Services, Matt Tyler, similarly likens a 'punishment-orientated mindset' to a 'race to the bottom'. He says this serves neither the parent nor the child: 'The young person then just punishes the parent.' This chimes with what we've observed in our own parenting peer group. An ongoing joke among parents who punish the most is that they're running out of devices to confiscate!

How does punishment make you feel?

If you're still not convinced that punishment will doom your efforts to build strength of character, Dr Shefali Tsabary suggests you ask yourself: How do I feel when I am punished?[7] Let's consider a grown-up version of punishment. Imagine you stuffed up at work. Maybe it was an accident, maybe it was carelessness or maybe you did it on purpose. It doesn't really matter, because, as with children who are punished, the 'why' is often secondary. You are called into your boss's office. Think about what your number-one priority might be in that moment. To have an honest conversation with your boss, take responsibility for your actions and earnestly reflect on your behaviour and the learning opportunity that you've been blessed with?

That might be how you'd spin it in a LinkedIn post or a performance review, but in real life it's far more likely you'd be feeling defensive and thinking about how you can cover your butt. That might include minimising your role in the error or deflecting responsibility onto something (a faulty process or piece of equipment, for example) or, yes, even someone else. Imagine your boss ranting and raving about how incompetent you are, then 'punishing' you by giving you a poor score on your performance review or withholding the discretionary component of your bonus this year.

How would you feel? Would you be inspired to reflect on your mistake and make amends? Would you be emboldened with self-belief and a renewed commitment to excel? How would your goodwill and loyalty to the company fare in that moment? You'd likely be pissed off, embarrassed and resentful, and the first thing you might do is log on to Seek.com to find a new job so you don't have to work with your ungrateful prick of a boss anymore.

What punishment really teaches

This isn't to say that punishment has no effect whatsoever. On the contrary, punishment teaches children all kinds of lessons. It's just that they're probably not the lessons you were aiming for. With painful, aggressive, humiliating or scary forms of discipline, the child is no longer thinking about themselves and their behaviour. Instead they are thinking about us and how we are hurting them.[8]

Let's imagine that a boy throws his toy truck across the room and it smashes against the wall. Our first instinct is probably to yell at him, 'DON'T THROW YOUR TOYS! THAT'S NOT HOW YOU TREAT YOUR THINGS!' In response to the yelling, the boy might pick up another toy and throw it, pushing every one of his parent's buttons.

Sound familiar?

It's really hard when our children disobey us – and it can feel incredibly embarrassing when they do it in public. In response to a situation like this, you might be tempted to grab your son, pull him across the room and sit him in the corner for a timeout so he can think about what he's done.

What do you think the chances are that this little boy will sit in the corner reflecting on why throwing a toy is a poor choice and vowing to never do it again?

We'd bet zero to none.

It is far more likely that the boy is contemplating one of two things: how unfair and mean his parent is, or how bad he is. The only things being developed here are resentment and shame. And what happens when boys experience resentment and shame? It corrodes their character.

Firstly, the shame and resentment build in them like a pressure cooker until they burst out in the form of dysfunctional behaviour, like, say, throwing a toy across the room. And then, over time, this turns inward and becomes self-loathing. Punish often enough and your boy will naturally assume that he is fundamentally flawed and irreparably bad. How we speak to and treat our children lays the soundtrack for the self-talk that will play in their mind for their whole lives. Do we really want that self-talk to be 'I am bad, I am unworthy?' While we might have been told that a dose of shame might do a little boy some good, make no mistake – nothing good comes out of shame. And we really do mean nothing.

Shame makes us feel unlovable and unworthy and, according to Professor Brené Brown, is linked to violence, aggression, depression, eating disorders and addiction.[9] 'Shame corrodes the very part of us that believes we can change and do better,' writes Professor Brown.[10] When boys and men feel ashamed and have limited ways to express this, it often bursts out of them in the form of aggression.

More passive forms of punishment, such as emotional freeze-outs or the silent treatment, are just as ineffective and shame-inducing as more active or physical forms of punishment. Not only are these passive aggressive, they can also wound just as deeply as physical punishment. A boy may interpret them as a withdrawal of love, and believe he is so bad his parent has stopped loving him. It's pretty hard to like yourself if you think your mum or dad can't even like you.

Parenting author and former teacher and counsellor Maggie Dent says that not only are physical punishment, sarcasm and exclusion ineffective, the shame they create is also dangerous. 'I can say without a doubt that all the boys and men I have worked with who have planned, attempted or expressed suicidal ideation, had deep layers of shame,' she writes in *Mothering Our Boys*.[11]

When it comes to responding to your son's behaviour, a simple rule of thumb is: if you would feel shame if a certain thing was said or done to you, your son will feel shame if you say or do it to him.

Getting disciplined about discipline

Does that mean we shouldn't be disciplining our boys?

Not at all. We are certainly not suggesting that you should raise your boy with no boundaries or limits and with low expectations. Quite the opposite. Discipline is extremely important in building strength of character. In fact, it is an act of love. But let's be really clear on something: discipline is not the same as punishment.

The word 'discipline' has a second meaning that is different from punishment. This meaning is 'to learn'. This is why we sometimes refer to Olympic sports as 'Olympic disciplines' and university fields of study as 'academic disciplines'. Both Olympic sports and university studies require many hours of instruction and learning to perfect.

If you think about it this way, discipline is an opportunity to strengthen character. It's about helping your boy understand why his behaviour was inappropriate, and supporting him to develop the courage to apologise and take responsibility for making amends, and *learn* to do better in the future.

While punishment might shut down poor behaviour immediately, any benefit is most likely temporary. Discipline, on the other hand, is about teaching and skill-building to support our children to manage their impulses and emotions, act according to good values, and consider the impact of their behaviour on others so they will do the right thing when nobody is watching as well as when everybody is watching.

Discipline as a learning opportunity

When you think about discipline as a learning opportunity – an opportunity to increase strength of character – it opens up a different way of thinking and talking about what we might do. It means creating an environment in which our boys can learn lessons not just in the moment but for their whole lives

Think about how you learn best. Is it when you're angry, resentful or scared of the teacher? Is it when you're afraid you'll be physically or emotionally hurt? Of course not. We learn best when we are guided and supported in a safe and nurturing way. We are more open to receiving advice and guidance from someone when we know they have our best interests at heart, not from someone who we fear is going to yell nasty words at us and take away our screen. The same applies to boys.

The good news is that wonderful life lessons and strengths of character can be developed through the right sort of discipline. And it doesn't have to take more time out of your already busy day. We're not talking major interventions here. To discipline effectively and maintain your connection with your boy, follow this rule: make sure your words and actions are helpful rather than hurtful.

Instead of yelling at your boy for throwing blocks at his brother then sending him to the corner for a timeout, then setting your watch and yelling at him some more to stop kicking the wall, discipline him positively to help him learn from the experience. It doesn't take that much longer. It's very often a conversation that takes only a few minutes.

For example: Walk over to your boy and calmly but firmly enforce your boundary: 'It is not okay to throw blocks at people.'

41

Build his empathy by asking, 'How would you feel if that was done to you?' and 'How do you think your brother is feeling right now?' Keep in mind that empathy is a skill that takes time to develop, so this is probably going to require some patience from you. Your boy might need some prompting and encouragement initially.

Simultaneously reinforce his self-worth and teach him to take responsibility for his actions by confirming that you know he's not the sort of person who would deliberately want to hurt someone, and by asking what he can do to make this better. This might be apologising, picking up the blocks, or fixing his brother's tower if he broke it.

Finish up by empowering him to do better in the future and further building his self-worth by showing that you have faith in him to improve by asking, 'What can you do next time so this doesn't happen again?'[12]

While punishment focuses on present behaviour and keeps your boy stuck in the problem, focusing on what to do next time encourages your boy to learn from the situation and do better in the future. If he is given the opportunity to come up with a plan for what to do next time he will be more invested in it and therefore more likely to do it. This step is also the antidote to shame. It's reinforcing to your boy that *he* is not bad. He simply *did something* that was bad, and because he has strength of character, next time he can try to make a different choice. Note the word 'try'. We need to have realistic expectations about how long it takes boys to learn self-control and good choices.

Every child is different and a discipline approach that works wonderfully for one child may not work for another. Or, as any parent knows, what worked yesterday may not work today. So it may take some trial and error and some creativity on your part to find a good approach. But even though the execution may vary, the goal of discipline is the same for every child and every situation: instilling the lessons required to build character so they can grow up liking themselves.

Discipline isn't a transaction

We were at the park one day and there was a boy around the age of four on the swing. He'd been on the swing for a long time and his dad was ready to leave. His dad had obviously read the parenting manual because he called out the five-minute warning. 'Five more minutes, buddy, and then it's time to go.'

Buddy snapped back 'No' and kept on swinging.

Dad exhaled a frustrated sigh and set the timer on his watch.

When the alarm beeped, Dad said, 'Okay, buddy, time to go.'

'No', came the reply.

'I'm serious, mate, get off the swing now, it's time to go.'

No response.

'If you get off the swing, I'll buy you a babycino.'

The boy thought about it. 'Hot chocolate?' he said.

'Okay, then,' Dad said.

Dad turned to us, rolled his eyes and said, 'You can't get kids to do anything without bribing them.'

A boy with strong character must learn self-discipline, internal motivation and a sound moral compass. But this development is jeopardised when we try to manage our children's behaviour with external rewards. We are inadvertently teaching our kids that everything in life is a transaction and that they should only do the right thing if there is some external pay-off.

Other common examples of seemingly innocent rewards that can rob children of the opportunity to develop their internal motivation and strength of character are dollars for good marks, lollies for goals scored and treats for cleaning up a mess in the lounge room. These may manipulate your child to do what you want in the short term, but in the long term they jeopardise their strength of character because they are building children up from the outside rather than the inside.

A boy with a strong character will get good grades because he is motivated to try hard and do his best; he will strive to score goals because he wants to contribute to his team and because it gives him internal satisfaction; and he will learn to clean up the mess in the lounge room because he is responsible and considerate.

We are guilty of bribing our children too. There are times when you do need immediate compliance and you use whatever method you can to get it. But as a general rule, try to avoid making good behaviour a transaction, because it's buying big trouble in the future. If it costs us a hot chocolate to get our boy off the swing when he's four, what's it going to cost us to get him to come home on time when he's a teenager?

If your boy does see good behaviour as a transaction then it might take a little while to ween him off it. But with time, patience and practice this can be done. Start by acknowledging his feelings. For example, the dad in the park who was trying to get his boy off the swing might say: 'I can see that you want to stay longer.'

Walk up to him. Drop to his level and make eye contact. State the situation calmly and with authority.

'I gave you a five-minute warning and now it's time to go.'

Take the boy's hand and guide him off the swing. If he resists and throws a tantrum, give him a cuddle. Yes, seriously! A cuddle might seem like a strange response in this situation, but cuddles are calming and bonding. It is amazing how many things a cuddle can solve.

What happens next is going to be different for every child. There are no guarantees with parenting. But just keep in mind that short-term behavioural manipulation through bargaining could be creating long-term pain, so avoid that if you can.

At a later stage, when your boy is calm, perhaps when he's in bed, you could have a chat about what happened at the park. You could tell him that you really like taking him to the park because he's so much fun to be with, but that he has to leave when you say it's time. If he doesn't, then you won't be able to take him as often. Be careful not to threaten what you cannot deliver. For example, don't say that he will never go to a park ever again, because it will undermine your authority.

Let logical remedies and natural outcomes be thy teacher

When we told a mother that we have not punished our oldest daughter, Violet, since she was three years old, and have never punished our younger daughter, Ivy, she was shocked.

'But you have to give consequences?' she said.

This is another idea that comes out of the 'Good Parenting' handbook. Enlightened parents don't punish, they give consequences. But what is the difference between a punishment and an enforced consequence? Not much, we would suggest. And as far as the child is concerned, probably nothing at all. 'Consequences' such as taking away screen privileges or cancelling birthday parties are still external ways of inflicting pain (in this case emotional pain) and shame on a child in an attempt to control their behaviour. Very often the consequence is totally unrelated to the behaviour that the parent is trying to stop.

For example, if your boy steals post-it notes and pens from the stationery cupboard at school and you cancel his birthday party as a 'consequence', what will he actually learn? It's hard for even an adult to connect stationery theft with a party due to happen two weeks in the future. How can we expect a child to learn anything from this other than how unjust his parents are or how he must be really bad to be unworthy of a birthday party?

If you want your child to not steal again, it is far better to use a logical remedy that he can understand and learn from. For example, the logical remedy for stealing from the stationery cupboard at school would be to replace what was stolen. If your boy still has the stationery then he needs to return it to the teacher

45

and apologise. Or maybe he needs to save his pocket money to buy replacement stationery. What's important here is that we are not inflicting pain or shame on our boy as a deterrent, by, for example, grounding him, yelling at him or taking away his device. Instead, we are supporting him to own the problem that he created and to take responsibility for fixing it. And then, having hopefully learned his character-building lessons about stealing and taking responsibility for his actions, he can be forgiven by his teacher. And his parents! Giving your boy the opportunity to make amends for his poor behaviour allows him to let go of shame and move on. He can learn a lesson, build his character and still like himself.

Little lessons prevent big stuff-ups

There are going to be times when our boys are irresponsible and make dumb choices as they grow up. That's natural and normal. After all, adults make dumb decisions all the time. Why should we expect our boys to fly through life making none? Boys at least have the excuse that they are still learning how the world works. But it's the *big* bad decisions our kids could make that can keep us awake at night – the kinds of decisions that can't be fixed with an apology and that can change their, and other people's, lives forever. The single best way to minimise the chances of your son making really bad decisions about big stuff is to allow him to experience the natural outcomes of bad decisions about little things. Outcomes are not punishments. They're not punitive. Nor are they something we inflict on our children.

The natural outcome of your son mucking around in the morning and not packing his lunch box is that he doesn't have lunch that day. This might be a horrifying suggestion to you. Our instinct as parents is to rush in and rescue our children from these types of outcomes. What sort of parent lets their son miss his lunch?

In our early days of parenting we would have gone home to get our child's lunch and been late to work as a result. Frustrated by how this had disrupted our day, we would have ranted and raved about personal responsibility. But how confusing is that for a child? We *tell* them about personal responsibility, but our *actions* say the opposite. We tell our child that they need to remember their lunch, but then when they don't, we fix the problem for them. No child ever starved when they missed one lunch. And this means that in the short term they are unlikely to forget their lunch box again; and that, in the long run, they will have learned a valuable lesson about personal responsibility.

If your child breaks his favourite toy in a fit of frustration or carelessness and you protect him from the outcome by buying him a new one, what has he learned? That he doesn't need to bother caring for his things because Mum or Dad will fix it. Now imagine your son in the future with a mobile phone, computer, house keys or even a car. You want him to have learned to take responsibility for his little things long before he gets the big things.

When to walk away

Another way to use outcomes is when dealing with rudeness or disrespect. When our kids are rude to us, this might trigger us to punish them. If you were raised in a house where such behaviour resulted in your mouth being washed out with soap, you might be tempted to do the same. (Yes, this still happens.) Other parents might be tempted to yell and lecture, to send their child to their room or to remove privileges such as screen time or playdates. But if our goal is to teach our boys not to be rude, these strategies are likely to do the opposite. If they worked, you would only need to do them a few times. But generally parents who punish for rudeness are always punishing for rudeness. A more effective way to teach your son not to be rude is to rely on the natural outcome of being rude, which is simply that when you're rude you don't get want you want. Kids will stop being rude very quickly when they realise that being rude doesn't work.

One effective way to respond to rude behaviour is to stay calm and say, 'That's not how you get what you want. Do you want to try again?' Or if your boy is demanding something from you in an entitled way, you might say, 'I don't feel like helping you when you speak to me like that.' Depending on the situation, you might take the opportunity to reinforce the character strength of empathy by asking your boy to reflect on how he feels when people speak to him like that. Ask him: 'Do you feel like being kind and generous when people talk to you in that way?'

If your child is not yet ready to learn this lesson, you always have the option of walking away. For example, simply tell your child, as calmly as possible, that that's not how we speak in our family. Invite him to come back and speak to you when he's ready to be respectful and polite. The key here is that you're giving your child time to calm down, rather than shutting him out and essentially giving him the silent treatment, which would be shame-inducing. By calmly inviting your boy to try again, this time without the rudeness, you can achieve the objective of teaching him not to be rude and also avoid shaming him and inflaming unnecessary conflict in your home.

Our friend used this approach with her son when he got frustrated while playing computer games and hurled his controller across the room. She could have yelled at him about losing his temper, essentially modelling the exact behaviour that she was trying to stop in her son. She certainly felt like it. She could have punished him by taking away some privileges, which would have inflamed the situation and created shame and resentment. But instead she took a deep breath, calmly walked over to the other side of the room, picked up the controllers and walked out of the room with them. When her son had calmed down, he came to his mother, apologised for losing his temper and asked for his controllers back. They had a calm conversation about how it's okay to be angry and frustrated but how chucking things across the room is not the way to deal with frustration. It became an opportunity for learning and connecting with each other, rather than punishment and shame.

Taking responsibility and showing accountability

Everyone stuffs up from time to time. We all hurt people, are careless or impulsive or just plain forgetful. We all occasionally have a reason to apologise for something we have done, or not done.

Having strength of character means admitting when you've done something wrong and having the courage to make amends. In general, men apologise less frequently than women, so there's a good chance your boy has seen women apologise, but not so many men.[13] We therefore need to work extra hard on teaching our boys that taking responsibility for their actions and apologising is not only good for other people, it's good for them, because it's not possible to have close and trusting relationships without accountability.

Accountability needs to be learned. You may need to explicitly teach your son that if he hurts someone by accident he is still required to apologise. Help him to build the strength to say the words 'Sorry that I hurt you.'[14]

Apologies that go something like 'Sorry if you got hurt' are fake apologies. They're missing a key ingredient – namely acknowledging one's own behaviour. In these kinds of fake apologies, there is no admission of responsibility. There is no accountability. Instead, there's just the recognition that something happened that upset the other person, and the implication that it's most likely their fault for being oversensitive. If you've ever received an apology like this, you'll know that it does nothing to resolve the conflict or repair the relationship. Most likely it just left you feeling resentful. If you want to spare your boy from a life of resentful and broken relationships you need to support him to learn to take real responsibility for his actions. Even when it's just an accident or mistake.

Help your boy understand the difference between a real apology and a fake one. For an apology to be genuine, your boy must do three things:[15]

1. Acknowledge that his behaviour hurt the other person ('I hurt Henry when I threw a ball at his head')
2. Recognise that he made a poor choice ('I should not have thrown the ball at Henry when he wasn't watching')
3. Focus on his behaviour and not on what the other person said or did ('I made the mistake – it was not Henry's job to dodge the ball').

Taking responsibility for bad choices and poor behaviour is hard. It takes a strong character. As parents it can be really difficult to stand by and watch our kids do it. We may get the urge to rush in and alleviate their discomfort by making excuses, by talking about extenuating circumstances or even blaming ourselves. We can't tell you how many times we have seen parents excuse their son for hitting another child by saying that he is tired. 'It's my fault,' we've heard parents and carers say – 'I didn't get him into bed on time last night' or 'He missed his day sleep'.

We think we are helping and protecting our kids when we do this, but we are doing them a disservice. As Maggie Dent says, 'Becoming someone who blames others and who refuses to accept responsibility for his actions is setting your boy up to be an irresponsible man who has a weak character. The need to blame external sources is surely delaying the development of emotional competence, of accepting responsibility for one's own actions, both of which could have serious repercussions later in life.'[16]

Don't punish yourself

If you are reading this chapter worried because you have been punishing your child, don't feel bad. How could you have known? The idea that children, especially boys, must be punished to build their character has been passed down through generations. There is also a lot of advice out there that is dressed up as modern and progressive but that simply doesn't work. Such as timeouts.

But our children's brains can be changed. They're not hardwired. It is not too late to change your discipline approach from inflicting external punishment to using discipline to build internal character. Focus on your relationship with your boy so you will be the person he chooses to come to when he is in trouble or has done the wrong thing, because he knows that you will help him (not hurt him!), teach him and, most importantly, still love him.

The strength to feel

One biggie that traditional masculinity got wrong about old-school strength of character was that men of character don't do emotion. We might not say it in so many words, but boys – and the men they become – are often policed to deny or ignore what they're feeling. At best, male heroes are brooding, stoic types. At worst, they veer into dysfunction. If they are prone to emotion, it's likely they're considered out of control. See Batman versus the Joker, for example. The caped crusader is a model emotional desert while the Joker is an excess of volatile emotions.

Emotional repression is the running gag – and underlying lesson for boys – in the hugely popular kids' show *PAW Patrol*. If you're not familiar with the show, think cute cartoon puppies saving the day by fulfilling emergency service roles such as a police officer, a firefighter, and an air rescue pilot. It all sounds pretty harmless, but watch a couple of episodes and you'll soon realise that it's essentially teaching kids that boys shouldn't demonstrate care and concern for others.

For example, in one episode, after the bulldog Rubble learns that a kitten is stuck on a boat drifting out to sea, he says, 'Oh no, the itty bitty kitten.' He then stops himself when he realises that he's expressing empathy. He quickly corrects himself and in his serious, all-business bulldog voice, says, 'I mean we have to save her.' It's not an isolated case. After Skye, the girl dog, performs a daring air rescue, Chase, the male dog in charge, says, 'Skye, I was so worried.' Realising that he's broken the unspoken rule that boys don't express empathy or concern, he corrects himself and says, 'I mean excellent flying.'

There are also plenty of programs that depict emotionally stunted male characters. A 2020 study conducted by the Geena Davis Institute on Gender in Media looked at the top twenty-five most popular television programs among boys aged seven to thirteen, and found that male characters are less likely than female characters to show emotions such as empathy (22.5 per cent compared to 30.6 per cent) and happiness (68.3 per cent compared to 75.2 per cent). Male characters were so emotionally repressed that they were even less likely to show negative emotions, such as anger (28.8 per cent compared to 36.6 per cent). Male characters also committed 62.5 per cent of violent acts against another person.[17]

And then we get to the problem of boys policing boys. How do we get our boys to have the strength to express their emotions when they face barbs such as 'Don't be a wimp/pussy' or 'Harden up' or 'Keep it together, mate' from their peers? We will cover how to help your boy handle this pressure in chapter six.

There is no doubt that we have a massive fight on our hands to build boys' emotional management skills, but the good news is that very often, consistency – the slow, unremarkable, everyday lessons of life – wins out. And that is reason for hope, because if positive lessons are laid down early, this means that these ideas are forming when parents are the most influential voices in their sons' lives. It means that we can get in first to intentionally build strength of character in our boys, which will give them the best chance to withstand the unhealthy masculine values that they will encounter.

Is it really such a big deal?

Is it such a big deal that boys are taught to repress their feelings? After all, they've been doing it for generations. The answer, as you might have guessed, is yes – it matters a lot. People who cannot deal with their own feelings suffer in almost every aspect of their lives. Professor Marc Brackett, who is the founding director of the Yale Center for Emotional Intelligence and a professor in the Child Study Center at Yale University, says if you want your children to concentrate, learn and be creative, they need to be able to deal with their emotions. 'If your child can't regulate or handle their emotions, if they are sitting in class all wound up, they are not learning.'[18]

Poor emotional management often prevents kids from reaching their potential, because they can't deal with the feedback they get. They are too brittle to tolerate the feelings of discomfort, disappointment and frustration that are essential for achieving success. 'They give up, not because of their ability, but because of their inability to deal with their feelings,' says Professor Brackett.[19] Poor emotional management also prevents people from developing and maintaining healthy relationships, affects sleep and physical health, and even damages career prospects.[20]

The other problem with repressing emotions is that it doesn't work. If feelings are not confronted and dealt with in functional ways, they leak out in dysfunctional ways, such as withdrawal, poor mental health and anger.[21] We also have men escaping feelings they lack the skills and strength to tolerate though alarming rates of suicide and addiction. And we have men refusing to see a psychologist or a relationship counsellor, even when they are clearly in crisis. They use toughness as their excuse. They don't need help. But as we have already seen, toughness and weakness go hand in hand. It takes strength to fearlessly face feelings head on.

Emotions featured heavily in responses from parents regarding their concerns about boys. Some parents were afraid because their boy was not expressing any emotion and they did not know what was going on in his head or heart. Other parents spoke of their boys' anger. This is not surprising given that, according to the rules of unhealthy masculinity, anger is one of the few emotions men are 'allowed' to feel and express.

As parents it is normal to want to spare our children from difficult emotions. We feel their pain and frustration as if it's our own, so it is very tempting to do what we can so our children don't have to face the pain. It's the forgotten homework at the bottom of the bag that we help them finish off. It's the phone call to another parent to intervene in a friendship dispute. It's the request that the teacher give our kid the weekly award. We know of a school that rewrote the script of a musical to create more speaking parts, because parents complained that their child didn't get a lead role. The parents argued that missing out on a lead role would damage their child's self-esteem.

But how damaging will it be when these children become adults and miss out on jobs they apply for, houses they want to rent, or people they want to date, having never had the opportunity to develop the internal resources to cope with difficult feelings?

To raise a boy with strength of character, we need to support and help him to develop the internal resources to be able to deal with the world around him as it is. As the saying goes, we need to prepare the child for the road, because we cannot always be there to prepare the road for the child. We will not always be there to change the environment to make life easier for our boys.

Boys with strong character must learn through experience and practice that unpleasant feelings are an unavoidable part of life. Their emotional pain is *theirs* to tolerate, manage and resolve. Nobody can do it for them. And it is only through experience that they will come to realise they are strong enough to endure it.

Naming is taming

The good news is that it doesn't have to be this way. We can help our boys to tolerate and express their emotions in simple, everyday ways. One particularly powerful way is expanding your boy's emotional vocabulary. This means getting him to name his emotions.

'There's 400 different emotions. Most people – particularly men – can only name a handful', says executive director of The Men's Project, Matt Tyler. What are the few emotions people can name? Anger, sadness and happiness.[22]

A concrete way to encourage and instil emotional expression in your boy is to ask him 'How are you *feeling*?' This is a different question to 'How are you doing?'

Equally as important as asking the question is listening for the answer. And insisting on an answer. As with most things when it comes to kids, this is unlikely to work on the first go. Or the second. In fact, it might take roughly 238 goes (or more) before you get anything useful. So get ready for some blank looks, shoulder shrugs, 'I dunnos' or a grunt.

Matt Tyler says to not let your boy respond with non-answers. As hard as it might be, insist that he identify and describe his emotions. Wait for him to put them into words. If he's having difficulty naming and describing his emotions, parenting educator and author Michelle Mitchell recommends asking him: 'If you couldn't call it anger, what would it be?' Of course, this applies to other emotions as well, not just anger.

If that doesn't get him talking, then use an emotion wheel to help him identify and name emotions. If you've never seen an emotion wheel, it's simply a wheel with common names for emotions in the centre, which fan out to more specific, precise labels for emotions. (We've included an example in the appendix.) Encourage your boy to move from the centre of the wheel to the outer ring so that he is being specific about his feelings. Instead of saying he's angry, for example, he might say he's frustrated or jealous. Or perhaps he says he's sad, but further reflection reveals his sadness is due to feeling lonely or disappointed. The important part of this process is getting him to identify and give specific names to the emotions he's feeling. By starting the process, you are opening opportunities for your boy to have what so many miss out on – the capacity to identify and name emotions – and enabling him to expand his emotional repertoire.

Matt Tyler says you can start to build an emotional vocabulary and promote empathy in very young boys through simple play activities such as creating a story with two toys, and asking how one toy feels if the other toy acts in a particular way – either positive or negative. 'Ask the question: "How do you think that makes Dumbo the elephant feel?"' says Tyler.

The benefits of naming and describing emotions are many, for both your boy and the man he will become. Drawing on work completed by Zac Seidler and others, Tyler says, 'Men who are able to describe their feelings can shortcut the link between distress and anger.'[23] By simply correctly identifying and naming what he's feeling, your boy will have gone most of the way towards dealing with it. Just think about how simple yet powerful that is. Spend a few moments getting your boy to identify and express what he's feeling, and you can mitigate his anger as well as resolve his distress. You are also opening up space and time for the development of character. The key to this process is being curious and compassionate so your boy is able to be authentic. Don't assume you know what your boy is feeling, or you'll risk prescribing an inaccurate emotion that your son will just go along with. When you misidentify an emotion you are not able to properly manage it.

Safe arms

If our boys are going to reveal their true and authentic feelings, we have to make it safe for them to do so. This is the opposite of how many of us were raised. It's approaching our boy's emotional outburst with curiosity instead of judgement. Rather than telling him to toughen up, get over it or stop crying, take a moment to sit with him, hug him if he'll allow it, and be okay with whatever comes next. He might talk or he might not. It doesn't matter. Your role is to be a calm, stable presence. That calmness gives him the space and, hopefully, the permission to feel.

These are moments when our boys really need us to be emotionally strong. Due to past trauma, many women can be afraid of male anger, so when they see it in their sons their first reaction may be to shut it down.[24] We tell boys to 'cut it out' or 'just calm down'. We send them to their room or threaten to take away their devices. But think about what message that sends to our boys. We are effectively telling them that they need to repress their emotions even within their family. On the other hand, being brave enough to be curious and empathetic about the emotion that triggered the outburst allows us to get below the surface to find out what's really going on.

When we focus on the immediate behaviour rather than what prompted or provoked it, we are missing opportunities to build emotional regulation. Yelling at, threatening or punishing a boy who's losing it doesn't help him resolve the emotion or develop effective strategies that will allow him to behave differently next time. In fact, punishing a boy for emotional outbursts will likely make him feel ashamed. When the feeling of shame grows, it will create a cycle of lashing out in what looks like yet more anger. That's right: our way of managing anger can create the breeding ground for more anger.

Sometimes it can be really hard to sit quietly as our child experiences difficult emotions. We will be tempted to rescue him, minimise his emotions or even completely contradict him so *our* discomfort will end. We might even be tempted to distract him from his pain with lollies or other treats or jokes. But if our boys are going to find the strength to experience and tolerate their authentic emotions, we need to have the courage to allow it. If your boy is sitting and struggling with big and scary emotions, reassure him that what he is feeling is temporary. It will pass. No feeling, no matter how strong or overwhelming, lasts forever. And whatever happens, he will be okay and you will be right there with him all the way.

Have you actually met a boy?

At this point, you might be thinking that all this advice about getting boys to talk about their feelings is well and good – but, you might want to ask, have we ever actually met a boy?

There is an assumption that largely goes unquestioned in many parts of society, that girls and women can naturally talk about their emotions, whereas boys and men are simply not capable of it. But this turns out to be, well, complete nonsense.

As Professor Marc Brackett says, 'These myths around biology and gender differences, they are myths. Boys aged five and six years old are just as capable as girls of expressing their emotions. They are also just as willing.'[25] When young boys are given permission to express their feelings in a safe and non-judgemental environment, they *want* to do it.

Differences in how boys and girls express their emotions start to emerge around the age of eight.[26] And while it might be tempting to say that a biological switch is triggered around the age of eight and that boys go on a different path, there's no evidence of any such switch. The reality is far more mundane. It's just that by age eight, boys have been boys for long enough to have learned that they aren't 'supposed' to show emotions. Professor Brackett says, 'These gender differences are created. It is a nurture issue, not a nature issue.'[27] Our society teaches boys in a thousand different ways over thousands of different days that expressing emotions is not part of masculinity. This is why our boys need us to counteract these messages and intentionally create the space and time within our homes and families for them to express their emotions safely.

Good deeds

Character doesn't develop in a vacuum. A necessary part of character is developed through interacting with others. It's about recognising the worth in other people and, in turn, having your value recognised by others. A great way for boys to develop and hone character is by engaging in their communities. But our society often gives boys the opposite message. As one eleven-year-old boy told us, 'Kindness is weak; it's something women do.' For this boy, the kindness that motivates good deeds is for suckers. And he wasn't going to be a sucker.

While this attitude is disturbing, it's not entirely surprising. Our society tells boys that being a 'real' man requires being a self-sufficient individualist. We admire men who go it alone. 'Somewhere throughout our history we all fell in love with the image of the lone cowboy riding over the range,' says Dr Sue Johnson, the American Psychological Association's 'Family Psychologist of the Year', and author of Hold Me Tight.[28]

The belief that kindness and good deeds are for 'chicks and losers' is obviously not great for society or families. It's also a disaster for boys. Men who don't give help are unlikely to ask for it either. And if your boy isn't kind and generous he's likely to struggle to make and keep friends. Research published in the peer-reviewed scientific journal PLOS ONE that surveyed 400 kids aged nine to twelve showed that kids who are kind have more friends and greater acceptance from their peers. They also have greater wellbeing.[29] 'Our study demonstrates that doing good for others benefits the givers, earning them not only improved wellbeing but also popularity,' the authors wrote.

To be clear, being kind is not the same as being a self-sacrificing doormat. It is important that your boy knows and maintains his boundaries, or, as we discuss in chapter six, his 'no-go zones'. Unfortunately, some boys can interpret overt acts of kindness towards them as slights or insults, and this can lead to a kind boy becoming a target for bullying. For example, your boy offering to help another kid with his maths could be interpreted by the other kid as a dig at his abilities. So while it's in your boy's best interests to be kind in his community, family and friendship groups, there will be some occasions where overt acts of kindness will backfire.

Boys are not born with an unwillingness to help others and do good deeds. Little boys are just as eager as little girls to help at home and at school and kinder. This shows that not all character strengths need to be built. Some of them just need to be preserved. We can't tell you how many parents have said that their little boy is sweet, kind and gentle and they just want him to stay that way. So how do we preserve the natural tendency in boys to be kind and helpful?

The first step is to value it. Research shows that parents who praise their preschoolers' good deeds are more likely to have generous, helpful children.[30] You may have to explicitly point out to little boys that doing good deeds will make them feel good. 'Boys experience the good feelings from being kind to others as much as the girls,' says Kate Hall, director of Neighbourhood House in Albert Park, who has forty years of experience in early-years education. 'But you have to keep it going. Keep talking about it in families. Encourage them to help in their communities in age-appropriate ways and point out that it makes you feel good when you help someone,' says Hall.

The other way to teach this is to model it. As the saying goes, you can't be it if you don't see it. Boys seeing parents, particularly dads or significant men in their lives, being of service to others is important in ensuring they see good deeds as central to their lives. This service might include taking part in school fetes, community sports or volunteer organisations such as Nippers, or just helping neighbours. Explicitly tell your boy that you, or another adult, are giving up your time and energy to be of service to the community. Point out other adults and older kids who are participating in volunteer work and make sure your boy knows how much you admire this. The benefits of being kind and doing good deeds are lifelong. A twenty-year study published in the *American Journal of Public Health* found that kindergarten children who cooperated with peers, were helpful to others, shared, played fair and resolved problems were more likely to be successful and happy later in life.[31]

Make sure these are good deeds for which there is no expectation of a return. Of course, benefits will likely come back to your boy for doing good deeds. But this should not be his motivation for doing them. This is not a transaction, after all.

If talk of being of service to others sounds like a traditional masculine ideal, once again, that's because it is. It is key to developing character because it is about doing something beyond yourself, which is critical for good mental health.

Just tell me what to do!

Toughness does not prevent weakness – in fact, it causes it. Toughness shatters in the face of adversity. And life is full of adversity! Instead, we should be aiming for strength of character – building our boys from the inside out so they will be strong enough to do the right thing when nobody is watching and when everyone is watching.

- Let your boy experience the natural outcomes of his behaviour so he can learn from them, as an alternative to punishing him. Try not to protect him from the consequences of his own behaviour, or make excuses for him. Let your boy experience difficult emotions so he will learn from experience that they are a normal part of life and that he is strong enough to withstand them.

- Naming is taming. Help your boy identify and name his emotions. Instead of asking him how he is, ask him how he is feeling. Refer to the Emotion Wheel in the appendix to help name emotions.

- Be your boy's safe pair of arms and let whatever he tells you be okay. Guide him to recognise his mistakes and teach him to do better next time. If you want him to come to you with his troubles (instead of going to social media for answers), hold off on the shame, judgement and punishment.

- Encourage your boy to be kind and to do good deeds for other people. Helping others is good for them, but it's also great for your boy's emotional wellbeing and friendships and even his future career success.

- When in doubt, hug.

3

A boy who likes himself has body confidence

A few years ago eight men stripped down to their underwear and posed for photos to encourage men to stop hating their bodies as part of Britain's Mental Health Awareness Week.[1] The campaign was run by men's health and grooming company Manual and looked a lot like the body-image campaigns that beauty companies have been targeting at women for years. You know the ones. They tell women that they are all beautiful and to love the skin they're in while simultaneously pushing them to buy some product to urgently fix their 'flaws'.

Leaving aside the obvious agenda of such campaigns, seeing these men in their undies was a shocking indicator that the commercially driven body hatred women have endured for decades is now infecting men – and boys. A 2018 study of 101 six-year-old Australian boys found that a third (32.6 per cent) wanted a more muscular body shape than their current figure.[2] Other researchers suggest that as many as 50 per cent of preadolescent boys, including boys as young as eight years old, are concerned about both leanness and muscularity.[3]

When it comes to gender equality, having men suffer as much as women was surely not what we had in mind. But body insecurity is big business, so of course it was only a matter of time until boys and men became the targets. Manual's campaign spokesperson and charity worker James Makings said that his body insecurity had dominated his life. 'I would think about how much I hated my body about 80 per cent of the time, if not 100 per cent of the time,' he said.[4]

Right about now you might be thinking of skipping this chapter, with the assumption that body confidence is one thing that is easier about bringing up boys versus raising girls, and that you don't have to worry about it. Your boy may not have even mentioned the appearance of his body before. But that doesn't mean he's not worried about it – or won't become worried in the future. Maybe the signs are already there if you know where to look for them. Perhaps he doesn't want to take his shirt off at the swimming pool or is flat-out refusing to go to the school swimming carnival. Maybe he's become picky all of a sudden and is cutting out a food group or eating in secret. Another warning sign that is particularly hard for parents to spot in our sport-focused culture is an unhealthy fixation on exercise.

In some ways, building body confidence in boys is even harder than building it in girls, because issues often fly under the radar. Boys and men tend not to speak about their body insecurities. As a society we often dismiss men's body-image concerns as trivial, or think they are 'tough enough to handle it'. But make no mistake, a poor body image can suck the joy out of a boy's life just as it can a girl's life. It can similarly damage his confidence, mental health and physical health, and in some cases can lead to suicidal ideation or even death.

In this chapter we are going to show you how to build a solid foundation of body confidence in your boy to help him navigate a world that is increasingly setting unrealistic and unhealthy expectations about how boys – and the men they aspire to be – should look, so he can grow up liking himself.

Why has body confidence become such a problem for boys?

One of the reasons that discussions about body image don't arise so often for boys is that the kinds of ideal bodies that are presented to boys appear to be 'healthy'. From muscular AFL and NRL footballers to *Men's Health* cover models, greater muscularity is regarded as a sign of peak health. Emeritus Professor Sarah Grogan notes that:

> Boys ma[k]e frequent use of sports and physical ability-related social comparisons when talking about their bodies and the bodies of others ... [T]his focus on sport and physical abilities reflects gendered trends in children's social comparison that are promoted through socialization processes; boys are trained to expect to be evaluated in relation to strength and athleticism, whereas girls are socialized to expect to be evaluated on their appearance.[5]

It also seems that boys regard media images of highly muscular men as inspirational or aspirational rather than as daunting and depressing. Professor Grogan notes that research shows 'that when viewing media images, preadolescent boys tended to view them as inspiring rather than deflating, identifying with their favourite celebrities and wanting to emulate them'.[6] In one study she cites, a boy says that looking at pictures of favourite celebrities 'would make you feel good because you could be slowly looking like the person, just say it's the person you want to look like, well you're starting to look like them'.[7]

This is in spite of the fact that these male celebrities' bodies are often no more attainable than those of female celebrities. The most extreme case here is Marvel hero the Hulk. The Hulk is supposed to be big – hence the name. In the late 1970s and early 1980s TV series *The Incredible Hulk*, bodybuilder Lou Ferrigno played the Hulk wearing cut-off jeans and lots of green paint. Ferrigno is no couch potato. He rivalled Arnold Schwarzenegger for one of the biggest bodybuilding competitions, the Mr Olympia, during the 1970s. His body was only attainable through genetics, hours upon hours in the gym, and obsessive dieting.

Fast-forward to the 2003 movie *Hulk*, and there was no man alive who was colossal enough to portray Marvel's angry green giant. Instead, computer-generated imagery had to be brought in to create a humungous Hulk. There was still a spot for the bulky Lou Ferrigno in the updated *Hulk* film – it was just that he was demoted to a cameo appearance as a security guard, inadvertently highlighting how unrealistic the new Hulk had become: not even a heavily muscled man could play him. In each sequel in the Marvel Cinematic Universe, the Hulk seems to get bigger and more muscular. While the Hulk is an extreme example, superheroes from Thor and Captain America to Batman and Superman have progressively gotten more defined muscles over time.

The same unrealistic body type can be seen in boys' action figures. While it's not uncommon to hear parents refuse to give their girl a Barbie or a Bratz doll on the basis that it promotes an unhealthy body ideal for girls, you rarely hear the same concerns expressed about the action figures presented to boys. But were they real people, these toys would have body-fat percentages in the single digits. The only way to achieve this muscle-to-fat ratio would be to use drugs such as anabolic steroids or human growth hormones.

Over the past decades, these toys have become steadily more extreme. For example, in their book *The Adonis Complex*, Harvard psychiatry professor Harrison G. Pope, Jr., Brown professor of psychiatry Katharine A. Phillips, and Harvard lecturer in psychology Roberto Olivardia compare the Star Wars and G.I. Joe figurines from the 1970s and 1980s with those produced in the 1990s. The differences are striking. Where the original Luke Skywalker, Han Solo and G.I. Joe look like regular – if physically inflexible – men, their updated versions appear to have been abusing steroids and spending hours in the gym. Their shoulders are barn-door wide and matched by similarly developed pecs and biceps set atop tiny waists. While many of these toys have shrunk down a little in recent years from their gargantuan proportions in the 1990s and early 2000s, they retain muscle-to-body-fat ratios that are anything but healthy.

'But aren't they just toys and movies?' you might be thinking. 'Surely kids understand that this is not real.' No doubt kids do have some understanding that these male bodies are the stuff of fantasy. But that doesn't mean kids aren't affected by what they see as the ideal body shape. For example, a 2018 study of boys and girls aged 9–14 found that 90 per cent of boys prefer hyper-masculine action figures as opposed to more regularly muscled action figures.[8] And it wasn't just the boys. Eighty per cent of the girls expressed a similar preference. When the kids were asked to explain their preferences, the children that preferred the hyper-muscular action figures gave a reason that was related to physicality (e.g. more muscular, larger) whereas those who preferred the more regularly muscled action figures would say 'other'.[9] The researchers suggest that the 'internalization of the muscular ideal body among young boys is not benign – evidence is mounting that internalization of the muscular body ideal contributes to the development of body image issues and eating disorders among adolescent boys and young adult men.'[10]

And it's not just superheroes who are being muscled up. Remember the 'Rob the dentist' TV commercials? If you don't recall them, they were a series of commercials for Oral-B toothbrushes that first aired in the 1980s. They featured a man, shown from the back, with a towel around his waist brushing his teeth, while a voiceover said, 'This man is a dentist so we can't show you his face.'

The adverts were so successful for Oral-B that they kept the Rob the dentist character throughout the 1990s and 2000s. But something changed over the course of the decades. In the first 1980s Oral-B commercial, Rob's back was lean but otherwise unremarkable. As a society we were much more interested in what our male medical professionals said and did than in how they looked. Rob the dentist later returned, this time advertising electric toothbrushes. But that wasn't the only change to the rebooted commercial. Rob's back was now a ripple of muscles, and in one of the commercials he even flexes his massive biceps at the end. The message is that all men must have muscle definition to be worthy – even in professions such as dentistry, where muscle definition is completely irrelevant.

Not just a problem affecting girls

At the other end of the spectrum, actual men's bodies are treated as a bit of a joke. Terms like 'dad bod' and 'man boobs' are thrown around with humour and are part of men's ribbing and bonding through banter. Psychologist Sarah McMahon, director of BodyMatters Australasia, says that these 'jokes' can do harm. 'The message is that these characteristics are defective and undesirable, resulting in increased body anxiety for people who possess them,' says McMahon.

As for girls, fat stigma and body shame can have a disastrous effect on boys' mental health, physical health and relationships. 'Weight-loss dieting is the most common path to an eating disorder,' says Dr Rick Kausman, who is a world-leading expert in healthy weight management. Body stigma is also a real risk factor for eating disorders. Dr Deb Mitchison, a researcher and clinical psychologist from Western Sydney University specialising in eating and body-image disorders, says, 'It [body stigma] is a risk factor for developing anorexia nervosa, because you are hearing negative comments about your body so frequently, or you are comparing yourself to your peers.'

We don't often think about boys as being at risk of eating disorders. But it's estimated that boys and men account for around 20 per cent of anorexia cases and 30 per cent of bulimia cases.[11]

In Australia, eating disorders appear to be increasing more rapidly among males than among females.[12] There is also some evidence to suggest that even though body dissatisfaction affects more women than men, it has a greater detrimental effect on men's psychological wellbeing as compared to women.[13]

Chris's story

When I was sixteen years old, I weighed about as much as a ten-year-old.

A ten-year-old girl, that is.

I was a boy with an eating disorder. It had been a long time coming. I had always been the fat kid at school, living in constant fear that my weight would be called out. Weight had been an ongoing and ever-present topic of conversation in my household and among my extended family. I'd been on a succession of weight-loss diets throughout upper primary school and on and off throughout high school.

In Year 11, something clicked. My first-term results were unexceptional and I was stressed. These final years of school counted in a way that earlier years didn't. And in the holidays between terms one and two, I decided to do something. I started exercising and obsessively controlling what I ate.

At first, regulating what I put in my mouth felt like magic. It seemed to be the key to controlling everything. My rapid weight loss was a source of pride. Late in the second term, a teacher took a moment at the end of class to praise my dramatic weight loss in front of all the kids. I was walking on air. Finally, my body had been commented upon in a positive way.

However, the warm glow that emanated from that first positive response didn't last long. As I controlled my eating, my world contracted into a narrow focus on food, eating and exercise, and the initial joy I had felt at the weight loss was smothered by my eating disorder. I lost the capacity to enjoy or laugh at anything. And I was too tired to socialise and was constantly numb with cold.

My parents and siblings could see what was happening. My restrictions had become obsessive and destructive. They implored me to eat. But anorexia doesn't listen to reason. All they could do was care for and support me. Their love and support are a large part of why I'm still alive.

I was never properly diagnosed, nor did I receive formal treatment. The one time I did visit the doctor, after falling off my skateboard, he couldn't conceal his look of horror. He muttered something about me looking like an inmate of a concentration camp. After stitching my chin back together, he suggested I hit the gym and put some meat on. As far as advice goes, it was about as helpful as telling someone who is suffering from clinical depression to look on the sunny side of life and cheer up already. I don't blame the poor man. I hardly fit the profile for an anorexic.

The winter that had set in at the beginning of Year 11 only started to thaw at the end of Year 12 and into my first year of university. With the pressure to perform academ- ically released, I felt able to release control of my dieting habits and gradually returned to a regular weight.

This is the thing about anorexia: it's not just about food. Food is often a means of asserting control over anxiety or depression or a situation where you feel out of control.

Warning signs to look out for

A recent study found that men who seek medical help for eating disorders 'are sent away from their physician's office, or are told to "man up" by their physician'.[14] When it comes to treating disordered eating, early diagnosis is important, which means that we all need to be on the lookout for warning signs and then advocate for our boys so their illness is taken seriously by medical professionals.

Psychologist Sarah McMahon says that weight changes – either increases or losses – are the most common warning signs of eating and body-image issues. But she cautions people not to rely on weight changes in isolation. 'Weight fluctuations can be a sign of any number of things, ranging from normal growth and development to any number of serious medical conditions. So relying on weight changes alone is narrow-minded and danger- ous,' says McMahon. Instead, she recommends also looking for other changes that sit alongside unexplained weight loss or gain. 'These might include changes in personality, interpersonal style, friendships, interests, hobbies and so forth,' she says. 'Often by the time weight changes are observed, behaviours contributing to these weight changes have become truly embedded.'

Keep in mind that your boy doesn't need to be skinny to have an eating disorder. Dr Deb Mitchison says that people with larger bodies can also be suffering from undernourishment and the psychological illness that comes with eating disorders. Dr Mitchison notes the emergence of 'atypical anorexia nervosa'. 'That's when they [the sufferer] have everything of anorexia nervosa – you know, they're losing a lot of weight, can be medi- cally unsafe and unwell, restricting their eating – but they're not yet underweight.'

When we think of eating disorders we tend to think of people not eating enough. But binge eating can also be an eating disorder. Australia's National Eating Disorders Collaboration reports that men are now suffering from binge eating at almost the same rate as women.[15] McMahon says that 'binge eating is associated with body shame and is often triggered or exacerbated by the engage- ment of unhealthy weight loss practices.' There will probably be times when your boy seems to eat everything he can see, and that's perfectly normal. However, if your boy is binging for emotional reasons or it is associated with distress then you may have cause for concern and it may be time to seek professional help.

Don't talk about appearance

The first step to building our boys' body confidence is to focus less on what they are putting into their mouths and more on what's going into their ears. This means focusing on what we're saying to our boys about their bodies and their eating. This advice might sound obvious, but research shows that the majority of boys receive comments about their body size and shape from their parents. Seventy-one per cent of boys say they receive positive comments about their body size and shape from their mother, and 51 per cent say they receive compliments from their dad.[16] But parents don't hold back negative comments either, with approximately a third of boys reporting negative comments from both parents.[17] When it comes to their eating, 57 per cent of boys say they get negative comments from their mum and 43 per cent get negative comments from their dad.[18]

You might think these comments are not such a big deal. You're not raising a snowflake, after all. Or perhaps you think you're helping your boy by bringing up concerns about his body and eating habits. The assumption might be that if you shame a boy about his body enough, then he'll be motivated to change it.

But the research shows that negative comments or teasing about your boy's weight, shape and eating are associated with kids gaining *more* weight. Not less! They're also associated with binge eating and unhealthy weight-control behaviours and mental health problems such as shame and depression.[19] [20]

Remember also that from toddlerhood to adolescence, your son's appetite is likely to expand and contract enormously according to his needs. As such, what may seem excessive to you might be just what his growing body needs.

If you're still not convinced that shaming your boy about his body is a bad idea, you might want to glance back to our chapter about strength of character (chapter two) to see how absolutely nothing – and we mean *nothing* – good comes from shaming a boy, and that includes shaming him about his appearance and his appetite.

With all this in mind, the bottom line is to stop talking about how bodies look. Full stop. This applies to all bodies – yours, family members' and friends', strangers', those of people you see on TV, and especially your boy's. It also applies to both negative and positive comments. As Dr Mitchison says, 'Talking about bodies at all and placing an overall importance on how you look and your appearance, even if it's very positive, can be unhelpful for the development of this kind of over-valuation of weight and shape. You learn that my self-worth hinges on how I look. That's not healthy for a boy or a girl.' Whether your son wants to be bigger or smaller, by not commenting on bodies either way, you are sending the message that body size just doesn't matter. In our house we have a rule that we never comment on how bodies look – good or bad. We only ever focus on and talk about what bodies *do*.

The secret to real body confidence

Our friend's ten-year-old is a natural at sport. He's one of those kids who just has to look at a ball or bat and then he's effortlessly kicking or hitting with it. He's a talented athlete, always one of the first to be picked for any team sports. He also has a classic athletic look. On the surface, he's the last person you'd expect to have body-image problems.

And you'd be wrong. This boy would cry himself to sleep because he did not like his body. He wanted to be taller, broader and have more muscle definition. His body hatred triggered both anxiety and depression. His parents could not understand why their boy was so dissatisfied with his appearance. He was a good-looking kid, so they figured body image was surely the last thing they all needed to worry about.

This is perhaps the biggest and most dangerous myth about body confidence: that if you look 'good' you'll have body confidence. This myth can lead parents with kids who come close to society's current ideal of attractiveness to dismiss their boys' body-image concerns and not treat them as seriously as is needed. But, even worse, it can lead parents to try to 'fix' their boys' bodies, in the hope that if they make their boys look 'better' they'll feel 'better'.

But, as our friend's boy shows, real body confidence has *nothing* to do with how we look. That may sound counterintuitive, but it's true. You could look like Michelangelo's statue of David and still have poor body image. The secret to real and enduring body confidence is not being attractive or even believing that you are attractive – it's not caring that much whether you are or not. We wrote in the introduction that many aspects of traditional masculinity were healthy and empowering and that we should not toss it all out. Body confidence is one aspect of traditional masculinity that we should absolutely cling to. Throughout history, we have cared way more about what men do, say and think than we have about how they look. If we are to give our boys body confidence we need to instil this old-school value in them once more. When they assess their worth we want them to turn inward to their strength of character (chapter two) and all their other strengths (chapter seven), and not their – or anyone else's – measure of their physical appearance.

Whether your boy is showing signs of being overly concerned about his physical appearance or not, it's worth beginning conversations about realistic body shapes as early as possible. This might be as simple as pointing out that the bodies of the heavily muscled movie stars he looks up to or the action figures he plays with are not real and can only be created through lots of injections, spending countless hours exercising and being deprived of a wide range of foods. Take every opportunity you can to reinforce the message that bodies come in all different shapes and sizes. Some are taller, some are shorter, some have curly hair, some have straight hair, some have darker skin, some have lighter skin, some have more muscles and some have more fat. We are all different and all bodies are good bodies.

But what about health?

Every time we talk about the benefits of not caring that much about how bodies look, someone will say that we're promoting unhealthy lifestyles and obesity. So let's nip that one in the bud. The leap from not caring that much about appearances to the assumption that we are endorsing obesity is a symptom of just how warped discussions about body image have become. This thinking assumes that there are two options, and only two options – that either you focus on appearance, which seems to mean ripped abs, defined shoulders and pecs and all the rest of it, or you are unhealthy. There is no third, fourth or even fifth option. The very fact that the 'discussion' is reduced to two choices should tell you that something is wrong with this picture.

Secondly, the idea that physical appearance and health are inextricably linked is based on the mistaken assumption that if you look good in the mirror, then you must be healthy. This is not the case. Physical appearance and health are not the same thing. And the ideal of health and fitness that is served up to boys – a body-fat percentage in the single digits, bulging muscles, broad shoulders and a tiny waist – is not just unattainable for most boys and the men they become, it is also only possible by engaging in some pretty unhealthy activities, including obsessive exercising and steroid use.

There is no question that a healthy lifestyle that includes eating well most of the time and exercising regularly is good for boys' physical and mental health and more likely to produce a boy who likes himself. But your boy does not need to fixate on his appearance, or feel like he needs to change his body, in order to have a healthy lifestyle.

A healthy lifestyle is the *process* of living well. It is not an *outcome* of meeting some external definition of attractiveness or a number on a scale or six-pack abs. And your boy is far more likely to maintain a healthy lifestyle if he's doing it because it's fun and makes him feel good rather than because he feels (or is told by others) that there is something wrong with his body that he needs to fix.

Teach critical thinking

From social media, YouTube, TV and advertising, boys are learning that there is only one right way for them to look. If you don't address this assumption head on, it's likely your boy will believe this too, and if he doesn't look like this – or doesn't believe he looks like this – he may struggle to like himself. This is why we need to get in first and arm our boys with critical-thinking skills so they are better able to deal with these messages.

When your boy is playing with ridiculously muscular toys, point out how unrealistic they look, and that people in real life don't look like that. Maybe make a joke about how the poor Hulk looks so swollen it's like he's been stung by a bee. Ask your boy if he thinks Luke Skywalker needs a six-pack to use the force.

The 'swimmer's body illusion'

As your boy approaches his tween years, you might want to start talking to him about why certain athletes look the way they do. For example, you could ask: 'Have you ever noticed that rugby players look big and chunky, that marathon runners are often thin and willowy, and that soccer players are somewhere in between? Why do you think that is?'

You might be thinking that the reason these athletes look different is that they train differently. Rugby players lift weights, whereas marathon runners often don't. Up to a point, you'd be right. But why does a rugby player, a marathon runner or a soccer player persist with their sport when others give up?

The answer has to do with what's called the 'swimmer's body illusion'. If you've never heard of it, the swimmer's body illusion was introduced by Nassim Nicholas Taleb in his book *The Black Swan*, as a lesson in how biases of perception arise in particular communities. The idea was popularised by personal trainer James Smith, author of *This Is Not a Diet Book*, as a response to fitness influencers who claim that anyone can achieve the same results as them by following their programs.

'Imagine someone, if you will, who wants to get in shape,' says Smith on TikTok.[21] 'They think that bodybuilders look too swollen and stupid. And they think runners look too skinny and miserable. They go, "Ah swimmers. They've got amazing physiques. I'll start swimming." Three, four, five months in they realise they don't look like a swimmer.'

The reason? Smith says that 'Swimmers don't look the way they do because they swim. They swim because of the way they look.'

Think about that for a moment. It's not that someone persists with a sport and then their body develops a certain way. It's that their body shape makes them suited to some sports and not so well suited to others. The reason successful swimmers have the same kind of body shape is not that swimming leads to this kind of body shape. It's that people who don't have bodies well suited to swimming stop swimming.

As Smith explains: 'People think I'm big and broad because I played rugby. No, I played rugby because I was big and broad. When my whole school year went to play rugby, only the big guys and the fast guys and the athletic guys actually enjoy[ed] it. And then they continue doing it and getting better. Those that don't, don't.'[22] This is the reason you don't see too many professional basketballers who are less than six feet in height, or cyclists who look like rugby players.

The lesson here is that your boy (and you) will have the kind of body that is well suited to some activities and not to others. Sure, you can try to change this with effort, but if you have the kind of body that's suited to playing rugby, then you're likely going to find long-distance running a chore. Of course, if your boy likes the challenge and sheer joy of a particular sport or activity no matter what, then we say go for it. We should absolutely support our kids in trying and playing any sport that interests them – regardless of their body type. But if your boy is doing it because he thinks it will radically change the shape and proportions of his body, then he's likely to be disappointed.

Remind your boy that all bodies are good bodies because they keep us alive, and allow us to do the things we enjoy, such as playing sports, mucking about with friends and hugging the people we love. Assure your boy that if he is living a healthy and active life then his body is exactly how it is supposed to be.

The rules around food

Nutritionist and family therapist Ellyn Satter, who is an internationally recognised authority on eating and feeding and the author of *Child of Mine: Feeding with love and good sense*, tells a story about when she was working as an outpatient dietitian. She was referred an eight-year-old boy and was told he had 'weight issues'. The little boy cowered in front of Satter, looking miserable. His mother was angry and frustrated. 'What am I supposed to do?' the mother asked. 'I have one at home who doesn't eat enough. And I have this one who eats too much. So what am I supposed to do? How am I supposed to get one to eat more? And the other one to eat less?'[23]

Satter had realised through years of experience that the prescriptive model of dictating exactly how much a child must or must not eat or how much a child should or shouldn't weigh doesn't work in practice, so she wasn't going to tell the mother to do that. 'There's so much that goes on today in the medical and nutrition world that is predicated on child deficit,' says Satter.[24] So, instead, she went with trust. She told the mother to trust her boys to know what they needed. Satter said to the mother, 'I don't think it's your job to get this boy to eat less and the other one to eat more . . . Your job is the one you're already doing. And that is doing a good job with choosing food for these kids, putting meals on the table. And after that, it's up to them how much they eat and how they grow.'[25]

Satter calls this approach the Division of Responsibility in Feeding,[26] which has now been adopted by doctors and nutritionists all around the world. Australian medical doctor and weight-management expert Dr Rick Kausman explains the approach as 'Parents provide and children decide'. Essentially, our job as parents is to provide a wide range of healthy and nutritious foods (and some treats too), and our children's job is to decide how much of it they will eat. And that's it. Do this, and your job is done.

This approach will empower your boy to trust his body. Tell him that his body knows when it is hungry and when it is full, and get him to practise tuning in to those internal messages. The other benefit of this approach is that you can avoid any power struggles or conflicts around food.

'Over and over again, I hear from these parents who talk about the struggles they're having with their children around eating,' says Satter.[27] 'And then they embrace the Division of Responsibility in Feeding and within days, the child becomes happier, more relaxed, and willing to come to the table. Family meal times become enjoyable for the first time in however long, and the parents say, 'He feels better, I feel better. And together we feel better all day long.'

Satter admits that it does take steady nerves and a leap of faith for parents to adopt the Division of Responsibility and to trust their child to eat as much or as little as they wish to eat.

But consider the alternative. If your boy is a light eater you could be setting yourself up for years of cajoling, nagging and power struggles. If your boy is a bigger eater and you are essentially putting him on a diet, you are setting him up for failure and potentially lifelong shame. Fifty years of research tells us that weight-loss dieting does not work in the long term in 95 per cent of cases. And this is among adults. If adults can't stick to diets, how can you expect a child to? You will also break your boy's little heart. He will come to think that there is something so wrong with him that even his parents feel he needs to be fixed. And he will likely assume that you will love him more if he is different to how he is now. In the face of all this, maybe trust isn't so hard after all?

Food is just food

For the Division of Responsibility in Feeding approach to work we need to remove any moral judgements around food. Food is food. It's yummy stuff we eat to give us the energy and nutrients we need to grow and live fun, active lives. Dr Deb Mitchison says, 'I do think that we have to be careful with how those healthy messages are portrayed in schools and elsewhere. It's particularly things like the labelling of foods as "good" and "bad" – this moral kind of association with how you eat.' Try to avoid terms like 'good foods' and 'bad foods' and instead use the morally neutral terms 'everyday foods' and 'sometimes foods'. This means that no foods are ruled out and there is no shame associated with eating or food choices.

Our role in the Division of Responsibility in Feeding is to fill our cupboards and tables with mostly everyday foods, so that when our children choose to eat as much as they like they are selecting from foods that are mostly nutritious. But make sure you are not too restrictive with 'sometimes' foods. 'Children whose sweets intake is restricted become food preoccupied and eat more when they get the chance and are heavier over time,' says Satter.[28]

Given it is very difficult for adults to deprive themselves of treats, it is too much to expect this of a child, and by enforcing this expectation you risk turning them into a closet eater. They will binge on forbidden foods in secret, or at a party or playdate when you're not there to stop them, and then likely feel ashamed afterwards. It is very difficult for a child to like themselves under these conditions.

In order to keep food as just food, we need to limit its use as an emotional regulator (as in, 'You're upset, have a cookie') or as a behavioural management tool (as in, 'If you do what I say I'll buy you an ice cream'). We are the first to admit that we have used food to control our girls' behaviour – sometimes you just have to use whatever works. But, as much as possible, try to keep food as just food.

What to do if your boy is teased for being fat

As a parent it's heartbreaking to see your child being teased for being fat, and it's very difficult to know what to say and do. For *Raising Girls Who Like Themselves* we consulted three experts for their advice on what parents should and shouldn't do if their daughter is teased for being fat. We have reproduced some of their advice here because it is gold for boys too.

Sarah McMahon, psychologist and director of BodyMatters Australasia
Do: Take your child's concerns seriously
Check in with your child to find out how they feel about their body. Try to do it in the same way you would make time to discuss any other concerns they have, such as how they're getting on with their friends or their studies. Parents can be powerful agents in building body confidence and body trust. Be mindful of how you talk about your body, their body and other people's bodies. People should never be shamed for their bodies. Ever.

That includes you. Be kinder to yourself. Avoid 'fat chat' or 'diet talk' about your own life and those of others.

Don't: Encourage weight loss or dieting
Encouraging weight loss will serve to validate the opinion of body bullies. It will send the message that yes, your child's body actually is defective, ugly, unhealthy, overweight and cannot be trusted around food.

Avoid dieting yourself. It models and normalises this unhealthy behaviour and can pass on body anxieties to your child. After all, if a child thinks there is something wrong with your body, they might assume there is something wrong with theirs.

Dr Rick Kausman, medical doctor, former board member of the Butterfly Foundation and author of *If Not Dieting, Then What?*
Do: Understand that weight and wellness are not the same thing
Contrary to popular belief, you cannot judge a person's health just by looking at them or calculating their BMI. Kids grow at different rates, bodies change over time, and all bodies are different. Instead of worrying about your child's shape and size, put your energies into providing the best environment you can to help your child be as healthy as they can. Focus on the process of living a healthy life, rather than weight loss as a goal.

Don't: Put your child on a diet
Nothing good can come from weight-loss dieting. The research is very clear: if a person focuses on weight and changing weight, it doesn't last. Very often it results in more weight gain.

Don't treat your children differently based on their weight. Don't allow the skinny child to have an extra serve of chocolate while denying the child with a bigger body. Children will rebel against that, sneak food and become 'closet eaters' full of shame around their eating.

Michelle Mitchell, parenting educator and author

Do: Remind them of the big picture

It's easy for kids to become fixated on the one 'mean' kid who is giving them a hard time. Tell your boy that it's okay if someone doesn't like him. Remind him that he has other friends, even if those friends are outside of school, or siblings.

Don't: Encourage your boy to push back with meanness

Calling another kid names, threatening not to be someone's friend, spreading rumours or hurting someone back are all ways kids try to stand up for themselves. One way that kids can detect if they are pushing back with meanness is by asking themselves, 'Would I be comfortable saying this in front of a trusted adult?'.

See chapter six for strategies to help your boy stand up for himself the right way.

Make your home a safe haven

The world can be a cruel place and you largely cannot control how your boy is influenced or treated outside your home. But you can try to make your home a place that builds your boy's body confidence rather than yet one more place that will try to corrode it.

The following is a checklist borrowed from *Raising Girls Who Like Themselves*, to identify factors that can help or hinder body confidence. It's not a test but it may prompt some conversations with the adults in your family to ensure that your home is a safe haven for your boy and his developing body confidence.

Protective factors

1. Do you focus on what bodies do rather than how they appear?
2. Do you talk about food in morally neutral language (such as 'everyday foods' and 'sometimes foods')?

3. Do you model exercise as something you do regularly because it's fun and you want to take care of your body?
4. Do you teach your boy to trust his body and to listen when his body tells him that he's hungry or that he's full?
5. Do you talk to your boy about the negative and unrealistic portrayals of bodies in the media and our culture more broadly?
6. Do you protect your boy from people who will police his body, or do you stand up for him when it happens?
7. Do you refrain from 'fat chat' with your friends in front of your boy?
8. Do you make an effort to talk about how people are different and that we come in all sorts of colours, shapes and sizes? We all have different qualities and talents.
9. Do you try to keep the negative thoughts you have about your own body to yourself?

Risk factors

1. Are you or your partner on a weight-loss diet?
2. Is your child on a weight-loss diet?
3. Do you or other people in your boy's life talk negatively about people's body size and shape?
4. Do you give compliments about people's weight, such as 'You look great, have you lost weight?'
5. Do you remark on your boy's appearance?
6. Do you remark on or shame your boy if you think he is eating more than he should? Or less than you think he should?
7. Do you force your boy to finish all the food on his plate rather than letting him decide how much he wants to eat?
8. Do you use food as a reward or a punishment (such as 'If you clean your room you will get a lolly')?
9. Do you use food to help your boy regulate his emotions (such as 'Don't cry, have a cookie')?

10. Do you talk about food using moral language, or label food as 'good' or 'bad'?

11. Do you talk about food in terms of calories and what's fattening and what's not?

12. Do you talk about exercise in negative terms, as a punishment for overindulging or as something you must do to correct a wrong body?

13. Do you tease or give your boy nicknames that relate to his physical appearance, such as 'chubby', 'shorty', 'big ears' or 'carrot top'?

14. Do you consume media in your house that convey negative messages about bodies (such as magazines, reality TV shows or diet books)?

Just tell me what to do!

When it comes to tackling the toxic messages our boys are going to receive about body image in today's society, we have a massive fight on our hands. But with everyday parenting tweaks we can build the essential foundational pillar of body confidence in our boys, to help them withstand the negative body-image pressures they will face, and thrive.

- Poor body image and disordered eating can suck the joy out of your boy's life. This is not just a girl problem, so take the issue seriously.

- Seek out everyday situations to help your boy understand that all bodies are good bodies, and remind him that many of the body types he sees portrayed around him are unrealistic. His body keeps him alive and is exactly how it is supposed to be.

- Take the pressure off food and eating. Your job as a parent is to provide a range of healthy, yummy food (and some treats too!), and your boy's job is to decide how much of that food he wants to eat. Help him tune in to his body and listen when it tells him he is hungry and when he is full.

- Make your home a body-confidence safe haven. Flip back to the list of protective factors and risk factors on page 83 to make sure your home life is building rather than corroding your boy's body confidence.

4

A boy who likes himself has balance

It was open-class morning at our kids' school and we and other parents were invited to the classroom to see the kids' projects. This particular term, the kids were doing the weather cycle, and the class was filled with posters and dioramas made from cardboard, papier-mâché and countless weird and wonderful household objects. As we looked around the class, it was clear the kids had poured themselves into their projects, and they were beaming with pride.

One boy had built his weather cycle out of Lego. It was a masterpiece that would have made The Brickman proud. We could see the anticipation on his little face as his mother walked over to look at his project. She folded her arms, shook her head and said, 'You spelled "precipitation" wrongly. You really need to work on your spelling.' The little boy's whole body slumped as his confidence, pride and self-belief whooshed out of him.

There is no doubt that this mum made her comment with the very best of intentions. In her mind she was helping her son to improve, she wanted what was best for him. But it's also likely that she was beholden to the myth that boys need to be 'pushed' in order to reach their full potential. People sometimes like to use softer words like 'extended' or 'challenged', but the idea is the same: that boys, especially, need to be propelled through their education rather than being permitted to develop at their own pace and take challenges as they come.

This thinking is exacerbated by parental anxieties about boys being left behind. On average, boys start school with less developed social, emotional, language and communications skills than girls.[1][2] Hearing this can make conscientious parents determined to ensure that their boy won't be left behind.

And parents don't just feel pressured to push their boys academically. The pressure also extends to areas such as sport, music, martial arts and other extracurricular activities. Not only might you feel that you have no choice but to push your boy, you might also see enrolling him in as many extracurricular activities as you can afford as the gold standard of good parenting. The alternative – not packing your boy's schedule with extra activities – might seem, in contrast, scandalously lax to the point of being negligent. At the very least, you might worry that your boy is missing out on all the opportunities that his friends are undertaking.

Our aim in this chapter is to convince you to resist the pressure to push and prod your boy, and to instead aim for balance. When we talk about boys having balance, we are not referring to children who are super Zen; quiet little angels who are perpetually obedient and obliging. Your boy may be that by nature, but many boys are not. By 'balance', we mean creating a life where boys have time and space away from the self-improvement treadmill to enjoy more unstructured time, where they can be children rather than being treated like learning machines who are pressured to succeed in each new stage of their academic life and life in general.

You may be asking, 'Why?' After all, isn't self-improvement a good thing? Don't we care about excellence? The short answer is: if this is your goal, then pushing boys is counterproductive. The research tells us that cajoling kids through education and rushing them from one extracurricular activity to the next will likely produce a burnt-out child who loathes learning, taking you further away from your goal rather than closer to it.

We're going to suggest that you give yourself permission to take the pressure off – both him and you. If you're concerned that he will be missing out if you don't sign him up for every class and activity that his friends are doing, we want to suggest that he may well be missing out on something far more valuable and important to his development and wellbeing. (Hint: it's play – free play. And no, this isn't some hippie-dippie idea about raising kids to be free spirits in nature. Play is actually really important to a boy's learning and development.)

To be clear, we are not suggesting that schoolwork is unimportant and will just take care of itself. Kids who are struggling with schoolwork need support and help. Nor are we saying that children shouldn't do any extracurricular activities. What we're arguing against is hothousing kids and pushing them many years ahead of their capabilities, because, as we are about to show you, it is unlikely to end well – for them or for you. It's about getting the balance right – a balance that will be different for every child and every family.

Our argument is with the lie that parents have been (and are still being) sold: that good parents must drag their boys through their education and that more extracurricular activities are always better, no matter how much they disrupt a family's daily routine or downtime. In this chapter we're going to show you why parents need to find the courage to push back against the culture of intense parenting. In essence, we need to ease up and slow down, because a boy who likes himself is not overtired, overstressed, overextended or overscheduled. A boy who likes himself has balance.

The cautionary tale of the tiger parent

The idea that pushing your boy through his education may do more harm than good might come as quite a shock. The notion that good parents must push their sons is so strong in today's society it is rarely questioned. We can't tell you how many loving and devoted parents we have heard fretting that their son's teacher or school does not push their boy enough. Schools and the ever-growing tutoring industry tap into parents' anxieties about children falling behind by promising more homework, extra tutoring and extension programs.

What the shiny brochures and sales pitches for tutoring services and extracurricular activities don't mention is that pushing boys through their education doesn't lead to better academic results. These pitches are also silent about the fact that it can cause serious damage – not just to boys' education but also to their mental health, their self-worth and their relationship with their parents.

You may be thinking: 'Yes, it's tough – but that's the point. Boys are tough enough to handle this level of pressure. And if they're not, after a couple of weeks of constant scheduling they soon will be. After all, the world is often a competitive and unkind place, so it's best boys get used to dealing with pressure so they can thrive academically.'

It's a nice idea. But that's all it is: an idea – and a flawed one. In reality, the evidence suggests that this approach doesn't produce the results parents want. Take, for example, tiger parenting, which is perhaps the most extreme form of 'pushing' kids. The term 'tiger parent' became prominent in 2011 with the publication of Amy Chua's *Battle Hymn of the Tiger Mother*. Chua argued that rather than respecting and nurturing children's individuality, the best way to raise high-achieving children is 'the Chinese way'. She advised parents to be strict and unrelenting, to use shame, fear and disapproval to push their children to succeed academically and in sport and music.

It turned out that Chua's book was based on a large helping of wishful thinking rather than evidence. The few studies that existed at the time showed that tiger parenting produced lower academic performance in children.[3] An eight-year study that tracked children who were pushed hard by authoritarian parents

90

found that this approach led to lower academic achievement, worse mental health and poor relationships with their parents. Rather than excelling, the poor little tiger cubs were suffering from a sense of emptiness and burnout. The reward the parents received from all the blood, sweat and tears was struggling kids who resented them.

Pushing before he's ready

While most parents are not as extreme as tiger parents, milder versions of pushing kids are also unlikely to produce the intended results. This is partly because many boys (not all, but many) are just not developmentally able to do some of the tasks that are asked of them.

For example, parents may compare their boy's stage in his learning – whether academic or social – to that of girls the same age, and conclude that their boy is falling behind. But the comparison is unfair, and doing a disservice to boys, who may simply be developmentally incapable of performing fine motor tasks, such as writing or using scissors, sitting still in class, and learning to read, at the same level. 'If we want to judge little boys and little girls in the same way at that transition point, we are usually going to see our boys not doing as well,' says Maggie Dent. While boys usually catch up on their own, forcing them to acquire social and academic skills before they are physically, cognitively or emotionally capable is likely to backfire. 'The mindset is if you force them to do stuff, they're going to do it better, but it's actually the opposite,' says Dent.

Another argument for pushing boys is that it builds their self-worth. The theory goes that if parents push their kids, they will achieve more and therefore have higher self-esteem. In reality, the opposite is likely to be true. Kids who grow up with too much parental pressure are more likely to have low self-esteem.[4] They are also more likely to suffer from depression, negative self-talk, eating disorders, trouble in school, aggression and anger

91

management issues, and to have difficulty maintaining relationships.[5] Suniya Luthar, former professor of psychology at Arizona State University, says that the evidence for children's poor mental health points to one cause: 'the pressure for high octane achievement'.[6] 'Kids are finding it impossible to keep up with our unrealistic expectations of success, and adults must accept blame,' writes Dr Michele Borba in *Thrivers*.[7]

What happens when you stop pushing?

The pushing strategy also has a limited shelf life. What happens when you stop pushing your boy? Quite possibly he will stop achieving, because his achievement has always been driven by external forces. That external force might be to please you or to avoid shame and punishment. He may have never developed self-direction or learned to be self-motivated.

Worse, it may kill his desire to learn before it really puts down roots. Clinical psychologist Dr Shefali Tsabary cautions parents that unwanted help and constant correction can not only damage a boy's self-confidence, but can also rob him of his love of learning. 'In the final analysis, the manipulation we think is going to motivate ends up killing the child's spirit,' Dr Tsabary writes in her book *Out of Control*.[8] In short, trying to fast-track your boy's education and development is likely to produce the opposite result. 'It's precisely this kind of attitude that taints the learning process,' writes Dr Tsabary.[9] Rather than raising a boy who likes himself, you will be far more likely to raise a boy who feels pessimistic and helpless and who goes through life feeling like nothing he does is ever good enough.

If not pushing, then what?

It can be hard for parents to permit their sons to step off the self-improvement treadmill. Even in the face of overwhelming evidence to the contrary, as a society we still think propelling boys towards success by all means available is the measure of 'good' parenting. It takes courage to raise a self-motivated learner because in many respects we have to let go of some of our control and put more faith and trust in our sons. Happily, there are a heap of alternatives to pushing that will lead to a much happier and more successful boy.

Connect effort to accomplishment

Children love to know that they can influence the world around them. And when they know this, they tend to want to keep doing it. Think of how a toddler delights in pushing a button on a toy (or an emergency exit!) that triggers a noise or movement (like a stampede of people). That's a game he'd like to play for hours. It's not the noise or movement that motivates the boy to keep pushing the button. It's that he made something happen. Harness your boy's natural delight in making things happen to create a can-do attitude.

When your boy achieves something, take the time to explicitly and clearly link his achievement to his actions. While he may take delight in the outcome, whether it's kicking a goal, climbing a tree, tying his shoelaces or learning his times tables, explain to him that his achievement was a direct result of his effort. This might be as simple as saying the following:

- You climbed the tree because you tried hard and didn't give up.
- You tied your shoelaces because you practised every day for a week.
- You aced your times tables because you worked really hard to memorise them.

The relationship between effort and achievement might seem obvious to adults, but the connection may be lost on kids. Understanding this connection from an early age has lifelong benefits. For example, high-performance coach Alyson O'Shannessy, who specialises in helping clients maximise their potential by understanding their thinking styles and the origins of the beliefs that underpin them, says that if you want to bring up your boy to be self-motivated and achievement-focused, empower him with the understanding that his effort makes a difference.

'Children need to know that when they act they can influence outcomes in their life, rather than just being passive bystanders,' says O'Shannessy. This doesn't mean your boy will always be successful in the first instance, or even the second or the third. But with practice and experience he will come to understand that it is through his own actions that he can move towards his goals – and 'this knowledge will motivate him to want to act more', says O'Shannessy. Achievement breeds more achievement. If your boy understands through his own experience that his efforts can influence his chances of arriving at a certain goal, he will be more likely to be motivated to continue to put in effort. This understanding is the antidote to helplessness and laziness, because he knows that even if he doesn't always get the outcome he wants, his effort makes a difference.

Value behaviour, not outcomes

What mark did you receive for your Grade 2 maths test? You know the one – the big one that you were super nervous about. The one in second term.

Can't recall?

The reason you likely don't remember is that it's not that important. It has had exactly zero impact on your life.

In spite of this, today's society suggests that 'good parenting' requires us to be intensely interested and emotionally invested in every little mark our children receive. We know of children in the early years of primary school who have vomited before tests and who are riddled with anxiety when their school report goes home.

They are terrified about disappointing their parents, getting in trouble or being punished for underperforming.

Parents are 'taught' to focus on the outcome of their children's performance. Intense scrutiny of every little measurement or mark starts even before kids are born, and continues as they develop, as we measure them against where we think they're supposed to be at each developmental milestone.

But focusing on the result (the outcome) sends the message to kids that we think their worth is determined by an external measure, and that one bad test result is a disaster. And we wonder why we have a mental health crisis in children.

An antidote to this way of thinking is to make sure your boy knows that you value behaviour far above the outcome. Our aim should be for our children to know it's the trying and the learning that matter, not the score. The added benefit of not caring too much about our children's test results is that they're far less likely to have test anxiety. This not only makes for a much happier childhood, it also ironically often makes for higher grades, because they don't psych themselves out before a test. They are also less likely to get burnt out, cheat, develop a fear of failure or become reluctant learners. Encourage your boy to embrace the process of learning, and the test results will take care of themselves.

If you think that this approach will lead to mediocre performance, then it's good to know that parents of bona fide champions use it. Rob Barty, father of Australian tennis superstar Ash Barty, tells a story about raising his champion daughter that perfectly illustrates the power of focusing on behaviour rather than outcome.[10] Barty was playing the under-twelve nationals and her dad tried to motivate her by promising to buy her an iPod if she won the tournament. She made it to the finals of the tournament but she didn't win. As Rob was watching Ash play the final, trying so hard and behaving so well, he realised he'd made a mistake. Instead of rewarding and celebrating winning, he should have been celebrating her behaviour – her effort and striving.

When she came off the court, Rob told Ash he'd buy her the iPod.

'But I lost, Dad,' she said.

Rob replied, 'Darl, it's not about winning now, it's about how you behaved and you behaved brilliantly.'

The lesson here is that behaviour is something your boy can control (most of the time) whereas the outcome isn't. Winning first place, acing a test, or getting a trophy are frequently based on factors that can't be controlled. Sure, practising or training hard increases your boy's chances of winning, but this still requires his opponent to be inferior to him, which he has no control over. If your boy is driven only by outcomes, and feels he might not win or get a good mark or score a goal, then he might well see no point in trying. For kids who value winning over trying, very often not trying is less painful and therefore preferable to not winning.[11]

The answer to this issue is to value and celebrate behaviours such as trying hard, persisting and taking initiative. That way, you increase the chances that your boy will naturally demonstrate these behaviours, especially since he will know for sure that he can succeed at them. When your boy does win or does well, get him to think about what he actually did to achieve that result.

What effort did he put in?

What strategy did he apply?

What can he do even better next time?

These are actions that he has some capacity to control – and to repeat.

Teach him to achieve for himself

Money for marks, lollies for laps, or presents for placing first.

Rewards like these might motivate your boy in the short term, but in the long term (and possibly even the medium term) they're training him to focus on the wrong thing: namely external validation and reward rather than the internal satisfaction of trying and achieving. Essentially, they're teaching your boy that achievement is a transaction: he will perform when you pay up, rather than in pursuit of his own personal satisfaction.

We're not saying you should never give external rewards, but try to frame them as a celebration for trying rather than making them a transaction, a payment for perfection.

To post or not to post

Posting about our children on social media has added another dimension to how parents acknowledge and celebrate success. Parents use their social media accounts to share news of their children's every success, whether academic, athletic or something else entirely.

As to whether this is a welcome or an unwelcome development, well . . . it's complicated. These posts come from a good place. You want your child to know that you care about their achievements and that you are proud of them. And social media apps have become the go-to platforms for proud parents to share pictures of their kids standing tall with medals. But what about when kids don't succeed, come first or even get a place? Do you post, or not?

Judging by our own social media feeds, which are filled with kids who seem to have unbroken streaks of successes, both academic and athletic, many parents only post when their child wins. If you only snap the picture or tell the world when they win, but are studiously silent or uninterested in documenting their achievements when they don't, they may well come to the conclusion that you're only proud of them when they're winning.

If you do use social media to share news about your boy, celebrate all of his efforts and achievements – whatever the outcome. We've all seen the post where the boy came second and there's a long caption about why he didn't reach the centre of the podium because of an injury or a slight cold. These posts are less celebrations and more justifications for a child not coming first.

Ditch the justifications. If you're going to celebrate your boy on the socials, just celebrate already!

The other key to success

Snap quiz: Aside from a capacity to deal with failure, what is the other essential ingredient in building persistence, resilience and a can-do attitude?

Don't know?

Hope.

That's what Professor Angela Duckworth found after she studied thousands of people to find out what makes some people persevere in the face of adversity, while others give up.[12] It makes sense that hope is important to success. After all, the people who keep going are the ones who are hopeful that their efforts will eventually pay off and they will succeed. And what gives these people hope? Duckworth says it is a track record of success. The reason resilient people get back up and keep trying is not that they have a 'resilience gene' or are stronger or more capable than those who give up. Resilient people bounce back because persevering has worked for them in the past. This faith in themselves comes from a track record of past success. By success, we don't mean massive record-breaking achievements. What's required are small everyday challenges that are a stretch for your boy in this moment, but that are within his capability now or in the near future. This might include him learning to pour his own milk or to hang up his own coat. Small everyday challenges that are initially difficult but eventually lead to success will build a foundation for your son so he will expect to triumph over challenges and succeed. And once he expects success he will be more likely to pursue it.

By contrast, pushing your boy to take on activities or meet standards that are well beyond his current capabilities will have the opposite effect. If he fails too often he will come to expect failure, lose hope in his ability to achieve, and become demotivated.

98

Isn't this just a recipe for mediocrity?

At this point you may be thinking that all of this sounds like a recipe for mediocrity – that if we don't push our boys, then we're allowing them to settle for 'good enough'. Or, alternatively, you may be thinking that this might be okay for other boys, but that your boy needs pushing, and that if you don't push, he'll never excel at anything.

Of course, it's perfectly okay to have high standards and to want the best for your boy in all spheres of life. But it's another thing entirely to present this as the only acceptable option or outcome. As we've seen, ratcheting up the pressure in the hope that your boy is always on top frequently has the opposite effect or comes with costs to mental health. The reality is that not everything has to be pursued to the highest level all the time. If your boy gets a disappointing test result, tell him that's okay and help him put it into perspective. One disappointment does not define him. If he doesn't place well or comes last, celebrate the fact that he turned up and gave it a go. Nobody does well all the time – and the world doesn't end. We need to take the pressure down.

Competition

'It's so hard to raise a boy,' says Anita, who has two older daughters and a boy who is seven. She's particularly concerned about how competitive her son Max's basketball team has become. Every game ends in tears because Max hardly gets any match time – he spends most of the games sitting on the bench. Max is not a natural athlete but he tries really hard. Anita raised the issue of court time with the coach and was told that performance is rewarded and that her son needs to try harder.

'Do you know how much courage it takes for Max to go out on the court knowing that he's one of the weakest players?' Anita said. 'Why isn't that courage rewarded?'

Anita asked the coach how the weaker kids were supposed to learn and improve if they weren't given any match time. The coach dismissed her concerns. As far as he was concerned, he had to keep the best players on the court because the team needed to go up the ladder.

At this point, it's worth pausing to ask: Why does the team need to go up the ladder?

This isn't a rhetorical question. It's a prompt to stop, think and question society's obsession with winning. Why is it important that a basketball team of seven-year-olds climbs the ladder?

We like to think of competitive sport as unquestionably good, and there are no doubt great lessons for boys to learn through playing sport. They can learn teamwork, a love of exercise, the satisfaction of pushing themselves outside their comfort zones and striving for their personal best, and how to win with humility and lose with grace. Every single one of those lessons can be taught without going up the ladder. Do we really want to teach our boys that winning is so important they should cut their weaker mates loose?

This is a poor lesson because losing is inevitable. No matter how much court time these naturally gifted seven-year-olds get and how high their team sits in the rankings, there will always be someone somewhere who is better than them, and a team who will beat them. How will these boys feel about themselves then? How will they be able to like themselves when they have been taught that winning is the only thing that matters, and they have not won?

We saw just how counterproductive this winning-at-all-costs mentality is at our local surf lifesaving club. Each week the eight-year-old Nippers were forced to engage in an elimination flag race. The kids lined up in small groups and ran on the sand to collect a flag. The kids who got the flags went back to race again. The kids who didn't get the flags – the less physically fit children and those with disability – had to sit out. Before long, most of the children were sitting on the sidelines, bored out of their brains watching the same few boys battle it out in the finals. And this happened week in and week out.

The outcome of this was that most of the kids were not learning or building their skills. So what did this competitiveness teach the vast majority of them? It didn't teach them how to be Nippers, because they spent the time sitting on the sand. The message was that they didn't belong at a surf lifesaving club. For the vast majority of the kids, the competition demotivated them and limited their growth.

There are a lot of people who would be disagreeing with us right now. Many people believe that, far from being harmful for children, competition is good for boys, that it breeds excellence and builds self-esteem. The rationale is that it's a dog-eat-dog world, so boys just need to toughen up and get used to it.

Early-years educator and director Kate Hall, who has forty years of experience, says that boys are more likely to be compared with other boys and to be raised in a competitive environment than girls. In addition to formal competition, such as a basketball tournament or a Nippers flag race, parents create competition in their families. They will try to motivate a boy by comparing him to his siblings, cousins or friends by saying things like, 'Ethan got more goals than you, Lucas,' or, 'He got a better mark on his test.'

Hall says that instead of motivating boys to do better and strive for excellence, this creates insecurity and self-loathing. 'They grow up filled with shame and feeling like they can't do anything right,' she says.

Decades of research support Kate Hall's experience. US education expert Alfie Kohn, who has been studying the effects of competition for more than thirty years, says competition creates self-doubt and risks mental health.[13] That's hardly surprising when you stop to think about it. When you divide children into winners and losers, the brutal reality is that most of the time our kids are going to be losers.

Think about the surf lifesaving club. Every week one kid is a winner and almost twenty other kids are losers. So one boy gets to feel good about himself while nineteen other kids feel like they don't belong. Wouldn't it be better for all twenty kids to have fun and develop their skills and corresponding sense of self-worth in a supportive environment?

Even if your boy is a massive overachiever who wins most things, competition can still be harmful to his self-worth, because if he is trying to seek validation by comparing himself to others, he is one bad race or slip-up away from feeling worthless. '[Winning] just lets a child gloat temporarily,' writes Kohn. 'Your value is defined by what you've done. Worse – you're a good person in proportion to the number of people you've beaten.'[14]

The 'why' of competition

We are not saying that there is no place for competition at all. It depends on the motivation behind your boy's competitiveness. Alyson O'Shannessy says there's nothing wrong with participating in competitive activities that are internally motivating, satisfying and fun. But if your motivation is to be better than someone else so you can feel validated, then competition comes at a cost. 'The need to be seen and noticed as being better than others is often driven by a deep belief that one's value and worth is determined only in reflection to others,' says O'Shannessy. 'Constant comparison to others is exhausting and utilises cognitive and emotional reserves that could be far better spent.'

Competitiveness is also a disaster for connection and relationships. It's really hard to be friends with someone if you're constantly comparing yourself with them and believe you have to be better than them in order to feel okay about yourself.

O'Shannessy identifies three motivations for competition: to look good, to be good and to do good. Only one of these will aid your boy in liking himself.

If a boy is competitive because he wants to *look good*, then he is externally motivated. His drive to succeed is to impress other people, and to be seen and noticed. He is also relying on being better than someone else in order to feel okay about himself. What happens when he's not the best? Measuring his value by how many people he's beaten will lead to a shallow and brittle existence. You want your boy to like himself all the time, not just when he's thrashing his mates.

Competitiveness in order to *be good* is when winning is about securing the love and approval of a parent or a significant other. A boy may see himself as a worthwhile person or deserving of love only when he is better than someone else. But once again, what happens when he's not winning? His self-worth will likely take a hit, and it's less likely he'll like himself. One of Australia's leading parenting educators, Michelle Mitchell, sums up this form of competitiveness by saying, 'When I look at competitiveness in a boy, what I'm actually seeing is insecurity.'

Healthy competitiveness is when a boy *pushes himself* to achieve because he wants to *do good*. He is intrinsically motivated and takes joy not from beating an opponent, but from learning and achieving. Not only does this motivation for competition lead to happier and healthier boys, it also leads to more successful ones.

A common factor among people who achieve excellence in any field, whether it's sport, music or scientific discovery, is that they are self-motivated. Their achievements have not been motivated by winning for winning's sake, nor by looking good for parents or coaches. These people achieved excellence because they enjoyed what they were doing and they took personal satisfaction from improving.[15]

Most importantly, healthy competitiveness means a boy can lose or fail to meet his expectations and still like himself. His identity and self-worth are not linked to winning or being superior to his peers. A boy who is motivated to *do good* is already good enough. Winning is a bonus.

If you want your boy to develop a healthy sense of competition, where his motivation is to *do good*, then try not to give him the impression that you will love him more if he wins. Make sure he knows that you are already proud of him and that he does not need to be better than someone else to earn or maintain your pride. Tell him that the only person he should compete with is the person he was yesterday.

Self-control, persistence and play

A surer path to many of the benefits that parents seek to instil in their boys through pushing and competition can be found through play. And by play, we mean pure play or free play. Free play is child led. It's when your boy is in his own little world. He might be playing by himself or he might be playing with friends, but either way there is no learning objective or outcome other than the fun of playing. Or there might be a goal that he and his friends have come up with on their own. The good news for parents who are anxious about their boy's screen time is that the right sort of computer games also count as play and will deliver many of the benefits of play in real life. We'll tell you more about these games later in this chapter.

Free play is distinct from 'play-based' learning activities. These are activities that are dressed up to look like play, but are actually adult-devised activities that have a learning outcome or a desired end goal. Free play, by contrast, is devised and led by the child and typically springs from spontaneous activities.

There is so much pressure on us to overschedule our kids with activities like tutoring, music lessons, organised sport and martial arts. We think that by doing this we are giving our kids a head start in life. However, what the research consistently shows is that one of the very best 'head starts' we can give our kids is to allow them time to play. A recent longitudinal study published in *Early Childhood Research Quarterly* shows that kids who are allowed unstructured play have better self-regulation two years later.[16] The researchers looked at the play patterns of 2213 toddlers and preschoolers and found that the more time children spent in unstructured play, the better their regulation was when they got to school age.[17]

Self-regulation is one of the strengths most highly correlated with success. It's a better predictor of academic success than IQ and it influences every aspect of a child's life.[18] As Dr Michele Borba writes in her book *Thrivers*, 'Do you hope your child is mentally healthy, excels at school, has healthy relationships, and a productive career? Then make sure that your son or daughter learns self-control.'[19] It may sound counterintuitive, but it is through play, not pushing, that your boy will learn the life skill of self-control. Professor Angela Duckworth also found that people who develop perseverance and self-control strengthen their 'grit muscles' by persisting at something *they* choose to do.[20] It is a myth that you can teach your boy perseverance and persistence by forcing him to do something he is not passionate about, or even worse, something that he hates.

Play is protective

A hobby can quite literally change the trajectory of a boy's entire life. Hobbies have been shown to work as a buffer against childhood trauma associated with divorce, family violence and living through natural disasters.[21] Research shows that kids who have experienced enormous adversity, yet go on to be well-functioning, caring, competent and kind adults, have something in common. They had a hobby that they loved and that they could retreat to when times were tough.[22]

As Dr Michele Borba says, 'Those kids had hobbies, they had something to fall back on or they enjoyed their own company. So when the stress really came, they went to the music or they went to the book or the art . . . It doesn't mean they're going to win a Nobel Prize from it, but that's not what it's about. It's about helping your child figure out what he enjoys.'[23]

This makes sense because it is in hobbies that children (and adults) get to exert some measure of control over their lives. The world might be spinning out of control around them, but if they have an activity that allows them to determine how they spend their time and energy, they will not feel so helpless and powerless.

And how do kids find that hobby that engrosses them and makes their little hearts sing? Through play.[24] Borba recommends that every parent look at their child's schedule and deliberately carve out some downtime for play. Every child she interviewed who was highly stressed and felt they were running on empty was overscheduled. 'And when I said, "What do you do for a hobby?", they all looked at me like, What the heck is a hobby?'[25]

Now, think about your boy's life for a moment. How much control does he have over how he spends his time? In the mornings he's likely following your schedule to get him up, ready and out of the house in time for preschool, childcare or school. Unless his pre-school or school is play-based, it's possible that he's spending the day following school rules and his teacher's instructions. If he goes to after-school activities, he's then also likely following the rules and expectations of his coach or teacher. When you get him home you're up against the clock again, so he has to follow your rules about dinner, homework, bath time and bedtime. A boy could easily go a whole day without having a single significant moment that he controls. Time that children can spend as they like is very often treated as a luxury that they can have only if all the 'important' things get done first. But make no mistake, play is important. In fact, it's essential. Play is one of the most important things in your boy's life.

Still not convinced about the benefits of play?

If you're still unconvinced that play is more beneficial for your boy than packing his schedule with structured activities, let's compare the two boys we introduced you to earlier. Sam's life has balance. Liam's does not.

Liam is super busy with adult-led activities every day after school and on the weekend. He trains for football one night a week and plays a match on another night. He also has a karate lesson, a piano lesson and a swimming lesson, and he's just started diving on the weekend.

Sam is in Liam's football team, so he trains and plays two nights a week too. But he spends his other afternoons in free play. His weekend is also free.

Liam is learning a lot of skills, there's no doubt about it. But let's look at what he's not learning because he is so overscheduled he rarely gets time to play.

First off, he's not learning how to behave when adults are not around to micromanage, intervene, mediate and control. This includes skills like independence and creative problem-solving without adult rules and instructions to follow, negotiating with peers and standing up for himself without relying on an adult to step in, and how to lose and win when adults aren't watching. Through play your boy will also have more freedom to unself-consciously try new things, explore different personas and make mistakes without feeling watched or judged. And, as we've just discussed, Sam is most likely developing way more focus and persistence through play than Liam is developing through his adult-led activities.

The research on grit shows that you don't develop it by having someone stand over you and make you practise scales, or bark orders at you from the side of a court or pool, or make you run another lap of an oval. These things very often just teach kids to perform when someone is watching them or making them do it. As soon as the person in authority's back is turned, many kids will have little motivation to continue.

Grit muscles are developed and strengthened when we are self-motivated – when we spend time focusing on something that we choose to do. Think of the boy who will spend hours perfecting his model train or spaceship, or the boys who are so engrossed in building their spy headquarters out of tree branches at the park that they don't notice it's gotten cold and dark and the mosquitos are biting their ankles. Focus and perseverance develop through play. So do personal responsibility, time management, initiative and intrinsic motivation.

In play, kids learn to please themselves. With structured activities they learn to please adults. They're also often getting the message that something is only worth doing if it leads to a grade, a trophy or some other external measure of success.

So while it's impressive that Liam can break a board with a karate chop, can sightread music and bash out some Bach, and has just got into a diving squad – all things Sam cannot do – it's also worth considering what critical life skills Liam may be missing out on because he does not have the opportunity to play.

Prepare yourself for your boy's boredom

When you introduce balance to your boy's life he may at first struggle with not being constantly occupied and entertained by activities and external stimuli. Downtime and play are what he *needs*, but if he's forgotten how to engage in free play, they may not be what he wants! It's likely he will tell you he's bored. Our generation of parents has been led to believe that boredom is a bad thing and should be avoided at all costs. In the quest to create perfect childhoods for our boys, we can feel pressured to remove our child's boredom with more adult-led activities, by entertaining them ourselves, or by buying yet more toys.

At the very least, we often see boredom as wasted time and think that a child could be engaging in some sort of developmental activity instead. Parents tell us they are worried that their child is bored at school, and assume it is a problem they or the school should solve, rather than an opportunity for their child to grow.

Boredom is part of life. If our children are not given the opportunity to deal with it in productive ways, they risk going into their teenage and adult years handling it in unproductive ways, such as with alcohol, drugs, shopping or other escapist behaviour. Dr Shefali Tsabary says that if we rescue our children from boredom they will not develop the emotional sturdiness to manage their emotions without external assistance, nor will they learn to find contentment from within. She recommends we tell our bored children, '[I]t's okay to be bored. There is nothing wrong with feeling bored. Keep being bored.'[26]

When our family jumped off the extracurricular treadmill and deliberately scheduled time for play, this initially did not go well. Let's just say our kids had a few complaints they put to management. But knowing how important free play is to their development and overall wellbeing, we pushed through the discomfort of boredom – ours as well as theirs! And then something amazing happened. They started to create, explore and imagine. Fifteen minutes after their cries of boredom they were in their room teaching their toys how to sit quietly in an imaginary class, or creating inventions out of the items in the recycle bin, or working on their handstands and somersaults. What our children needed most was for us to get out of their way and to trust them to be children.

To be clear, free play doesn't always go this well in our house. As any parent knows, there is no perfect strategy that's going to work every time. We certainly don't want to give the impression that we are perfect parents with perfectly behaved children. We are just as likely as any parent to switch on the TV for our kids to get a moment's peace! But, in general, we try to find the strength within ourselves to allow our children to be bored. When this leads to complaints and pushback, we remind ourselves that it's not our job to create a perfectly pleasant childhood for our kids, free from discomfort. Our job is to prepare them to be well-functioning adults who like themselves. And a very important part of that quest is allowing them to learn how to entertain themselves.

Keeping them out of trouble

Parents tell us that, aside from trying to cram as many skills as possible into their boys as quickly as possible, they also pack their boys' schedules with adult-led activities to keep them occupied. The theory is that if boys are kept super busy and tired they won't get themselves into trouble. Maggie Dent says that this attitude is understandable but that it can do more harm than good. 'The implicit message here is that you don't trust them,' she says. 'We need to be working with our boys, not inflicting things on them.' If our boys grow up believing that even their own parents don't have trust and faith in them, how will they ever be able to believe in themselves and feel good about who they are?

The reality is that you may well be borrowing time. What's going to happen when you stop scheduling them and send them out into the world on their own without their ever having had the opportunity to learn the life skills that come from play and unsupervised time? We don't know about you, but we'd much rather our kids stuff up and learn from their mistakes when they are young and the stakes aren't so high.

But won't he spend all his time on screens?

Another concern that we frequently hear from parents is that if they don't fill their boys' schedules with self-improvement activities, they'll be on their screens. The underlying assumption here is that screens are bad by definition and should be avoided at all costs. For years we've been warned that screens ruin our kids' attention spans, corrode their social skills and jeopardise their physical and mental health. This makes parents riddled with guilt when their kids inevitably use screens. At worst, it makes us terrified we are harming our children.

But here's the good news.

Once you get past the panic and parent shaming and look more closely, the evidence for the dire effects of screens on kids starts to fall apart. Professor Stephen Houghton from the University of Western Australia has conducted research on adolescent mental health and time spent on screens. He says many of the claims about the harmful effects of screens on kids are 'questionable'.

'I was looking at the data [allegedly] saying that if you spend too much time on screens it's going to make you depressed, anxious, lonely,' says Professor Houghton. 'But I couldn't really find any evidence showing that.'

In a study on the links between screen time and depression in adolescents, Professor Houghton and his colleagues found 'no substantial evidence for a longitudinal association between screen use and depressive symptoms'.[27] They conclude this 'undermines the likelihood that there is a causal link between screen use and subsequent changes in depression, or vice versa'.

They did, however, find that increasing screen time may indicate that some adolescents are using screens to cope with poor mental health.

Ah yes, you might be thinking, but then why does the World Health Organization (WHO) recommend that parents limit screen time for children aged three to four to no more than one hour per day, and recommend no screen time for children aged one and under?

It's true that the WHO does make these recommendations, but even the WHO acknowledges that the evidence for this advice is poor. On the very same page where the WHO makes its recommendation, it also says: 'Strong recommendations, very low quality evidence.'[28]

Dr Amy Orben and Professor Andrew Przybylski, who at the time were part of the University of Oxford's Department of Experimental Psychology, compared the effects of using digital technology on adolescents' wellbeing with other everyday activities, such as regularly eating potatoes and wearing glasses.[29] While they found a small association between technology and a decrease in adolescent wellbeing, using the same measures, they also found

111

that other everyday activities, such as eating potatoes and wearing glasses, were just as 'bad'. In fact, it turns out that wearing glasses is apparently slightly worse for adolescents' wellbeing than screen time. Nobody is suggesting that children shouldn't eat potatoes or wear glasses, because we apply perspective and common sense to these findings. We need to apply the same perspective and common sense to advice about screens. Writing in the journal *Nature Human Behaviour*, Dr Orben and Professor Przybylski concluded that this 'suggests that the effects of technology might be statistically significant, but so minimal that they hold little practical value'.[30]

And just in case you're wondering, no, these studies were not funded by the games industry or social media companies – or anyone else who stands to benefit from kids spending more time on screens. Given the lack of conclusive evidence, the Royal Society for Paediatrics and Child Health (RSPCH) in the UK has stated that it is unable to recommend a cut-off for screen time. According to the RSPCH, 'the evidence base for a direct "toxic" effect of screen time is contested, and the evidence of harm is often overstated.'[31]

Psychologist Jocelyn Brewer has a special interest in the psychology of technology. She says what's far more important than the time your kids spend on a screen is what they are watching or doing. 'Giving a ten-year-old a device that has unlimited access and not keeping an eye over what they're actually doing is really, really different to saying, "Okay, we're going to watch *Mister Maker* and then we're going to make the stuff,"' says Brewer.

The upside for screen time

In fact, keeping children off screens may do more harm than good. The reason for this is that children who do engage in online environments develop a range of digital skills – including crucial skills such as managing online privacy.[32] As the researchers for UNICEF's 'Growing up in a connected world' report – which includes interview surveys of 14,000 internet-connected kids from eleven countries – write, 'when parents impose restrictions, children engage in fewer online activities overall and tend to have weaker digital skills.'[33]

The researchers go on to say that the focus should be on the quality, not the quantity, of the screen time:

> The aim, therefore, should not be to restrict the quantity of screen time or the activities children engage in, but rather to improve the quality of children's online experiences – by focusing on what children are viewing or doing online, and on helping them to become more critical and knowledgeable in their internet use. This is where parents can exert a lot of positive influence.[34]

Fortnite and chemo

'How's your mum? She still doing chemo?'

This was a conversation a friend overheard between her son and one of his friends while they were playing computer games. The boys were playing and idly chatting and, during the game, her boy expressed empathy and care for his friend whose mum was undergoing treatment for cancer.

The game they were playing was – wait for it – Fortnite.

It's not an isolated case. Another mum told us that if it weren't for online games like Fortnite, her son would have very few friends. He'd started at a new school and most of the other boys his age played online computer games. If she had limited or banned him from playing, it would have been very difficult for him to make friends. In this case, far from causing social harm, online computer games were the gateway to friendship. And after listening to her son's conversation with his friends while online, she says that games have helped him form deeper connections with them. 'It's unlikely my son would ever talk about his feelings

113

while sitting face to face with another boy,' she said. 'But when they are engaged in an activity like gaming it is easier and safer for him to go there.'

Yes, yes, yes – we know. Reading something positive about online computer games, especially games like Fortnite, in a book about parenting boys likely goes against everything that you've seen and heard. Computer games are supposed to be *the worst* when it comes to developing social skills – particularly for boys. Parents are told over and over again that computer games have robbed generations of boys and men of their social skills and emotional lives. Fortnite has been described as 'an epidemic, a pestilence' and been accused of turning children into 'zombies'.[35] A report in the *Times of India* went one step further, claiming that some parents had compared the addictive nature of the game to cocaine.[36]

If they're not condemned for destroying boys' social skills, then computer games are held up as cesspits of sexism, misogyny, rape culture, violence and cyberbullying. These lessons in hate are arguably reinforced within online gaming culture itself, where boys come together to normalise toxic attitudes and police any deviation from the norm.

To which we say . . . quite correct. All of this can be true.

There are computer games that expose boys and men to a barrage of highly sexualised images of girls and women. And it's true that there are computer games with immersive storylines that revolve around and glorify violence, up to and including torture and sexual violence against women. (Grand Theft Auto V and its imitators, we're looking at you.)

Given all of this, why on earth would we want our boys anywhere near computer games?

The answer is that computer games and gaming communities are not all sexist, misogynistic breeding grounds for bullying. The same charges could be levelled at organised sports – almost every sporting code and club is guilty of aggressive and sexist behaviour. Almost every other week a sporting hero who was held up as a role model for boys is revealed to be a violent misogynist. And it's not just our sporting clubs. Our parliaments, boardrooms, media and educational institutions suffer from the same kinds of problems.

None of this is to say that this is okay. The point is that in spite of the truly alarming frequency of awful behaviour and attitudes in sport, politics, business, the media and education, you never hear people seriously making the case that our boys should avoid these areas of life. For example, no one suggests that boys should give up football because of the latest player scandal. The same balanced attitude should be applied to computer games.

But aren't computer games addictive?

Can you imagine the parents of little bookworms fretting about their children being addicted to reading and worrying that it will ruin their impressionable young minds? When books were a new invention this is exactly what happened.[37] A similar degree of pearl-clutching also occurred with the invention of writing, radio and television. Pretty much every new technology inspires fear before it's accepted. History is repeating itself with screens and online games.

Children, especially boys, are spending long periods of time playing online games, such that gaming and other online activities have become a significant part of their social lives and their relationships. In Australia, around 62 per cent of 8–13-year-olds play online computer games. And more boys than girls play games – 71 per cent versus 51 per cent.[38]

Unlike reading, sports and other pursuits, computer games and screens are rarely seen as having any redeeming features. They are typically considered to have only downsides and it's generally believed they should be avoided or minimised at all costs lest our boys become addicted.

There are claims that online games in particular are specifically designed to activate the pleasure and reward centres of the brain, to keep kids playing. The American Psychiatric Association (APA) even has a name for this – 'internet gaming disorder'.[39] Similarly, the World Health Organization recognises 'gaming disorder' as a psychological dysfunction.[40]

However, what you may not have heard is that this is not an official diagnosis. 'Internet gaming disorder' is considered an area for further study. While there are concerns about gaming, the jury is out as to whether it's an actual addiction. And even those researchers who think there may be cause for concern acknowledge that the evidence isn't in yet.

The research that has been done isn't always reliable. For example, one of the problems with a lot of the research generating claims about the addictive nature of gaming is that it relies on people reporting how much time they – or their kids – think they spend gaming online. In other words, it is based on people providing their best guesstimates of time spent playing.

But it turns out that people are not particularly good at this. One of the few studies that has looked at how much time people think they spent gaming versus how much time they actually spend gaming (based on logs from game servers) found that, on average, players overestimated the time they spent playing by 0.5 to 1.6 hours.[41] That's right – they overestimated the time they spent playing online games. This is important because most of the claims about the addictive nature of computer games rest on arguments about excessive time spent gaming. But if the guesstimates of this time are wrong, then the whole addiction thing starts to look even less conclusive.

This is not to suggest that problem gaming does not exist. But we need to be careful about throwing around terms like 'addiction' and 'disorder' when it comes to computer games. Simply spending lots of time doing something that you like does not, in itself, make it an addiction. As Dr Richard T. A. Wood,

116

who specialises in gaming behaviour and addiction, says, 'there are lots of activities that people undertake for long periods of time that we do not usually regard as inherently addictive. Watching television, reading, playing a musical instrument, training for a marathon are a few of the more socially acceptable examples. There have to be some negative consequences before we can say that the behaviour has become a problem.'[42]

Psychologist Jocelyn Brewer, who specialises in cyber psychology, says that gaming becomes a problem when it starts to encroach on healthy functioning in other areas of life. 'This is where you're not going to school, you're not connecting with your peers, you're not holding down a job, you've ditched your offline activities, you're not sleeping, you're not doing any of those things, because you're gaming,' says Brewer. To meet the criteria for a gaming disorder diagnosis, Brewer says this pattern of problematic behaviour would need to go on for at least twelve months. She notes that around 1–3 per cent of gamers fall into this category of 'clinically significant pathological gaming', and that an estimated further 15–20 per cent are at risk of developing this.

And even then, these are not necessarily 'pure' cases of screen addiction. In some instances, screens are a way of coping with other problems that are going on in a person's life. 'Your behaviours might appear like you are "addicted" to the internet,' says Brewer, 'but you also might have undiagnosed ASD [autism spectrum disorder] or a parent with mental illness [or] have lost a grandparent and that's the reason that you've developed a reliance on escaping into games.' In this regard, gaming or screens can be a symptom of other problems.

Alternatively, it may be that games provide ways of satisfying other needs boys have that cannot easily be met in modern environments. Brewer says a developing male brain needs to learn to take mitigated risks and to have sensory and cognitive stimulation, which games provide in abundance, but there are limited socially acceptable ways to satisfy these needs in today's society.

117

Games are one avenue for this. 'So you have needs that are not getting met except in video games,' says Brewer, 'but then we (adults) want to call you an addict for seeking to have those psychological needs met.'

If your boy is engaging in screen activities that interrupt normal life or that verge on problematic gaming, then you may need to seek professional advice. It may be that your boy is using screen-based activities to cope with certain events or experiences or to meet needs that are not otherwise being met. But for the vast majority of parents, the principle should be balance. If your boy is doing what he needs to be doing with an appropriate level of effort (not just phoning it in!), and playing computer games is not interfering with other aspects of his life or development, then take the pressure off yourself and him; it's likely that his gaming isn't a problem (and in fact could be socially and cognitively beneficial!).

But what about the bad moods?

We've heard from parents that their boy never wants to get off his devices, and that when he is finally forced off, he's irritable and angry. Some parents are concerned that the immersive nature of computer games and the endless content available on YouTube brings out the worst in their boys.

Brewer says you're not imagining things: your boy is likely to be moody when he's forced to get off the screen. But it's not necessarily the screen itself that's the problem. It's likely the problem is the timing of your telling him to stop. Quite possibly he's moody and irritable because he was in the middle of something and he had to stop before he was finished.

Brewer likens this to eating a meal at a restaurant and the server coming along and taking your food away before you've finished, saying 'Okay – food time is up!' Or imagine that your boy is three-quarters of the way through the second half of a game of soccer, and you come onto the field and tell him, 'Okay, time is up! I think now is a good time to stop, so get off the field!' You'd likely be irritable too!

Parents are unlikely to abruptly end a real-life game like soccer, because we think these games are important and we understand how they work. But here's the thing: even though online games may not interest you, they are just as important (and 'real') to your boy as offline games. This is especially true of online games that are played in pairs or in teams. When a boy leaves a game before it's finished, he's not just missing out himself. He's also potentially letting his mates down. And some games penalise players who leave in the middle of a round – just like a soccer coach might bench your son if you randomly pulled him off the field. If he's playing a game in a persistent world like Minecraft or Roblox, where the 'game' continues even after he logs off, he may have just spent an extended period of time creating something that, if he isn't permitted time to secure it, may now likely be altered, ruined or even completely destroyed by other participants in the world. As our friend Anna, who is a mum of two boys, says, 'With some games, if you just shut it down you die or you lose everything. So of course they're going to be annoyed by that. I would too!'

Alternatively, it may just be that he's experiencing a flow state, and suddenly he has to break it. 'A lot of kids get into flow state [when they play games],' says Brewer, 'and that's why they get irritated, because somebody comes and breaks that amazing flow state that they feel like they possibly don't get into in any other area of their life.'

If we treat our boy's time, social interactions, sense of achievement and progress, and feelings of flow with such little respect and understanding while he's playing games, it's not surprising he gets annoyed.

The answer, says Brewer, is to check in with your boy when he's playing. That might be as simple as asking, 'Are you hungry/thirsty/angry/tired?' Or, before he starts or rejoins a game, you might even ask him what he is looking to achieve in this next half hour of gameplay. This shows you are interested in what he's trying to do, while also making it clear that there's an endpoint to the play.

You can also help your boy to break up his gameplay by mixing in physical movement. Brewer suggests getting him to pause the game after, say, 15–25 minutes of gameplay, and then getting him to do star jumps or go outside to run around in the fresh air or play on the trampoline before continuing with the game.

Another strategy is to set and agree on time limits for play. Our friend Celia, who also has two boys, says that her boys are only irritable after online gaming if she doesn't respect that what they are doing is important to them. 'I give my boys a warning that they are going to have to get off their screens soon and then I ask them how much time they need to finish their game,' says Celia. 'If they say they need another five minutes I let them have it and tell them they have to get straight off after that.'

Brewer also suggests having a hard finish time, and then allowing 'fade-out time'. To do this, you will need to set an alarm on your phone for the hard timeout, and then use a big hourglass timer for the fade-out time that your boy can see. When the alarm goes off, tell your boy that he now has to finish up. Then turn the hourglass over so he can see how much time he has to finish up the game. Brewer says that this gives kids a chunk of time where they can choose the most logical point to stop playing. This works not only for games, but also for YouTube. 'Imagine it's like allowing a young person to finish the page or chapter of the book they are reading,' says Brewer. 'Giving fade-out time is an opportunity [for them] to get to a reasonable finishing point that they feel a small level of control over, and can communicate with their friends and team.'

The good news about computer games

Not only are computer games fine in most cases, they actually also have benefits that you probably never expected. Perhaps most obviously, as we've already mentioned, there are social benefits to boys being online. As the United Nations Children's Fund (UNICEF) notes in a report called 'Child rights and online gaming':

> Studies of online social interaction indicate that gaming can enhance a child's social relationships, as those who play together are sharing experiences that can lead to strong connections and contribute to developing teamwork skills. In this sense, games can be seen as a digital space where children can pass time, develop relationships, learn, and participate in many important aspects of life.[43]

Our friend Anna started off by being very strict about online games, not letting her son play the games his friends were playing and also not letting him play for the same length of time. Initially she thought she was doing the right thing, but she quickly realised that her son was suffering as a result. 'He was missing out on all the conversations and connections that happen between boys when they play games. He was feeling left out and isolated at school because he wasn't part of the game that happened online and didn't know what was going on,' she said. Anna now considers online gaming not as a source of mothering guilt and something to be avoided, but rather as an important part of her son's social life and wellbeing.

In a recent UK study that looked at play in digital and non-digital environments, the researchers argued that we shouldn't get hung up about whether play takes place in digital or real-life environments.[44] Rather, the researchers concluded, it's about what children are doing in those environments.

Much of the resistance parents have towards online environments is based on a large serving of nostalgia. We seem to think that kids are missing out on the great outdoors. But as psychologist and author of *Free to Learn* Dr Peter Gray says, 'We would like to think that kids are attracted to the great outdoors, but they're really attracted to other kids.'[45] And if the kids are online rather than outside, then that's where they'll go. As Gray says, 'if they're not allowed outside to play, in my opinion, it's better that they play on the computer than not playing at all. And it's better that they communicate with their friends by social media than they not have friends at all.'[46]

The more important question is: Are children playing games where they can make their own rules within the game and express themselves through play, whether it's on screen or IRL (in real life)? Sometimes digital environments don't allow children to do these things. Games that are just about buying stuff or sticking to rigid rules are poor substitutes for play. That happens in some real-world environments too: the rules are laid down for kids and they have to conform to a series of adult-led objectives. It all comes back to free play: children playing for their own sake. In the words of the authors of the UK study, if we allow children to play on their own, we allow them to 'learn and grow through exploring, experimenting and making mistakes'.

Online games and activities named in this study[47] that allow for beneficial play include:

- Roblox – e.g. role-playing and playing hide and seek
- Minecraft – e.g. building and creating
- The Sims – e.g. building houses and interacting with others
- Nintendo Switch games that encourage movement and allow children more expression than just pressing buttons – e.g. performing certain movements to win
- Animal Crossing – e.g. creating worlds.

Non-games named in this study that encourage free play on the screen include:

- Zoom – e.g. using whiteboards on which kids can draw and write together.

It doesn't take too much imagination to think about other uses for digital tools that enable connection. This might be kids cooking together via video-conferencing software or playing with action toys and cars.

Our kids have the most wonderful free play online, on Minecraft or Roblox. They play these games while simultaneously talking with their friends via FaceTime. They chat away as they play, creating amazing imaginary worlds and scenarios. They sometimes fight, but if they want to keep playing they have to resolve the conflict, so they are working on key life skills as well.

If a fear of screens is the reason you are overscheduling your son, we hereby give you permission to drop the guilt and cross this one off your worry list. You're welcome!

Treat digital environments in the same way you treat physical environments

When we talk about free play, we are not saying that kids should be allowed to roam around any digital environment without any oversight whatsoever. Digital gaming environments should be treated the same way as non-digital environments. Just as you wouldn't drop your boy off at the local shopping centre, playground or park and leave him to make his own fun, you shouldn't let him loose in a game or on a digital platform without first knowing what he's getting into. As parents, we make sure that we go into these online environments and become part of these worlds as well. We're close by and alert to any dangers, just as we would be in a real-life situation.

Psychologist Jocelyn Brewer recommends spending some time in children's digital worlds. 'Some of the homework I give parents is to go and download a game like Fortnite or PUBG and go and play it and work out how hopeless you are at it. Be vulnerable to not knowing and not having the answers,' says Brewer. 'It's an opportunity to role model a range of skills like help seeking and problem solving.'

This is not to say that all your children's screen time requires intensive parental monitoring. We rely on our children's screen time as much as the next parent to get our own work done and to have a break. But we manage risk by having an open-door policy in our house, and by setting up parental controls and regularly monitoring and talking to our kids about what they are doing on their screens.

The report card on homework

One of the most contentious issues among primary-school parents and their children, and another big factor that can prevent your boy from achieving the balance he needs, is homework. Many parents believe that homework is necessary for their son to 'get ahead'. But this turns out to be another myth, and does little other than making parents stressed and children anxious and reluctant learners. In fact, with the exception of reading at home – which should be endlessly encouraged – homework is a dud.

'We know from the research that [homework] has very little value in increasing educational outcomes, especially in primary school,' says Maggie Dent. Dent points to a 2014 Victorian par- liamentary inquiry into approaches to homework in Victorian schools which found 'strong evidence and general agreement that homework at the primary school level has little impact on academic performance'.[48]

The ineffectiveness of homework is also backed by academic researchers Mike Horsley and Richard Walker, who write in their book *Reforming Homework* that 'homework has no achieve- ment benefits for students up to grade 3 [and] negligible benefits for students in grades 4–6.'[49] In spite of the research, however, parents often demand homework from schools. It's another way that concerned parents like to 'push' or 'extend' their boys. But yet again, the focus on pushing kids could be counterproductive.

One of the reasons homework is ineffective is that by the end of the day kids' brains are essentially full. Even if they do the homework diligently they may struggle to remember what they learned. Dr Brendan Bentley, a senior lecturer in the School of Education at the University of Adelaide, says that 'Younger kids have less capacity to hold things in their working memory. If you're really tired, your ability to retain items is reduced.'[50]

And it's not just the mental load of homework that can overwhelm kids. Children may not be sufficiently developed to complete homework tasks that are set. 'I have heard of four-year-old children getting an hour and a half [of homework]. They have to go home and colour within the lines,' says Maggie Dent, who states that many children, especially boys, lack the fine motor skills to successfully complete the tasks they're assigned. 'That horrifies me. You're asking children to do something that they're actually not developmentally able to do. And you're asking them to do it over and over again,' says Dent. 'We are stealing childhood in the hope that we're going to have academically bright kids.'

There is also the long-term emotional and physical toll that homework can take. It can be a significant source of stress and conflict within the home. We can't tell you how many stories we have heard about homework that also include raised voices, slammed doors and tears. There would have to be a very good reason for you to invite that level of conflict and stress into your home, night after night. Homework is not it!

That's not to say that children learn nothing from homework. It just may not provide the type of lessons parents are hoping their children will learn. Dent says that homework can instil a loathing of any kind of formal learning. 'Some of the kids are getting twenty-five new words to study, four nights a week. I'm sorry, that is not how the brain learns,' says Maggie Dent. 'All you do is make them hate words.'

125

Of course, some will point to other benefits of homework, beyond the academic. Homework, so the argument goes, teaches kids time-management and study skills while instilling in them good work habits. But there is precious little evidence to show that's the case. Take time management as an example. Maggie Dent says that in many instances the school sees the completed product without seeing what went into the activity. 'Some kids take two hours to do what is a set piece of 20 minutes. And then we have perfection-driven children who do the task over and over and over again, to an unhealthy level.' And if homework only gets done when parents nag, shout or bribe, then it's not the child managing time, it's the parents.

If homework is turning your home into a war zone, Dent recommends having a respectful conversation with your child's school about what you feel is best for your child and your family. Because, really, what's the point of tears, tension and late nights when homework has little to no educational benefit?

It's fair to say that most adults don't like to bring work home with them. It can cause stress, exhaustion and resentment and can put pressure on relationships. If *we* don't like it, why on earth would we think it's a good idea for young children to bring work home with them?

Sleep

If you have any concerns about your boy's mental health, impulse control, emotional regulation, resilience, friendships, appetite, physicality, energy levels, concentration, memory or academic performance, the very first place to look is sleep. That's right. Sleep. Get sleep right, and everything works better.

We mean everything.

While people are becoming increasingly aware of the need for a good night's sleep – and the adverse consequences if we

126

don't get it – sleep still is not given the priority you might expect for something that is so integral to all aspects of health and wellbeing. And when it comes to a choice between an enriching activity or an early night's sleep, sleep is often sacrificed. Professor Sarah Blunden, psychologist and director of the Australian Centre for Education in Sleep, says that sleep is becoming less of a priority and more something kids do after they have done all the 'important things' such as scheduled activities and homework.

'There is a lot more competition,' Professor Blunden says, 'and we tend to push [kids] harder and harder ... we do give up sleep for things that we find "better for us": better for our future, better for our intellect, better for our development and learning.'

But make no mistake, there is *nothing* better for your boy's development, wellbeing and learning than enough sleep. There is simply no class, tutor or activity that can make up for chronic sleep deprivation. In fact, prioritising these things over sleep is counterproductive. Your boy is unlikely to learn effectively or perform at his best if he does not get enough sleep.

And how much sleep is enough? Many parents are surprised by just how much sleep their boy needs. The Sleep Health Foundation recommends that toddlers aged 1–2 years get 11–14 hours per day, and that preschoolers aged 3–5 years get 10–13 hours. If your boy is in primary school, he needs 9–11 hours of sleep per night.[51]

How to get your boy to sleep

Some kids are naturally good sleepers. Others are shockers! But the good news is that sleep is a skill, and with the right strategies and daily practice, sleep can be vastly improved. 'Sleep is modifiable,' says Professor Blunden. She suggests making small changes, such as adjusting your boy's bedtime and wake-up time by 15 minutes every 2–3 days. When he's adjusted to the new times, move them by 15 minutes again, until he's getting the right amount of sleep.

Make sleep your number-one priority. Look at your family routine and work out what needs to be changed or cut so that your boy is in bed early enough to get enough sleep. We know life is busy, but the more highly we prioritise something, the more likely we are to do it.

For the best results, decide on your boy's bedtime routine and stick to it. Make it exactly the same, at exactly the same time every day. Ideally the routine should start about an hour before you want him to nod off, so he can relax and get ready for sleep. Your non-negotiable bedtime routine might include: bath, teeth, reading, toilet, bed. Crucially, this time should not involve screens, as the blue light and the stimulation of devices can work against your boy winding down for bed.

Balance takes courage

Building your boy's foundational pillar of balance takes courage and prioritisation. It is so easy to be swept up in the arms race of overscheduling and to succumb to the myth of pushing. We hope this chapter gives you the confidence to reject the pressure to push your son too hard. The best things you can do for your boy's wellbeing, academic performance and future success are to facilitate sleep, and to ease up and allow him to play freely (including online), and discover and pursue his own interests for their own intrinsic rewards.

If you're still in doubt, let us ask you to reflect on the current state of boys. We have been pushing and overscheduling children for years, and they are 'less happy, more stressed, lonely, depressed and suicidal when compared to any previous generation – and those descriptions were identified prior to COVID-19 and all the resulting anxiety it produced.'[52]

The first step in another direction when you're on the wrong path is always the hardest. You will feel as though you are breaking the rules. But know that in changing directions you are doing the right thing – and that you will have a better chance of arriving at the intended destination.

Just tell me what to do!

The idea that boys need to be 'pushed' in order to reach their potential is a myth that can sow low self-esteem, poor motivation and perseverance, lack of resilience and resentment towards parents. If you want your boy to thrive and reach his potential, it is far more effective to create a balanced life.

- Create a motivated and achievement-focused boy by helping him understand the connection between effort and achievement. Focus on behaviour that leads to achievement, rather than on outcomes, and help your boy set and strive towards achievable goals so he will have faith in his ability to achieve what he wants when he works towards it.
- Competition can be healthy and motivating when your boy is striving to 'do good' for his own internal satisfaction. Steer him away from competition that teaches him that he must compete to 'be good' ('I'll be lovable if I win') or 'look good' ('I will impress people if I win'). You want your boy to be able to like himself all the time, not just when he's beating someone else.
- The best way to develop your boy's motivation, grit, social skills, sense of purpose, wellbeing and capacity for learning is to make free play a non-negotiable part of his life.
- Allow him the space and time to develop and pursue his own interests and hobbies, away from the structures of formal lessons, coaching or training.
- When it comes to screens and online gaming, it's about quality, not quantity. Games that allow your boy to use his imagination,

control what happens in the game and foster social connection can actually be beneficial.

- Enough sleep makes every aspect of your boy's life better. Create the conditions for your boy to get adequate sleep and prioritise maintaining it.

5

A boy who likes himself has mastery and independence

While Ben was stuck at home with COVID he decided to build a card tower like the one he saw in his book. Things weren't working out as easily as his book made out. The picture in the book showed an impressive structure three levels high. So far, Ben had only managed to balance the cards together to make a couple of A-frames. When he added more cards to make another layer, all of his good work collapsed like, well, a house of cards. Understandably, Ben was getting more and more frustrated.

After a time he went into his parents' bedroom and threw himself on the bed and sobbed. Ben begged them to help him. If his parents hadn't both been exhausted and feverish with COVID they probably would have helped him build his tower, if not built it entirely themselves. Instead they gave Ben a cuddle and suggested some new techniques to try. Dad suggested using the rough side of the cards so there was more grip. Mum suggested Ben stand well back from the table so he didn't accidentally knock it and make the cards fall.

After Ben had calmed down and dried his tears he went back to the table to try to build his card tower again.

There was more frustration, more tears.

And then more frustration.

And more again.

And then, eventually, success.

Ben had built his own card tower. Three levels high, just like in the picture. And he'd done it all by himself!

'I did it! I did it!' Ben shouted as he ran into the bedroom to share his triumph with his parents. His face was lit up with pride, bliss and empowerment. This moment might seem like a drop in the ocean of a lifetime, but these small wins are the essence of building real and enduring self-esteem. What Ben was experiencing is mastery – the process of facing a challenge, struggling yet persisting through frustration and failure, and then eventually succeeding. Ben *wanted* a card tower. What he *needed* was the mastery and independence of doing it himself. In time Ben will most likely forget about his tower, but he now knows that persistence will bring success. And that lesson can last a lifetime.

If Ben's parents had 'helped' him build the tower, they most likely would have denied him the gift of struggle, frustration and failure. It might sound counterintuitive to refer to these things as 'gifts', especially since many parents (including us!) often feel an overwhelming desire to protect their children from unpleasant feelings. But the elation and self-belief that Ben felt only come from mastery. And the road to mastery is paved with struggle. You cannot give your child a shortcut to mastery. You cannot go there for them or carry them on your back. You can't give them mastery through praise, or through things. Mastery can only come from within.

Think back to the times in your life when you have achieved mastery. Perhaps one of them was the first time you rode a bike by yourself. Chances are you didn't sit on a bike for the first time and effortlessly pedal off into the sunset. If you did, then it's likely the occasion would not have been memorable. One of the reasons bike riding is such an important milestone in a child's life is that it can only be achieved through the struggle and frustration of skinned knees. It is something that a child must do all on their own. Your parents may have been there coaching you and cheering you on or filming you with their video camera as you learned to ride your bike for the first time, but it was something you had to do all by yourself.

As an adult, you might have experienced the high of mastery when you first learned to drive and then made it to your full licence. Or when you completed a half marathon, learned how to use tricky software, or taught yourself to knit. All of these achievements would have come after a period of struggle. The feeling of satisfaction that resulted probably made your day.

If your boy does not struggle he will not achieve mastery. And if he doesn't achieve mastery he will find it difficult to believe in himself and like himself. According to the godfather of positive psychology, Martin Seligman, depriving your boy of mastery is as damaging to his self-esteem as if you 'belittled, humiliated, and physically thwarted [him] at every turn'.[1]

In this chapter we are going to show you how building your boy's essential pillar of mastery and independence will bring him joy for life and real, enduring self-esteem. And how allowing your boy to struggle will inoculate him against being fearful and lazy. It can also reduce the likelihood and severity of anxiety and depression.[2]

We cannot anticipate all the challenges our boys are going to face in life. We will not always be there to protect them. Building your boy's essential pillar of mastery and independence will give him the inner strength and resources he needs to endure life's struggles and make the most of its opportunities.

But first, let's talk about what mastery is, and what it isn't.

Mastery does not have to mean a cabinet full of trophies

The word 'mastery' has become so warped it is almost unrecognisable. This is particularly the case when it comes to modern parenting. It sometimes seems that unless your boy is reading

133

Proust in French by age three, playing the violin by age four, intimidating a chess grandmaster by age five and being chased by scouts for the Olympic swimming squad by age six, then not only is your kid not a master, you're also parenting wrong. Things only get worse when you open up your socials and see newsfeeds filled with carefully curated posts about the stellar achievements of other people's kids, when your boy is, you know, just being a kid and doing kid things.

So, to be absolutely clear, when we talk about mastery, we are not talking about winning awards and external validation. Sure, those things can be nice, but they're not mastery. Mastery is about having the skills and the practice to do life.

There.

That's it.

And when we say 'do life', we don't mean *everything* in life. We're talking about age- and developmentally appropriate things.

Nor do we mean high achievers. In fact, high achievers can be at risk of low-esteem because they spend so much time training or studying to achieve excellence in one particular thing that they may not have much experience in other aspects of life. Dr Michele Borba, who interviewed high-achieving students and athletes for her book *Thrivers*, was struck by just how unprepared many of these high-achieving kids were for life. They were good at doing tests or kicking goals or jumping hurdles, but many felt unable to cope with life outside the classroom or off the sporting field. Borba found that many of these kids feared growing up and suffered from anxiety, depression and an overall sense of inadequacy.[3]

What these high achievers are missing is what psychologists call 'self-efficacy', which is 'a person's belief in their ability to succeed in a particular situation'.[4] Boys don't have to be child prodigies to have self-efficacy. Instead, they need to be able to persist and try new things, even when they find them hard or fail at them the first, second, third or the twentieth time.

These activities don't have to be earth-shattering achievements that you plaster all over your socials. They can be utterly mundane, everyday activities – like housework, for example. In fact, it's even better if they're mundane. Even now, sons do fewer household chores than daughters on average, which means boys are likely to be unprepared for being independent adults. A 2016 report by UNICEF found that girls aged 5–14 do, on average, 40 per cent more housework than boys. And this unequal time spent doing household chores is true even in countries with a reputation for equality, such as Norway and Finland.

It's crucial that boys learn these skills, since it's not only embarrassing to not know how to look after yourself – or to take care of the people you love – it's also disempowering. Life can feel scary and threatening if you have to rely on other people to take care of your basic needs.

What not to do

Many of us grew up with the self-esteem movement, which taught us that we can build a child's mastery through boosting their self-esteem. It was logical as far as it went. After all, the people who were most competent and capable seemed to have high self-esteem, and boosting self-esteem therefore seemed to be a shortcut to developing more capable and competent people. Tell a kid often enough how great they are, and, so the theory went, they will believe it. Then they'll be on the path to high self-esteem, which, in turn, will lead to high achievement.

In hindsight that turned out to be complete rubbish.

The problem is that it gets things the wrong way around, confusing the cause with the end result. It assumes that mastery comes from high self-esteem when, in fact, self-esteem comes from mastery.

The lesson here is that you cannot give a child self-esteem with word presents. (Actually, you cannot *give* a child self-esteem at all.)

135

We can tell our children that they are great or awesome at music, maths, football or skateboarding, but without mastery this is essentially a waste of time. When it comes to building your boy's self-esteem, your words count for very little. Real and enduring self-esteem, the kind your boy needs if he is going to grow up liking himself, can only bloom from within. The foundation of good self-esteem is the belief that you have what it takes to cope with what life throws at you.[5]

In fact, telling your boy 'You are awesome' all the time could do more harm than good. According to Martin Seligman, 'By emphasising how a child *feels*, at the expense of what the child *does* – mastery, persistence, overcoming frustration and boredom, and meeting challenge – parents and teachers are making this generation of children more vulnerable to depression.'[6]

The truth is that self-esteem is not an end in itself. It is an outcome of doing something well. Focus on helping your son to engage in action – to do well at the tasks of life – and the feeling of self-esteem will take care of itself.

The secret to mastery

If you want your boy to develop mastery, then get ready to watch him fail, spectacularly and often.

It sounds counterintuitive – wrong, even – doesn't it?

But the truth is that the most successful people fail and feel disappointment frequently. Legend (AKA thousands of internet memes) has it that Thomas Edison failed 10,000 times before he invented the light bulb.[7] Whether the figure of 10,000 is accurate or not, you can be sure that Edison didn't invent the light bulb the first time he sat down to try. And the first disappointment (and all those that followed) didn't prevent him from trying again. If he had never learned to tolerate disappointment we might still be using candles.

You can see the same ability to tolerate failure in basketballer Michael Jordan, who famously said: 'I've missed more than 9000 shots in my career. I've lost almost 300 games. Twenty-six times I've been trusted to take the game-winning shot and missed. I've failed over and over and over again in my life. And that is why I succeed.'[8]

Persisting, practising and failing – and (most likely) repeating the same process of persisting, practising and failing some more – are the secrets to mastery. Learning to tolerate disappointments rather than trying to outrun them or pretend they never happened or blame someone else is what it takes to succeed.

This is often difficult and frustrating for parents to watch. We want to get in there to help our boys. Sometimes we want to rescue them from feelings of frustration and disappointment. But we need to allow them to experience these feelings. This is because absolutely everybody feels this way from time to time. It's what people do next that separates those who thrive from those who flounder. Do you quit? Or do you endure the discomfort and accept this setback as an essential stepping stone on the path to mastery?

The best thing about this kind of self-esteem – real self-esteem that is built on action rather than empty boosterism – is that it is self-powering. Once your boy has proven to himself that he is able to tackle new challenges and can, in time, master them and cope with whatever life throws at him, he is likely to be a flourisher rather than a quitter. More likely than not, he will approach life with more confidence, persistence and bravery, which in turn will lead to further success and mastery and greater self-esteem.[9]

Create a bank of mastery experiences

Having life skills is a crucial part of mastery. But just having a list of skills is not, in itself, sufficient. What's equally important is for your boy to do hard things. Not only does this help him develop mastery muscles, it also builds a bank of evidence so that he knows with absolute certainty that he is capable of facing struggles head on. Psychologists call this 'mastery experiences'.[10] These are experiences from your boy's own life where he initially struggled with activities or challenges but eventually succeeded.

This knowledge – that he is capable of working at challenges that he at first found difficult, even impossible, and can cope with what life throws at him – is armour against insecurity and anxiety. At its core, anxiety is a fear that you won't be able to cope with something that hasn't happened yet. While stress is a physical response to an immediate threat or stressor, such as a barking dog or too much homework, anxiety – excluding trauma and complex cases – is triggered and amplified by a lack of independence and mastery.[11]

These fears might be more perceived than real. For example, your boy might be anxious about going on camp, not because he will actually be in danger, but because he *perceives* that he doesn't have the resources to cope with what may happen. If we genuinely believe that we are masterful and have the skills to deal with whatever life throws at us, we won't worry about not being able to cope with future events and therefore won't have any cause for anxiety.

You can use a bank of evidence of past successes to support your boy in facing challenges and turning his limiting tendencies into winning characteristics. You might say, 'Remember when you first got your bike, and it was really hard to balance, but you kept practising and now you just hop on and start pedalling?' Or, 'Remember when you were learning to read and you had to sound out every letter and look at the pictures to help you? Now you can read whole pages – even if there are no pictures.' These examples are all evidence that he can do hard things.

These don't have to be groundbreaking achievements. They might include your boy learning to crack an egg, folding a fitted sheet, doing his first ollie on a skateboard, reading a paragraph of text by himself or completing a multiplication table. What is absolutely crucial to mastery is that these are your boy's own experiences. They aren't stories about other people conquering their fears, or merely words of encouragement. While there is nothing wrong with either of these things – modelling persistence can be effective too – nothing beats firsthand experience. As social psychologist Albert Bandura puts it, these experiences 'provide the most authentic evidence of whether one can muster whatever it takes to succeed. Success builds a robust belief in one's personal efficacy'.[12]

These experiences are also transferrable from one context to another. If your boy is struggling to play a musical instrument, for example, you might remind him that he faced similar struggles with reading or with maths, but kept at it and succeeded. Or, if he is struggling with shooting hoops, you might remind him that he found kicking a footy hard at first, but he practised it and can now do it. Building up a store of these experiences is incredibly important to building mastery. The only way your boy will form the belief that he can cope with life's challenges is by facing challenges and creating his own bank of evidence about his capabilities.

What matters in building mastery experiences is that your boy does (age-appropriate) hard things that he's never done before. If he succeeds at a range of fairly easy tasks with little or no effort, it is unlikely he will learn what it is to really persist at more difficult challenges. And if he is used to succeeding with little or no effort, when he does encounter a more difficult challenge, he may well come to the conclusion that it is beyond him. In Bandura's words, 'If people experience only easy successes, they come to expect quick results and are easily discouraged by failure'.[13]

From reluctant reader to speaking dog

You may be thinking that your boy was just born a certain way and that there's nothing you or he can do about it. You might have a happy boy, a shy boy or an anxious boy. One parent told us that her son doesn't like to learn, that he's not a learner. Whatever the attributes, these are often presented as fixed and unchangeable – as if kids are born that way and there's nothing you can do to change it.

It makes sense that parents think this way. Children really do pop out with different personalities and characteristics. Some are naturally talented in one area, such as drawing, music or athletics. But this isn't the end of the story. The reality is that, far from having fixed attributes, kids just start from different places.

Take the Hallam family. They have two girls who naturally approached reading in very different ways. Yes, this example is about girls, but stick with us, because the lesson applies just as much to boys. Their older child, Issy, was one of those kids who wanted to read as soon as she could talk. Reading has always been her thing. Their younger daughter, Sienna, on the other hand, thought books were much more useful as things to chew on or to build towers with that could then be leapt off. When Sienna started reading, she'd invent all kinds of diversions to avoid having to even try. She'd make jokes, clown about or yawn really loudly. Or it would all just end in tears. To be clear, we're not talking about dyslexia or other learning disabilities here. This was just plain old reluctant reading. Unlike her sister, Sienna found reading hard, so she didn't want to do it.

Same parents, same household, totally different approaches to reading.

Sienna's parents realised that reluctant reading wasn't actually the core problem. Rather, it was a symptom of Sienna not having mastery and independence. The truth was that Sienna was afraid of failure. She didn't want to practise reading because she was afraid of making mistakes. So she just avoided it altogether. And she built it up as being harder and harder in her mind.

Her parents could have wasted hours and buckets of tears – theirs as well as Sienna's – trying to solve a reluctant reading problem, when what they actually needed to do was build up Sienna's mastery and independence. But the challenge was figuring out how to do that. Sienna had such an aversion to reading that she'd already shut that option down. As such, they couldn't use reading to build her mastery skills.

This is where Sienna's bank of mastery experiences came in. While she didn't have many deposits against reading in her bank of mastery, she'd built up considerable wealth in other areas, such as swinging on monkey bars, skateboarding and doing puzzles. These were areas in which, like reading, Sienna had struggled for a while, but had ultimately succeeded.

Rather than just telling Sienna that she could read if she practised, her parents presented her own experiences back to her as evidence that she could try hard things and succeed. They reminded her that when she started skateboarding she couldn't even stand on the board without holding onto something for balance. But she practised and, in spite of falling off a lot of the time, she kept trying, and now skateboarding is easy for her. Her parents told Sienna that reading was the same – that if she kept practising and trying, even when it was hard, she would succeed. They reminded her that she was really good at doing hard things.

The wonderful thing about a bank of evidence is that Sienna didn't have to take her parents' word for it that she was capable. Instead, she could see how she had mastered other skills in her life, and that if she applied the same tenacity to reading then she would succeed. It's much easier to convince a child (or an adult, for that matter) of something if they have personally experienced it themselves, rather than by just using words.

As well as making withdrawals from the bank of evidence and connecting them with her present challenges, Sienna's parents also changed the focus of their praise. Rather than praising her for sounding out words correctly or for finishing a reader, they'd praise her for trying hard words. (We'll talk more about motivation and praise later in this chapter.) Within a matter of weeks – that's all it took, weeks – Sienna had left her days of being a reluctant reader behind.

And then, a few months later, her parents saw just how powerful a bank of evidence can be in building a child's sense of mastery. Sienna was on a walk with her parents and she told her mum that she was going to invent an app to translate dog barks into human language. She took her mum through her plan, and then said, 'But I'll have to go to the library first because I'll need to read a book on how to speak dog.'

Here was a child who had gone from not wanting to read at all, to telling her mother that the only thing standing between her and her dog translator app was getting her hands on a book about dog speak.

If mastery is a superpower, fear of failure is kryptonite

Think back to when your boy first discovered the joys of climbing. If he is still in this phase then take a moment to observe him closely as he tries to climb something that is a stretch of his capabilities. You'll likely notice that the pathway for him to achieve his goal (climbing to the top of something) is punctuated by micro-struggles and failures. He'll fall over, he'll slip down and he'll fall off. Each time this happens he will experience feelings of frustration and disappointment.

Instead of giving up in passive helplessness or a fit of rage, he'll tolerate the uncomfortable feelings and try again. And again. And again. He will keep trying with laser-like focus and keep tolerating unpleasant feelings until he succeeds and achieves mastery. When he does achieve his goal, notice the look on his face (or, if your boy is older, try to remember the look he used to have). What you see is confidence, pride, real self-esteem, a boy who likes himself.

The ability to tolerate struggle and to persist in the face of difficulty seems to be innate in very young children. In fact, toddlers are often better equipped to deal with these kinds of difficult feelings than many adults. As they get older, though, children unlearn this crucial life lesson. They become self-conscious and fearful of failing. And sometimes they avoid the possibility of failure at all costs. This prevents them from achieving the sense of mastery necessary for them to like themselves. And while they may be spared the pain of failure, they will also keep their lives small and limit their potential – possibly with lifelong consequences. If mastery is a superpower, a fear of failure is kryptonite.

If you want him to learn resilience and be hopeful, let him fail

One of the main reasons that kids learn to fear failure and mistakes and decide that it's better not to try than to try and fail is inexperience. They often simply don't have enough experience with failure. And sometimes it is us parents who don't allow our kids to have these experiences. With the very best of intentions we might rush in and rescue our kids before they have a chance to fail.

This is understandable. We feel our children's pain as if it's our own and we want to spare them from it. We believe one of the biggest reasons our generation of parents is inclined to intervene in our children's lives more than previous generations is simply that we are there to see our children's struggles. When we were young and hanging out with the neighbourhood kids on the streets and at creeks and God knows where else, there were often no parents around. On lots of occasions there probably should have been! Many of us grew up with parents who didn't have to 'choose' to let us struggle. We struggled because much of the time adults simply weren't there to help us. If we let our kids wander off and get up to some of the things we did – such as swinging on vines over fast-flowing creeks, or hurtling down steep roads on bikes with no brakes or helmets, or setting grass fires in suburban

143

bushland (yes, one of us is guilty of this) – we'd likely get a knock on the door from Child Protection.

It is entirely appropriate for us to be more present and more protective of our children. But this means that our generation needs to actively choose to allow our kids to fail. And this is not easy. If you're there watching your boy fail, you have to make a conscious decision about when to and when not to intervene. You know your boy and his capabilities best, so you should make that call. Know, though, that while you may feel pain, there is a big upside to not intervening. In her book *Daring Greatly*, Professor Brené Brown writes that kids who are allowed to fail are more resilient, motivated and resourceful. They also tend to have better mental health and greater levels of self-belief than kids who have not experienced struggle and adversity.[14]

That's all well and good in theory. But it's much harder to do in practice. This is where there can be a clash between the head and the heart. Professor Brown also found that parents who worried about the potentially negative effects of children being rescued are the same parents who swoop in to rescue their kids.[15] In our heads, we understand that we need to let our kids fight their own battles and deal with their own failures. But in our hearts – and in the heat of the moment – we often struggle to do this. We confess to doing exactly the same with our children.

But we all need to be brave enough to allow our kids to fail, because protecting them from failure makes them think that failure is so bad their parents have to save them from it, and that it is to be avoided at all costs. Rescuing robs your boy of self-belief because you are effectively telling him that you don't believe he's capable of managing on his own. We could also be denying him the opportunity to experience hope. 'Hope is a function of struggle. If we want our children to develop high levels of hopefulness, we have to let them struggle,' Professor Brown writes in *Daring Greatly*.[16]

It sounds counterintuitive. Wouldn't struggle rob kids of hope rather than giving it to them?

The answer is no.

Hopeful people aren't the ones who sit on the sidelines of life revelling in feel-good platitudes and wishful thinking. Research shows that hopeful people have plenty of firsthand experience of failure and adversity. It is through overcoming adversity – not by being protected from it – that these people have proven to themselves that they can achieve their goals because they are persistent and can endure uncomfortable feelings. If things don't work out the first time, or even the fourth (or the 10,000th!), they have the courage to try again.[17]

It is through experience (not our pep talks) that kids fully understand that failure and mistakes are a necessary stepping stone to mastery and success. We are not responsible for keeping our children happy 24/7. Our job is not to protect them from life's failures and disappointments. It is to prepare them to be independent, capable adults who have learned how to cope with life's challenges so they can flourish.

What are the penalties for failing in your family?

One reason kids may learn to fear failure has to do with penalties for mistakes. We might tell our kids that it's okay to make mistakes, but if we lose our temper at them when they spill paint on the table, lose their shoes, forget their lunch or do poorly on a test, they will quickly learn that mistakes and failures are a source of pain and shame and should be avoided at all costs. As Maggie Dent says in *Mothering Our Boys*, 'We are much braver to make mistakes if we are still valued after we mess up!'[18]

Of course, we're all human, and adults make mistakes too. So it's very likely that you've responded to your child's mistakes in ways that would not be considered parenting best practice. We certainly have! But if we want our kids to truly be okay with failure, we have to show them that we are okay with their failings too.

When your boy does make a mistake, see it as a learning opportunity. Don't focus on what has happened, focus on what he can do next time. For example, ask him what he can do so it doesn't happen again. By asking him what he could do differently next time, you are helping him to fail well. By 'fail well', we mean using each mistake and failure as feedback and an opportunity for improvement. Some people fail and then get back up and do exactly the same thing again. This doesn't lead to progress or mastery. Successful people use failure as an opportunity to learn and develop. They say to themselves, 'Well, that didn't work out how I wanted it to – what can I try next time that might lead to a better result?'

This way of thinking is empowering and also hopeful. Both of these things are important if your boy is going to grow up liking himself. A caveat here: if your child spills milk all over the floor and you're late for childcare or school, it may not be the best time for a learning opportunity. Be gentle on yourself, too!

Change your boy's goal

If your boy has gotten into the habit of refusing to do something because he thinks he won't win or excel at it, help him to redefine his goal. An example of this strategy came from a mother who read *Raising Girls Who Like Themselves* and applied the principles of mastery to her son, who did not want to run the school cross-country. The previous year, he had refused to run the cross-country because he knew that he would not come close to winning it. His fear of failure meant that he decided it was better to not even try. For the next year's cross-country his mother talked to him about changing the goal from winning to participating. She said, 'Our family value is bravery. We have a go, even when it's hard and we're unlikely to win.'

The boy did run the cross-country. He didn't win or get a place, but that didn't matter. His mother celebrated his bravery in

146

having a go and told him he should be proud of himself for trying. The following week the boy got a school award for his sportsmanship. 'I just started crying,' his mother said. 'I couldn't believe the difference in him from last year to this year.'

Perhaps your family value (and your boy's goal) could be persevering, doing hard things, or improving on past performance. The important thing is that reaching the goal should not depend on external measures such as someone else's inferiority or judgement. The most empowering goals are internal and are within a boy's power to achieve.

Model mistakes

In our society, masculinity in particular is often presented as a mistake-free zone, as an uninterrupted series of success after success. Failure is often shown to be a weakness to be avoided at all costs. If failure happens, as it inevitably will, it is covered up and never spoken of again. But if boys never see adults, particularly fathers, father figures or other men in their lives, being at ease with making mistakes, then how can we expect them to be?

Share stories with your boy about times when you failed at some goal. This failure might be reasonably small, such as burning a meal or ruining the cupboard you were 'fixing'. But make sure your boy also knows you've failed at things that had higher stakes, such as missing out on something that you really wanted. This example might be from your school days, such as missing out on school captain, or it might be a new job or a promotion. While your son might not be old enough to understand the complexities of school or office politics, he will understand that it was something that you wanted and worked for but still missed out on. The message that you want him to learn is that all of us miss out on some things sometimes. And then tell him how you got back up and continued on regardless.

You want him to learn that failure is not a character flaw, but rather feedback about how to act. Failing at something is not a measure of self-worth, it is a problem that has not been solved yet. Help him understand that the problem is not a fixed character trait; it is a behaviour that can be worked on. It's the difference between being ('I'm a terrible speller') and doing ('I currently struggle with spelling'). One is an internalised assessment about who he is as a person. The other is something he does, and that he can work to change.

The season for planting the seeds of mastery and independence is now

You might be thinking that this is all fine, but that surely harsh lessons about failure and the struggles that come with mastery and independence can wait for some time in the future. Parents have told us that their kids are too young to struggle. Their kids, they say, should be able to enjoy their precious years of childhood – and, in any case, when kids are young they're unlikely to learn lessons of failure and to develop independence.

It's a nice idea, but remember what our end goal is. Our most important job as parents is not to curate 'perfect childhoods' for our boys. It is to build a strong enough foundation so our boys can thrive in life when we are not there to protect them. This foundation of mastery and independence takes years to build, so we need to start laying the bricks now so our boys are prepared when they really need these skills. Here are three small strategies to start using now that will give your boy the skills he needs to thrive in the future.

Use praise to motivate rather than to celebrate

Praise is powerful. But it can be a double-edged sword. Used the right way, it can strengthen a boy's sense of independence and mastery. Used the wrong way, it can corrode it. Praising your son for practising and trying, even when he didn't get the results he wanted, is far more valuable than celebrating the end result. It sends a message to your boy about what's really important. It shows that you value skills and character strengths like persistence and courage that he can apply to many other areas of his life beyond what he's being praised for. And, crucially, that he can replicate these behaviours.

If you only praise your son for the end result – the gold star, the trophy, the test result – this can diminish his motivation and sense of self-worth rather than building them. This is because, very often, children can't control outcomes. If you only praise your boy for the end result, what will happen when he doesn't get the gold star or when he moves up to a higher reading level but stumbles over new words? He may feel that he's no longer worthy of your praise – or, more worryingly, your love and acceptance. In some cases, he may not try at all, because not trying is emotionally safer than not succeeding and risking losing love and acceptance.

But if we praise persistence and courage, then our kids will always have it within their power to succeed on their own terms, so they will be motivated to keep striving towards their goal. To refer back to Sienna's reading, her parents made a really big deal about her trying. They celebrated her courage, persistence and willingness to have a go even when she didn't know the answer – in fact, especially when she didn't know the answer.

This doesn't just apply to informal types of learning. It also applies to school grades and report cards. Actually, it particularly applies to these kinds of formal reports. Parents can be so invested in the outcome that they can forget that effort, persistence and learning are more important.

Learning and behaviour specialist Noël Janis-Norton recommends a technique she calls 'descriptive praise' to foster good behaviour in your boy and reduce behaviours you don't want.[19] Descriptive praise can work for anything from instilling good manners and getting your boy to pick up his dirty socks, to reducing aggressive behaviour. It's also great for helping your boy to overcome his fear of failure and to try new and hard things.

Descriptive praise is as it sounds. You simply describe what your son is doing, or not doing. For example, if you are focusing on helping him overcome the fear of failure, you might say, 'You fell off your scooter but you got back on – that was brave.' These achievements don't have to be major accomplishments, but rather small behaviours that are heading in the right direction. If you want to help your boy master self-restraint, you might say, 'I noticed you waited your turn – that was patient of you,' or, 'You asked your sister if you could play with her doll instead of just taking it – that was considerate,' or, 'I notice you're feeling frustrated but you didn't yell – that shows real strength of character.'

To encourage independence, you might say, 'I noticed you wiped up the floor after you spilt your milk without me having to tell you – that was very responsible,' or, 'You carried your schoolbag to school without complaining – you're taking responsibility for your belongings.'

Our kids naturally want our attention and want to please us, so when we show them that we notice their good (or okay) behaviours and state exactly why these behaviours please us, our kids will be motivated to replicate them. The other benefit of descriptive praise is that you are helping to build an identity based on good qualities and values. The more your boy hears positive qualities attached to the things he has done, such as being brave, persistent, considerate, strong and independent, the more likely he is to see himself as that sort of person.

Taking responsibility for belongings

One small step towards mastery that you can implement right now is to get your boy to practise being responsible for his own belongings. This is a fairly simple lesson that will have a massive impact on your boy's self-belief and pay dividends as he gets older.

Begin with his kinder bag or schoolbag. In our research we were amazed by just how often educators and child-development experts talk about the benefits of children carrying their own bags. For starters, this is an antidote to entitlement. One school principal told us that she shudders when she sees kids running out the school gate with their parents trailing behind like pack-horses, carrying their bags. 'What message does that send to the children?' the principal asked. 'That Mum is their servant and it's her job to pick up after them?'

Making boys carry their own bags also teaches independence and responsibility for belongings. Parents sometimes tell us that their boy is too young or too tired to carry his own bag. If this is the case, then, within a matter of weeks, if your boy is non-disabled, he should be able to build up the strength and fitness to manage on his own. This is an excellent way to teach your boy that he is stronger and more capable than he thought, and to show him that you believe in his capabilities. Just remember that when we rush in and deny our kids the opportunity to do something for themselves, we are implicitly telling them that we don't think they are capable or strong enough.

Navigating space

At our children's primary school, children literally never go anywhere alone. They even have toilet buddies so they don't go to the toilets on their own. Then children get to high school and we throw them in the deep end, and expect them to get to their locker and to different classrooms without any practice and without any past evidence reassuring them that they are capable. Imagine how insecure you would feel and how scary the world would seem if you felt you were incapable of going anywhere on your own.

You can start teaching your boy to navigate space in age-appropriate ways through practical exercises such as getting him to point out landmarks in your neighbourhood so he knows where the shops, the library and the park are in relation to your house.

If you live in a neighbourhood where you can walk to a lot of places, get your boy to navigate to where you are going. For example, tell him that it's his job to find the shops or the library. You will likely need to help him at first – unless you want to make a day of what would otherwise be a 10-minute walk – and be there to make sure he is safe, but he will start to learn to take responsibility for where he is going rather than always relying on someone else to lead him. If it's not possible to walk to key places around your neighbourhood, you can help him develop the same skills in shopping centres. When you're doing your grocery shopping, send him to the end of the aisle that you are in to get a product, bring it back and put it in the trolley. As he gets older and more confident, send him to the next aisle and then the next. Eventually you can stay out the front of the shops and send him in to buy something on his own. In doing so you will be building his confidence and mastery through baby steps, so that when he's older and gets to exercise more independence, he will know, from his bank of experience, that he will be able to cope.

Talking to adults and other figures of authority

Another part of mastery and independence that kids need to master early on is speaking up for themselves. This is particularly important when it comes to adults and authority figures such as teachers, school principals and doctors. It is also a skill that you can help your boy develop when he is very young. As soon as your boy can speak, get him to speak for himself wherever and whenever you can. If a friend or relative asks him a question, encourage him to answer it on his own. You may have to translate his toddler words, but you are still showing him that he is capable of speaking for himself and that what he has to say is valuable. When you go to the doctor, assuming your boy is well enough, get him to give his name to the receptionist and then tell the doctor what is wrong. Practise this in the car on the way to the doctor. Ask him, 'When we walk into the doctor's and the receptionist asks for your name, what are you going to say?' If you get a blank look, turn the question into a joke and say, 'Well, are you going to tell the receptionist that your name is Mr Kafoops?' As you can imagine, this kind of comedy gold will almost always prompt a laugh. When he says 'nooooo', reply with, 'Well, what are you going to say?'

It might seem strange to get your boy to tell you his own name, but role-playing beforehand will help him feel more confident when he has to do it. You should also rehearse what he plans to say to the doctor when they ask what's wrong. Say something like 'So, when we go in to see the doctor, what are you going to say to them?'

This applies not just to the doctor's office, but to any situation where you meet with figures of authority. It might be a principal on a school orientation day. Or it might be the coach at tryouts for the local football team. Or it might be the receptionist at the play centre. Some parents have told us that in these kinds of situations their child simply refuses to speak, and they don't know what to do. One trick is to get your boy to practise speaking for himself in cafes or restaurants. Tell him that if he doesn't order he doesn't get anything. And stick to your guns, even if it ends in a tantrum and you have to leave. We've found that food is a great motivator!

What about when the stakes are higher?

You might be on board with allowing your boy to develop mastery and independence (by failing and struggling along the way) when it comes to tying shoelaces and playing at the park. But what about when the stakes are higher? For example, what about when it comes to activities such as schoolwork and projects?

You may be tempted to get in there and push your son – or even just help him along a little. We saw this a lot in the COVID lockdowns. During remote learning, our kids' school would send out weekly pleas to parents: 'Please don't do your child's work for them.' Sometimes the teachers found it necessary to send this request multiple times a week. Apparently some of the work that was being submitted, with its complex sentences, perfectly constructed letters and correct spelling and punctuation, had clearly been done by adults.

To be clear, we're not picking on parents here. High five to all of us for surviving remote learning. And we confess there were many times when we cut corners or intervened in our children's learning just to get through the day. But remote schooling shone a spotlight on the consequences of too much parental intervention in kids' learning. When parents micromanaged or even did their children's schoolwork during remote learning, teachers were unable to get an accurate picture of where the students were at so they could give the students the right support. But the problem was bigger than this. Every time Mum or Dad rushed in to micromanage their child's work, they were effectively telling their child that they weren't capable of doing it on their own.

One teacher told us that she noticed a drop in confidence in some children when they returned to the classroom. She suspected one reason for this was the overinvolvement of parents. These children had effectively developed learned helplessness, believing that they couldn't do any schoolwork without an adult sitting next to them micromanaging every pencil stroke. Additionally, these kids were effectively taught that they were not responsible for their own work. What's the point of trying when Mum or Dad will come along and fix your work for you?

Maggie Dent says that parents may think that they are helping their son by finishing his homework or assisting with his assessments, but they're actually doing the reverse. 'It is making them dependent on you rather than themselves and it can make boys quite lazy. It is also telling them, in an indirect and invisible way, that you think "they're not capable or not good enough" . . . Such a small thing that seems to come from a place of love can have such a negative impact long-term.'[20]

We are not saying that you should never help your boy with his schoolwork. The research clearly shows that when parents take an interest in their children's education, kids do better at school. But it's important to remember our role. We are the support crew. Our role is to support, not to lead or take responsibility for the work. In practice this might mean a trip to the shops to buy glue and pipe-cleaners for your boy's project. It might mean doing a practice spelling test, or assisting with a particular area of maths your boy is struggling with. But he must learn to take responsibility for the work, and he must feel the frustration of not understanding something and then develop the persistence and resourcefulness to learn it. We've already done school – it's their turn now.

It's not too late to start

If you're worried that you've been rescuing your boy and potentially thwarting his sense of mastery and independence, don't feel bad. You are far from alone and it's not too late to turn things around. And, let's face it, sometimes you just don't have the luxury of making every experience an opportunity for him to develop his sense of mastery. But, as far as is practical, from this day on focus on this simple guiding principle: Only do for your boy what he cannot do for himself. If your boy is capable of doing something (even badly at first) then encourage him to do it. This isn't about lazy parenting or ruining childhoods or making children grow up too soon. Rather, see it as a fundamental vote of confidence in your boy. You are encouraging him to do (and sometimes insisting he does) something for himself because you believe in him. This principle will help to prepare him to be a competent adult and will reduce the risk of learned helplessness, which can cause both anxiety and depression.[21]

You won't always get it right. We certainly don't! Just like every other parent, some days we're tired and stressed and are more focused on getting through the day. But if you can get it right enough, you can transform learned helplessness into determination, independence and mastery. As we covered in the introduction, brains are mouldable and it's never too late to undo an unhelpful pattern of behaviour.

Independence is bittersweet

Independence is not a gift our children unwrap on their eighteenth birthday. It's a destination it takes years to arrive at, with hundreds of baby steps along the way. And each step must be taken by your boy. We are essential as their guide, their coach and their support crew. We prepare them for the journey, nudging them on to the next step when they are ready, but we cannot complete the journey for them. And we must resist the urge to hold them back, because if our boys reach adulthood without having successfully journeyed towards independence, it will be very difficult for them to like themselves.

As parents we are constantly called upon to use our judgement as to when our children are ready to take their next step towards independence, and when it is appropriate to hold them back a while. Sometimes we hold them back because it can be painful to not be needed by them. Other times we hold them back for purely practical reasons. Learning independence is time-consuming and messy. Sometimes you just don't have a spare hour for him to put on his own seatbelt. But wherever possible, we need to prioritise the end goal of parenting – to raise our children to be so competent that they do not need us.

Just tell me what to do!

Self-esteem doesn't come from nice word presents; it grows from within. Our job as parents is to help our boy develop it by creating the conditions for mastery and independence.

- Be brave enough to let your boy struggle and fail so that he can feel the eventual satisfaction of mastery and independence.
- Use your boy's bank of evidence of past successes to help him realise that he is capable of doing hard things. Assure him that he can do hard things because he's done them before.
- Build your boy's independence with this rule: Only do for him what he cannot do for himself. If your boy is capable of doing something (even badly at first) then encourage him to do it.
- Praise the process, not the outcome. Notice and remark on your boy's persistence, bravery or creativity rather than the trophy, the gold star or the finished product. When you see him try something new, step out of his comfort zone, or make a mistake and keep trying, make sure he knows that you have noticed. Say something like, 'I noticed you found doing that new puzzle really tricky at first, but you kept trying – that was very persistent.'
- Help your boy be okay with failure by:
  - Normalising it. Help him to understand that everyone fails and makes mistakes. It's part of life. The most successful people fail often.
  - Trying to make sure there is no penalty for making mistakes in your house. If he spills the milk, loses his hat or fails a test and you crack it, then, no matter what you tell him, he will learn to fear failure, and this will prevent him from developing mastery and independence. Remind him that mistakes are a normal part of life and an opportunity to learn and be better next time.

- Telling him stories about how you have failed and been okay. When you make mistakes in day-to-day life, articulate them so he can see that it's normal to make mistakes. You are your boy's hero, so if *you* can make mistakes and be okay, then anyone can!

6

A boy who likes himself has strong relationships

Harvey was desperate to find a best friend, but he was going about it in all the wrong ways. A casual observer watching Harvey in the classroom or in the playground might have found it surprising that he didn't already have a friend. He's academically bright, funny and articulate, and a talented athlete. He always has a group of boys laughing and joking around him. Mostly the attention from other boys is due to Harvey's frequent disruption, rudeness and disrespect. Sometimes his rudeness is directed at teachers, but more often than not it's directed at kids he considers not as smart or athletic as him. His mum is mortified by frequent phone calls from the school and from other parents about her boy's behaviour, but she also knows that they don't have the full picture. Harvey looks like a cocky kid who is supremely confident about his place in the world. But at night his parents frequently find him crying because he doesn't have the thing he wants most – a friend.

After one of Harvey's 'poor choices', which prompted another trip to the school for Harvey's mum for another little chat with his teacher, she asked Harvey why he behaves the way he does. She just doesn't get it. On his own, Harvey is thoughtful, empathetic and kind. So why does he act up and become so rude and mean at school?

In tears of frustration, Harvey told his mum that she doesn't understand what it's like to be a boy. He said he needed to behave like this so he could fit in with the other boys. If he could fit in, Harvey figured, then he could make a best friend.

It's a familiar story. Boys will do all kinds of things to fit in and be accepted by other boys. Unfortunately, 'fitting in' is about one of the worst things you can do to develop genuine friendships. Brené Brown defines 'fitting in' as 'assessing a situation and becoming who you need to be to be accepted'. In a boy's world, that can mean behaving contrary to his own values to try to impress other kids, pretending to like things that other boys like, and faking who he really is. Harvey's efforts to 'fit in' meant that he was essentially changing himself to be what he thought the other kids wanted him to be. But, in the process, he was denying himself the opportunity of making a real friend. The foundation of true, meaningful and intimate friendships is authenticity. What Harvey really wanted was to belong, but he was unknowingly sabotaging himself. True belonging, writes Professor Brené Brown, 'doesn't require us to change who we are; it requires us to *be* who we are'.

Trying to 'fit in' is an indication of a boy not liking himself very much. If a boy genuinely liked who he was, he wouldn't think he needed to hide or change his authentic self. On the flip side, one of the most important qualities of a good friend is that they like your boy just the way he is. For your boy to know if he is accepted just the way he is, he has to be himself. Being yourself takes courage and strength of character, and it is the *only* pathway to real friendship. Spelling it out like this might sound obvious to adults, but these can be tricky concepts for some kids to understand – and they can be even harder to live by.

Although Harvey was going about things completely the wrong way, he was absolutely right in one respect – he did *need* a friend. Friendship is as important to boys' and men's wellbeing as it is to girls' and women's. And contrary to popular belief, boys' friendships can be just as complicated and drama-filled. Building the foundational pillar of strong relationships is so essential to bringing up your boy to like himself that it should not be left to chance. But building this pillar might mean rethinking some of the assumptions you've grown up with about boys and friendship.

The skill of friendship

Some kids (and some adults) are great at making friends. They can walk into any room and make a connection – the starting point of a friendship – almost immediately. But many other kids (and some adults) really struggle. One reason for this is that they mistakenly believe that friendship is largely out of their control. The process of making friends can seem to involve some weird mix of chemistry and serendipity, with a hint of magic thrown in. But the reality is that friendship is a skill. Those who have good friends are those with good friendship skills.

When it comes to boys, we tend to regard friendships as uncomplicated. Boys seem to manage friends just fine on their own, whereas girls' friendships are stereotypically considered almost as complex as navigating a minefield. If things get heated, boys seem to just shrug it off or sort it out on the sporting field. Boys, so the thinking goes, work friendship out on their own. This is so taken for granted that while lots of effort is devoted to helping girls navigate friendship, we mostly leave boys' friendships to boys themselves. Friendship and wellbeing educator Rebecca Sparrow, for example, says that she receives more invitations from schools to talk to girls about friendship skills than there are days of the year. In contrast, Sparrow can count the invitations she's received to talk to boys about friendship on one hand.[1]

But the reality of boys' friendships is more complex than is often assumed, and they need just as much support as girls do.[2] So don't assume that because your boy is not talking about his friendship struggles, he doesn't have any.

The costs of not learning friendship skills

Even when boys do manage to make friends (without the same level of help or support that girls may receive), they often struggle to keep them. Male friendships are often more a result of circumstance – attending the same school, belonging to the same sporting club or working for the same company – than intentionally formed relationships. In many cases, it's only decades later, when school is a distant memory, and injury or age result in sporting club or job changes, that the accidental and transient nature of many men's friendships becomes clear.

Research on boys from a wide range of ethnic backgrounds and social classes suggests that male friendships start to decline in middle to late adolescence.[3] This decline seems to continue throughout middle age.[4] A 2021 US survey found that 15 per cent of men said they did not have a single close friend, which is a five-fold increase from 1995, when 3 per cent reported the same. Those who said they had at least six close friends dropped by half – from 55 per cent in 1995 to 27 per cent in 2021.[5] (Full disclosure: the same study also found that women's friendships declined, but not nearly as precipitously as men's.)

The *New York Times* reports on a 'friendship recession' among men, with a 2021 survey of 2000 US men finding that fewer than half were satisfied with how many friends they had.[6] The study suggests that the reasons for this are tied to traditional masculine values such as competitiveness and stoicism. Many boys, and the men that they become, never really learn the skill of making and maintaining friendships. This has dire consequences. In his book *Billy No-Mates: How I realised men have a friendship problem*, UK actor and comedian Max Dickins writes that it wasn't until he was looking for a friend to be best man at his wedding that he realised he didn't have a single male friend he considered close enough to fill the role. And Dickins isn't alone. In his search for a best man, he discovered online discussions between soon-to-be-married men in the same position, trying to work out who could be their best man.

The problems of friendlessness among men go beyond finding someone to stand next to you in a tux. One long-term study in the US published in *Psychological Science* found that men who spent more time with friends when they were boys had better physical health in their thirties. Importantly, the researchers found that these health benefits were not explained by the men's health as children, their current levels of social interaction, or other factors such as income.[7]

The Australian Longitudinal Study on Male Health found that 'men who reported lacking close friends or relatives were around twice as likely to have thought about suicide in the past 12 months'.[8]

Developmental psychologist Professor Niobe Way writes that 'the significantly shorter life span of men compared to that of women and the spike in suicide rates of teenage boys right at the moment when the pressures to be manly – independent and stoic – intensify testify to the negative consequences of ignoring the importance of close friendships, trust, empathy, and emotionally supportive relationships more generally.'[9]

Boys can learn the skill of making and keeping friends

Professor Way and her colleagues are at pains to point out that boys are not somehow 'hardwired' to need friends less than girls. Prior to adolescence, boys express just as much need for close friends and intimacy as girls. In fact, Professor Ryan A. McKelley says that girls and boys are as emotionally expressive as each other.[10] And that's a good thing. It shows that there is nothing natural or inevitable about the decline in boys' friendships.

Research shows that children who develop good friendship skills grow up to have better adult relationships.[11] If we want to spare our boys loneliness and help them to grow into happy, healthy, mentally and emotionally flourishing adults, we have to be brave enough to actively reject the myth that boys don't get hurt by friendship problems and that they don't need help learning relationship skills. Because the truth is that making friends is a skill. It's not some magical gift that some boys get and others don't. And like any skill, it can be learned and improved with practice. You can teach your boy the skill of making and keeping friends, and, by doing so, provide him with lifelong benefits.

How to make a friend

This might sound strange to you, particularly if you are one of those lucky people who seem to develop friendships naturally, but unless you specifically tell your boy step-by-step how to make a friend, he may not know how to do it. Don't assume he's going to work it out on his own at some point in his life.

Here's a three-step plan inspired by parenting educator and author Michelle Mitchell's work, to teach your boy the skill of making friends. Think of friendship as a bit like a house. If you want someone to come into your friendship house, first you have to open the door. Next you have to invite them in. And thirdly, you have to make them feel welcome so they want to stay. Let's take these steps one at a time.

Step 1: Open the door

Children, like adults, are attracted to people who are fun and welcoming. So if you want to make a new friend, you have to let the other person know you're open to it. You can do this by making and maintaining eye contact, smiling and adopting open body language, as well as through similar non-verbal cues. Some boys find it hard to make eye contact with people, so you might have to practise this *a lot*. We've practised it with our kids by encouraging them to look people in the eye when they meet them. When they order in a cafe, we prompt them to look at the serving staff in the eye, and again when their food arrives and they say thank you.

Friendship expert Audrey Monke says that kids who think other children are excluding them or being 'mean' often aren't aware of how others perceive *their* closed-off and negative body language. 'Children need to learn that by smiling and presenting a positive demeanor, more people will be attracted to them as a potential friend.'[12] You may need to tell your boy that if he has a scowl on his face he is more likely to repel a potential friend than to engage with them. The same goes for open body language. When we are feeling shy and insecure we tend to hunch over and cross our arms over our chest. It's okay to feel shy, but we need to make sure that our body language is sending the right message to potential friends.

In addition to non-verbal cues, there are, of course, verbal cues. The big one is introducing ourselves. Tell your boy that this is how we open the door to our house of friendship, and get him to practise introducing himself. Get him to smile, look you in the eye and say what his name is.

Finally, get your boy to ask what the other child's name is. This bit is critical. If he doesn't ask the other child's name, it could be like slamming the door in his potential friend's face.

Practise role-playing all three parts of opening the friendship door. Make eye contact, smile with open body language, and say, 'My name is . . . what's your name?'

If talking is too confronting for your boy, or he's not good with his words, tell him to just join in the game. That's right – to go up to a group and start playing. This may come as a surprise to you if you were taught to ask politely before joining a group. But, as you may have experienced yourself when you were a kid, asking permission can be a risky strategy. It interrupts the game, and leaves nowhere to go if the other kids answer with 'no'. If your boy just joins in, his actions will speak louder than words. Of course, this won't always work, but it's good old parallel play and it's something that boys often respond well to.[13]

Step 2: Invite them into your house of friendship

The way we invite someone into our friendship house is by finding some activity or interest in common. The best way for your son to do this is by asking a question. The good news is that he probably only needs one or two questions that he can use at any time to make a friend. Your boy will have to work out what questions work for him, but here are a few examples to get you – and him – thinking.

> Have you seen the *Minions* movie?
> What superpower do you wish you had?
> Do you play any sports?
> What have you got for lunch?
> Do you play Minecraft?
> What school do you go to?
> Do you have any pets?

Once your boy has chosen his question(s), practise it at the dinner table, in the car or while you're going for a walk. Pretend you are a kid at school and get your boy to ask his question and then listen to your answer. The listening part is really important and some kids need this step spelled out for them. (You probably know a few adults who could have done with a lesson in listening when they were a child!) Once your boy has mastered asking and listening for the answer to his first question, get him to ask a follow-up question to keep the conversation going.

'Kids (and adults) who master question-asking, listening, and follow-up are well-liked because they give people the opportunity to share about themselves,' says Audrey Monke.[14] If your boy is reluctant to ask questions, explain to him that asking questions is kind. It is saying to the other person that they matter and that you are interested in them. And like everything, it gets easier with practice.

Step 3: Make them feel welcome

The third step is to make the other person feel welcome in your friendship house. How do we make someone feel welcome? We are fun, positive and enthusiastic – as well as honest, respectful and kind. This one is really important. We naturally gravitate to people who treat us well, and we feel good when we are around them. Kids are the same. If your boy wants good friends, then the best thing he can do is *be* a good friend.

There. That's it. Those are the three steps to making friends. These steps might sound obvious to adults, but for many boys, the process of making friends is a complete mystery. For example, we recently saw a little boy starting at a new school. He desperately wanted to make a friend. But he walked into school with closed-off body language, staring at his shoes and not smiling. Despite all these cues screaming that he wasn't open to friends, another little boy walked next to him with his friendship door wide open. The other little boy was looking over, smiling, trying to catch the new boy's eye. But the new boy wasn't just *not* opening his friendship door – he'd bolted it shut. He'd essentially put up a 'Trespassers will be prosecuted' sign and set the dogs on the other kid.

That night the new boy told his mum that he'd had a terrible day at school. He hadn't spoken to a single person other than his teacher.

You can see why, right?

His mum helped him practise his skill in making friends, and two days later – that's all it took, just two days – the boy made a friend at his new school. And then, a couple of weeks after that, his new friend invited him on a playdate outside of school.

If your boy needs help with making friends, talk to him about what he needs to do to open the friendship door, invite the other person in and make them feel welcome. Role-play the conversations with him to develop his skills and build his confidence.

Friendship is a choice

It was the first day of the school year, and the footpath outside the primary school was chock-full of nervous and excited children and parents. One little boy, dressed in his stiff, oversized uniform, looked up at his mother and said, 'I hope someone picks me as their friend today.'

Not missing a beat, his mother bent down to his level, locked eyes with him and said, 'No, buddy, *you* pick them.'

Give that mum a prize!

One thing to make very clear to your boy is that, unlike many of his other relationships, friendship is a choice. Specifically, it is *his* choice. Help him to understand that a friend is a person *he* chooses, not necessarily the people who choose him. And given that we are heavily influenced by the people we spend the most time with, it is a very important choice.

What makes a good friend?

We all deserve friendships that are good for us, but it can be tricky for boys (and sometimes for adults!) to know the difference between a friendship that is healthy and one that is unhealthy. The most basic place to start is to ask your boy to think about how he feels when he is with his friend.

Does he feel happy and energised?

Does he have fun?

Can he be honest and truthful with this person?

When we are in the company of friends who are good for us, we feel good most of the time. There is always going to be misunderstanding and conflict (we'll get to that later), but, in general, a good friend makes us feel good. A friend that is not good for us makes us feel angry, hurt, silly, small and left out.

The following is a good-friend checklist that we've adapted from the work of Brené Brown, Michelle Mitchell and Tanith Carey's *The Friendship Maze*. Work through it with your boy and explain to him that a good friend should be all of these things, most of the time.

A good friend:

- is fun to be with
- makes me feel happy and good about myself most of the time
- is kind to me
- respects me
- is trustworthy
- keeps my secrets
- takes turns and is fair
- listens to what I say and cares about my feelings
- stands up for me (even when I'm not there)
- notices when I'm upset and asks me why
- includes me in fun things
- doesn't expect me to like all the same things they do
- doesn't try to make me do things as a condition of staying their friend
- checks on me when I miss school
- likes me just the way I am.

Is he being a good friend?

Friendship is a two-way street. The good-friend checklist is also a useful way to talk to your boy about *his* behaviour as a friend.

After all, the best way to make and keep good friends is to *be* a good friend. If you suspect that your son might not be behaving in a way that a good friend should (which is completely normal and should be expected, because like all skills, friendship skills must be learned and practised), ask him what his friend would say if they applied this list to him. Often very basic things that are obvious to us are not at all obvious to kids.

One of our friends had to teach her son that poking someone in the chest is not the best way to entice them to play with you. This is obvious to adults, but he was oblivious to this point. If you see your son behaving in ways that do not support healthy friendships, gently prompt him to reflect on that behaviour. For instance, you might say something like, 'We know that a good friend is kind. Do you think taking Rory's toy was kind? How do you think Rory felt when you took his toy?' Always finish these conversations with empowerment rather than keeping him stuck in the shame of the present. For example, ask him, 'How do you think you could act next time?' Then praise him for his thought-fulness and commitment to being a good friend.

Don't give up on friendship

Where friendship is concerned, there are no guarantees. Your boy can use these strategies and still feel like he hasn't found 'his person'. But this is not a reason for him to give up on friendship.

Michelle Mitchell says that friendship can be found within many people. It will be there if your boy is willing to seek it out. As we discussed in our power perspective chapter, your boy can choose to be negative and focus on all the negative things about his peers and classmates, and all the reasons they cannot be best friends; or he can choose to focus on the positive qualities of his peers and classmates and see the opportunities for friendship that are right in front of him. 'Confident and optimistic kids find friendship wherever they go because they are open to it,'

170

says Mitchell. If your boy has already decided that there is no possibility for friendship in his peer group, then he is likely to retreat and stop trying and will make his fear of friendlessness a reality.

Some kids think they need a big group of friends like those they see on TV, and worry that there is something wrong with them if they don't have that. Assure your boy that he does not need a huge group of friends to be happy. Nor does he need to be in the popular group. 'Two or three good friends with whom they can share confidences is enough to enjoy school,' write Tanith Carey in *The Friendship Maze*.[15]

Dealing with peer pressure and the pressure to fit in

With friends comes peer pressure. Peer pressure and going along with the pack to fit in were two of the biggest concerns parents shared with us. Their concerns ranged from how to instil confidence in their boys so that they don't do dumb things to impress their friends, to helping their boys have confidence in their own judgements rather than those of their friends. Other parents were concerned about their boys crossing the line between being chilled and accommodating and being pushed around.

If this is you, then let us introduce you to go and no-go zones.

No-go zones

As adults, we might call no-go zones our boundaries. Essentially, no-go zones are behaviours that your boy is not okay with at this moment in his life. Help him to understand that everyone has no-go zones and that everyone gets to decide for themselves what theirs are. His no-go zones will change over time and depend on who he is with, but what's important is that he knows he is allowed to state what he is okay with and not okay with right now. No-go zones aren't just important from the perspective of safety and peer pressure – they are also an antidote to the kinds of behaviours that boys like Harvey, mentioned at the beginning of this chapter, engage in to 'fit in'. Remember: when it comes to friends and friendships, your boy ought to aim to belong – not just fit in. One way to tell if he belongs rather than merely fitting in is to see whether those around him respect and honour his no-go zones.

Some examples of no-go zones might include:

- I'm not okay with you taking my cookie out of my lunch box.
- I'm not okay with you calling my mum mean names.
- I'm not okay with you telling me that I can't play with someone.
- I'm not okay with you telling me I shouldn't like this or that.
- I'm not okay with stealing the lollipop out of your sister's bedroom.
- I don't do scary movies.
- I don't do sleepovers.
- I'm not okay with you telling me I can't talk to girls.
- I don't want to do that prank on that boy.

Respect is non-negotiable when it comes to healthy friendships. This includes respect for other people's no-go zones. In a world where we are up against peer pressure and bro codes, we need to explicitly tell boys that they are allowed to have no-go zones. And so are their friends.

Rebecca Sparrow says it is helpful to role-play enforcing these no-go zones.[16] She recommends getting your son to practise saying in a big, assertive voice:

- 'I don't do . . .'
- 'I don't like . . .'

When he's still young, while you are the most influential voice in his life, have conversations with your boy about the things he is not okay with. Validate his opinions so he knows that he doesn't have to be like everybody else. For example, his friends might like watching Harry Potter, but it's completely fine if he doesn't like it because he finds Voldemort scary. Your boy is allowed to say 'I don't like watching Harry Potter', and it's reasonable for him to expect his friends to respect that.

Go zones

The flip side of no-go zones is, you guessed it, go zones. These relate to behaviours and activities your boy enjoys doing or that are important to him, regardless of what other kids might think of them. When he's young these could include:

- I hug my sister at the school gate in the morning.
- I like doing gymnastics.
- I like playing Roblox even if other kids call it lame.
- I want to hold my mum's hand.

When he's older these might include:

- I'm going to study instead of going out to a party.
- I'm choosing to spend time with my family rather than my mates.
- I like doing X even though my mates don't get it.

It's important for your boy to understand that good friends respect his go zones, even if they don't like them themselves. You may have to explicitly tell your boy that he doesn't have to like all the same things as his friends in order to be friends – but he does have to respect his friends' choices. If your boy has a friend who is repeatedly trying to trample on his go zones, then it might be helpful to go through the good friend checklist (p. 168) and have a chat about what makes a good friend, and how he deserves to be surrounded by people who respect his choices, even if they are different.

Sometimes your boy may need to enforce his go zones with his friends as well as with kids who are not his friends. A really effective way to help him do this is to teach him the simple phrase: I like it.

For example, we recently saw a kid sucking on a squeezy pouch of pureed apple. A boy came over and said, 'That food's for babies.' The kid with the pouch just shrugged and said, 'I like it.'

It might sound like such a small thing, but that's a kid who knows their own mind and who has no trouble enforcing their boundaries. 'I like it' says 'I heard you, but what you said doesn't affect me because I like it. End of conversation.'

Developing and practising go and no-go zones

Sometimes enforcing go zones and no-go zones is hard, so, even with practice, it's likely that your son will feel uncomfortable doing it. This is why it's important to help our kids understand that difficult feelings are a necessary part of life, and that they need to learn to tolerate these feelings rather than avoiding them.

Make it clear that you expect your boy to enforce his go zones and no-go zones, even when it's hard. When you see him do it, praise him for it. You want this to become second nature – just how he interacts with the world. Don't wait until the stakes are high before you start having conversations about boundaries and having the courage to say no.

This is an investment for years to come. You don't want your boy to go into his teen years having had no practice with the kinds of discomforting situations that require him to define and state his go zones and no-go zones. Encouraging and equipping your son with the skills to enforce what he will and will not accept improves his chances of making the right choice when he is confronted with dangerous peer pressure later on. You want him to have well-practised skills when it comes to voicing potentially unpopular opinions such as 'I'm not okay with getting in that car with a drunk driver', or 'I don't do vaping', or 'I'm not okay with treating a girl like that.'

Respect is reciprocal, so explain to your son that in order to be a good friend, he needs to respect other people's go zones and no-go zones too.

Talking out misunderstandings

Even in the best friendships, there will be times when your son's friend tramples on your boy's no-go zones without realising it. As with adults, there will be times when friends make mistakes or misjudge situations and cause conflict and upset without intending to. Maybe Harry took your boy's Pokémon cards home and your boy wants them back. Maybe James is calling your boy a nickname that James thinks is funny but that your boy doesn't like. Or maybe Connor said he'd wait for your boy at the swing at lunchtime but never showed up.

Situations like this are best handled with what *Big Life Journal* contributor Rebecca Louick calls 'I messages'.[17]

An 'I message' is a non-judgemental statement which is effective because 'it doesn't blame or criticise and it keeps the listener from feeling attacked or defensive', says Louick.[18] It goes like this:

'I feel [insert feeling] when you [insert behaviour]. I would like you to [insert request].'

For example: 'I feel angry when you take my Pokémon cards. I would like you to give them back, please.'

Or: 'I felt left out when you started the game without me. I want to play too.'

Or: 'I feel upset when you call me "shorty". I'd like you to stop calling me that.'

The next step is for your boy to stop talking and wait to see what his friend has to say in response. In an ideal situation the friend will say that he didn't realise he was upsetting your boy and that he's sorry and he won't do it again.

But as with all human relationships, there are no guarantees that this will be the response. It's possible that the other kid will get defensive and strike back. Your boy's friend may never feel ready to talk about it, particularly if he has already learned brittle and unhealthy masculinity. But at the very least your boy will have boosted his own dignity and self-respect by standing up for himself, enforcing his no-go zones and trying to repair his friendship.

There will be times when your boy is the one hurting a friend's feelings or letting them down. Everyone screws up from time to time, especially kids who are still learning and developing social skills. Rebecca Sparrow says that when this happens, it is important to 'own the impact'.[19] This means your boy having the character strength to admit that he made a mistake or did the wrong thing, to acknowledge the hurt that he caused and apologise for it. As we explained in chapter two, it is very difficult, if not impossible, for your boy to have a deep and meaningful friendship (or romantic relationship, when he is older) if he is incapable of owning the impact of his behaviour and genuinely apologising for it.

Teaching your boy to stand up for himself (without violence)

Simon walked into his classroom and noticed that there weren't enough chairs. He offered the last chair to his friend and then went outside to fetch another one. This chair was different from all the others in the room. Noticing this, another boy, Kyle, called from the other side of the class, 'You have to get a special chair because you're so fat!'

When Simon got home that afternoon he told his mum what happened, and said that he might come home with some bruises tomorrow because he was going to beat Kyle up after school. Simon's mum didn't want to condone violence but her heart was breaking for her little boy and she didn't know what else to suggest.

Simon's mum is not alone. A dad told us that his boy was deliberately kicked by an opposing player during a soccer match. The referee didn't see it but the dad did, and he was worried that if his boy didn't fight back it would happen again. 'It's so hard,' the dad said. 'I don't want to encourage violence but I don't know what else to do.'

Even young boys are going to be confronted with behaviour we want them to stand up to. If Jacob calls your boy 'poo-head', for example, he is going to feel hurt. And if it's said in front of other kids, he'll be embarrassed as well and will likely want to respond. If Oliver laughs at your son's Batman costume for Book Week and tells him Batman is stupid – yep, your son is going to feel that too. And then there will be personalities that your boy just clashes with for no apparent reason.

Michelle Mitchell says there is an old-school belief that boys need to stand up for themselves with physical violence. 'Lots of parents I know believe their sons need to "push and shove" and be physically violent in order to defend themselves,' says Mitchell. Dr Marc Brackett says that no one wants their kid to be the one that gets pushed up against the lockers at school, so parents tell their boys, 'You can't cry if you're bullied, you've got to punch back.'[20] In many cases, the adults giving this advice are not pro-violence and don't want their boy to be a brawler. It's simply that they see their child in distress and don't know what other advice to give.

The problem with this approach is that the research shows that while it may work in the short term, it actually makes matters worse in the long term. One study found that '[o]f children who are bullied, those who hit back are more likely to be bullied six months later than children who don't retaliate'.[21] Far from being deterred, the kid who has just been hit now has a vendetta against your kid and will likely want to beat him up to settle the score. This can also be a traumatic experience for your boy. Imagine how you would feel if you were being pressured to do something where there was a good chance you would end up bruised and bloodied.

If you teach your boy to settle his conflicts with his fist, or to stand up for himself with physical violence, think about how this is going to work out if he takes the lesson into adulthood. Imagine him in a bar when he's twenty. Some guy calls him a pussy. And, as he was taught throughout his childhood, he throws a punch. That could potentially ruin your son's life. A milder consequence could be that he's charged with assault and potentially loses his job and employment prospects. But if his punch turns into a king hit and the other guy is seriously injured or even dies, your son could be spending the best years of his life in prison and having to live with the intolerable shame and regret of maiming or killing someone.

You might be thinking that this sounds a bit dramatic, and that there is one rule for the playground and another for the rest of society and adult life. But ask yourself: When and how is your boy going to learn that distinction? And is he likely to remember the distinction in the heat of the moment? Ask yourself:

- Would I be happy if my boy hit his mate when he's twenty?
- Would I be happy if my boy punched his boss?
- Would I be happy if my boy used violence to settle a dispute with his partner or with someone who is physically smaller or has less power than him?
- Would I be happy if my boy struck his own child?

If this is not how we want our sons to behave when they are adults, why on earth would we risk encouraging them to behave like this as children?

Ignore it and it will just go away. Or will it?

Another piece of advice out of the old-school playbook is the complete opposite to punching it out – and it's just as ineffective. It's that boys should ignore poor behaviour and that it will go away. The problem is that the behaviour we ignore is the behaviour we allow. If your boy just ignores bad behaviour, he is essentially telling the other kid, 'No problem. You can treat me like that.' Aside from being an invitation for the other kid to continue and to potentially do worse next time, it is also robbing your boy of the dignity and self-respect of standing up for himself.

Trying to ignore bad behaviour is also likely to breed resentment, which could possibly make things much worse. Repressed feelings get bigger and bigger until they explode out, which can make the conflict even worse.

So what should your son do instead?

While there is little evidence that punching or ignoring stops bullying, there is considerable evidence that standing up for yourself with the right verbal response reduces the severity of intentionally mean behaviour and the likelihood of it happening again.[22] [23] Kids who use correct verbal responses get bullied less than kids who don't – and that includes those who resort to their fists.

So what works?

The most effective way for your son to stand up for himself is with what educator and founder of Kids First Children's Services Sonja Walker calls a 'clever comeback line'.[24]

A clever comeback line is a short statement that lets the other child know that your boy heard or saw what they said or did, and that your boy is not okay with it. A clever comeback line should:

- be short
- be a statement, not a question (unless it's a rhetorical one)
- not be mean or nasty
- be able to be said with confidence.

Your boy will need to choose his own clever comeback line, but here are some examples to get you started:

- Not cool.
- That's not okay.
- Not funny.
- Yeah, whatever.
- Seriously?
- I'm not listening.

Getting the delivery right is essential. The clever comeback line needs to be said in a strong voice with a don't-mess-with-me posture. Role-play your boy's clever comeback line at home so in the heat of the moment he'll know what to say and how to say it. He needs to assert himself by saying it, and then he needs to walk away. You don't want your boy to stay there and have a conversation with someone who's being deliberately mean to him. Using the other kid's name at the end of the clever comeback line adds even more impact, because it shows that your boy is not afraid or submissive.[25]

Back to Simon, who was fat-shamed over the chair at school. A more effective response than beating up his tormentor after school would have been for Simon to use a clever comeback line. He could have said something like 'Yeah, good on ya, Kyle' and turned away to talk to someone else. This response would have given Simon the dignity and self-respect of standing up for himself. It also would have shown Kyle (and all the other kids in the class) that Kyle's behaviour was not okay. Simon calling out

Kyle's behaviour in such a way would likely have made Kyle less inclined to do it again, because he didn't get the pay-off he was hoping for.

Of course, it is a lot to expect of Simon to remain calm when another kid is being so mean to him. This is why it is critical that you practise the clever comeback line at home, so your boy is so familiar with it that in the heat of a moment he will be able to say it. Not only will this help him deliver it when he needs to, it will also create the expectation in your family that you all stand up for yourselves. Let your boy know that you expect him to stand up for himself – with words, not with fists. Making sure your son knows that you expect him to stand up for himself will reduce the likelihood of him developing a passive and victim mentality. It also shows your boy that you believe that he is capable of it.

This stuff works

The clever comeback line sounds far too simple to work. We've heard this a lot. We tell parents about the strategy and they give us a look that says 'That's it?' But that's the brilliance of the clever comeback line: it's so simple. Over-complication for the sake of over-complication doesn't get you closer to a solution.

If you are sceptical, let us tell you the story of William. We worked with William's mother after she told us William was getting picked on at school. The children had to line up in alphabetical order to walk into class, which meant that three times a day William had to stand in front of a boy called Henry. Each time they walked into class Henry would accidentally-on-purpose elbow William in the ribs.

William's dad wanted his son to turn around and deck Henry, figuring that one punch would sort things out. William's mum was not so sure. Firstly, Henry was bigger than William and most likely to come out on top in a physical fight. But William was also a gentle boy who had never been in a fight in his life. Fighting was likely to be a scary prospect for him (as it is for most people!). But perhaps the strongest reason that telling William to thump Henry was a bad idea was that it was unlikely to work. In fact, in all probability it would have made matters worse and Henry would have been even more motivated to menace and hurt William.

Instead, William's mother taught him about the clever comeback line technique. Together they brainstormed different comebacks until they found one that William felt comfortable saying. Then they role-played the delivery. William practised standing tall and saying in a big, assertive voice, 'That's not cool, Henry.'

The next time Henry got in William's face, William delivered his clever comeback line. Henry was taken aback and stopped elbowing him. When they lined up again after recess, Henry elbowed William again and William used his clever comeback line another time. By lunchtime, Henry had got the message. He didn't elbow William again and he hasn't done it since. In fact, William told his mum that Henry is now being super nice to him.

What about bullying?

No strategy is foolproof. And that includes the clever comeback line. While friendship skills experts tell us that the clever comeback line is the best way for kids (and adults!) to stand up for themselves and shut down deliberately mean behaviour, there are going to be times when it doesn't work.

Severe bullying is one such example.

Before getting to this, we need to be clear about what bullying is and what it isn't. The National Centre Against Bullying defines bullying as 'an ongoing and deliberate misuse of power in relationships through repeated verbal, physical and/or social behaviour that intends to cause physical, social and/or psychological harm'.[26]

A kid not playing with your boy at lunchtime is not bullying. A child taking your boy's pencil on one particular day is not bullying. Someone accidentally bumping into your boy in the playground is not bullying. Neither is not being invited to a birthday party.

With your support, these are issues that your boy should be able to handle on his own. Mild bullying, like Henry elbowing William, can also often be resolved without adults intervening directly.

As a general principle, when it comes to friendship and social issues, our job as parents is to coach our kids from the sidelines and support them to work things out for themselves. But if your boy has tried his clever comeback line and you are sure he delivered it well, and the bullying is continuing, then it's time for adults to get involved.

Every child has the right to feel safe, and some problems are simply too big for little people to solve on their own. In cases like this, talk to your boy's teachers to work out a plan that your boy is comfortable with to keep him safe. You can also help by making sure he has friendships and a support network outside of the environment where he encounters bullying. By making sure your boy has a friend outside of the situation, he will never feel totally alone. A good insurance policy against the harm of bullying is to prioritise your boy cultivating and maintaining friendships outside of the context where the bullying occurs, such as school. These friendships might be with a kid from a sporting club, a cousin or a child of one of your friends.

Pranks and teasing

Traditional male friendships have long been synonymous with pranks, practical jokes, sledging and roasting. There is nothing inherently wrong with good-natured banter between friends. It's a connection point for some people and actually makes them feel closer to the other person. But it's essential that everyone is a

183

willing participant in the joke. If they are not, then this behaviour is not on. As social scientist Professor Brené Brown says, 'Nothing that celebrates the humiliation or pain of another person builds lasting connection.'[27]

The consequences of boys bonding via pranks and ritual humiliation can be severe. When this 'bonding' is an abuse of power dressed up as humour, it can actually ruin lives. For example, a few years ago in Brisbane four teenagers were charged with raping their mate with a beer bottle after he passed out drunk at a party. It was 'just a prank', the lawyer for two of the young men said in their defence.[28] In fact, the teenagers were so caught up in the 'joke' that they even filmed it and shared it on social media with the caption, '[Our friend] passed out so we stuck a bottle up his arse and he just took it . . . Funniest thing I've ever seen, legit.' Three of the boys went to jail, one was given a suspended sentence, and the victim's life was changed forever.[29]

You might argue that it is a big leap from schoolyard pranks to committing sexual assault, but the basic behaviour is the same: boys degrading and humiliating each other for kicks and laughs as a bonding experience. Are you sure your teenage son will know where the line is in the heat of a moment if he has spent his primary-school years 'bonding' and being 'funny' with his mates via intense pranks and sledges?

It can be hard to teach a boy where the line is between harmless fun and cruelty. A guiding principle is: It's only funny if everyone is laughing. And by that, we mean genuine laughter, not laughing along with others because you feel you have to in order to avoid being the target of further pranks. Being able to laugh at ourselves is part of healthy development, but if the target of the joke is not genuinely laughing, it's not funny. Rather, it has crossed the line into spiteful (and potentially even criminal) behaviour. Another way to check that the pranks and teasing are acceptable is to see if they go both ways. If everyone in the group is pranking each other then it's probably fine, but if the target is always the same kid then it's starting to look a lot like bullying.

And to make doubly sure that it's 'harmless fun', before your boy does any prank or makes any sledge, get him to ask himself, 'Would I be happy if this was done to me?'

What if your boy becomes friends with kids you don't think are good for him?

If you don't like the friend or group your boy is hanging out with, we have bad news for you. We cannot pick our children's friends. And we mean that literally. Parents have been trying for decades, but in almost every case it backfires. Often spectacularly. You can orchestrate playdates, you can find other ways to push kids together, you can talk up one friend and talk down another – but ultimately your son is going to make his own choices about his friends.

If we are too controlling about our boys' friendship choices we risk diminishing their power perspective, because we're essentially saying to them that they're not capable of making their own decisions, and that they shouldn't trust their own judgement. It can be really damaging to a child's self-confidence and self-belief if we undermine them in something as intimate and personal as a friendship choice.

But what we can do is influence them. There are no guarantees here. But these are good conversations to have anyway. The first thing to do is to help your son understand that friendship is a choice and that he deserves good friends. Go through the good-friend checklist (p. 168) with your son and talk about whether or not his friends are good for him. And talk about whether or not his friends are respecting his go zones and no-go zones. This can be a really clarifying conversation.

As frustrating as it may be at times, our children need to be empowered to make their own friendship choices. When they make unwise choices, these can later become learning experiences. But in the meantime, friendships have to be something that our boys choose for themselves.

Meaningful connections with girls

We were at our friend's house when we saw her eight-year-old boy laughing raucously at TikTok videos. We asked what he was laughing at, so he showed us. It was a cute animated video with a far-from-cute message. 'If girls are so strong, why can't boys hit them back? If boys are uglier than girls, why do girls have to wear make-up?'

It was repetitive and hypnotic, and he thought it was hilarious.

It was also teaching an eight-year-old boy to disrespect – or worse, hate – girls and women. Is it any wonder that the research shows that by the age of six boys mistakenly believe that they are smarter than girls?[30] Even if the words don't come from their parents' mouths, the messages are everywhere. If boys show emotions, they are 'crying like a girl'. If they don't go in hard enough on the football field, they 'played like a pack of girls'. If they haven't worked out their ball skills yet, they 'throw like a girl'. If they complain, they're 'whining like a girl'.

And then there are the more subtle ways we tell boys that being like a girl is about the worst thing they can be. For example, while it's cool to dress a little girl in overalls or shorts, and we cheer when progressive parents ditch the dolls and glitter in favour of balls, trucks and blocks, how many of us would put our little boy in a dress or even a pink floral onesie?

Sure, we've seen the occasional boy turn up at library storytime rocking a tutu or nail polish, but it doesn't happen very often. And it's always met with some smirks and raised eyebrows. We have friends who happily dress their son in hand-me-down girls' clothes in the privacy of their own home, but to let him be seen in the street wearing that?

Nuh-uh.

Not only do we teach boys to never be like girls, we also teach them that girls are uninteresting and irrelevant. In fact, girls are apparently so boring and unimportant that adults spare boys from even having to think about them. For example, internationally bestselling and award-winning children's author Belinda Murrell, who speaks to thousands of children every year at schools around Australia, says that librarians, teachers and parents will often decide that only male authors have universal appeal. 'Often schools prefer to book a male author as they assume that their books will appeal to both boys and girls, while they may choose not to book female authors as they assume their books will only appeal to girls,' says Murrell.

And it doesn't stop there. Men and male characters dominate children's books, often leaving girls and women in the background. An analysis of Nielsen BookScan's 100 top-selling kids' picture books in 2017 shows that two-thirds of them have male protagonists[31] and that even animals and inanimate objects in children's books are 73 per cent more likely to be male than female.[32]

We are just as guilty as other adults of only buying books with male protagonists for boys. In fact, until recently, it had never even occurred to us to buy a boy a book about a girl. And yet our girls' bookshelf is full of Harry Potter, Geronimo Stilton, the Treehouse series, Diary of a Wimpy Kid, Percy Jackson . . . you get the idea. Without even realising it, we've been helping to teach boys that while girls should be interested in boys' experiences, they need not reciprocate. The implicit message is that the lives and experiences of girls are trivial and unimportant.

Some books go one step further and actively encourage boys to degrade girls. For example, book two in the wildly successful WeirDo series by Anh Do opens with the line: 'I was out shopping for a birthday present for the seventh-best-looking girl in the class.' Think about that: the seventh-best-looking girl in the class. Ranking, objectifying and dehumanising girls is presented to young boys as funny, acceptable and just what boys do. While this might be defended as a bit of fun, all the ways girls are diminished in the eyes of boys add up. And this has long-term effects that harm boys as well as girls. Add a few more years, and boys are getting expelled from school and being disgraced on the front pages of newspapers for precisely the same behaviour – ranking and dehumanising girls.

Here is just a small selection of the countless news headlines about sexist and misogynistic behaviour from the last few years.

'"This is Grammar, boys – that means nothing under a seven": Students at exclusive private school rate formal dates in degrading "Tinder boot camp" video.'[33]

'The boys who started the "Slut of the Year" got expelled. And that's exactly what they deserved.'[34]

'St Kevin's College students rating, sexualising female staff.'[35]

'Wesley College students reported for misogynistic March 4 Justice comments.'[36]

We read these headlines and wring our hands and wonder where these behaviours come from. But given all the ways, both subtle and unsubtle, we diminish girls' and women's experiences, it's surprising that *more* boys don't act this way. Our society actively teaches them in a thousand ways that girls are inferior, lesser beings, and not worthy of respect.

When boys grow up with this belief, it's obviously a disaster for girls and women. But it is also setting up boys for a lifetime of disconnection and, most likely, loneliness. It's impossible to have a meaningful connection with someone if you think they're inferior.

We know that men are suffering a crisis of loneliness. Even men who are married to women suffer from loneliness and disconnection. The tragedy for many of them is that they may well be sleeping next to someone each night who is desperate to be emotionally intimate with them, but they are unable to make this connection because they don't view their partner as an equal. They may well have women in their lives who would make wonderful friends, but true and emotionally satisfying friendship is impossible without equality and respect.

If we want boys to be able to form genuine and meaningful connections with girls and women, then we need to be very intentional in teaching them that girls are their equals. You can do this by:

- having zero tolerance for 'girl' being used as an insult to boys
- celebrating your boy if he wants to play with 'girl' toys or dress up in 'girl' clothes
- reading stories and watching movies and TV shows with active female protagonists
- pointing out female leaders and public figures in business, politics, education and the community who do good work
- watching and celebrating women's sporting and athletic performances
- calling out everyday sexism and the derogatory treatment of girls and women, and explaining to your boy in age-appropriate terms why it is wrong
- explicitly telling your boy that it is okay to play with girls and to have female friends – in doing so, we can begin to expand boys' horizons and help them avoid a future of loneliness and disconnection.

Positive male role models can also help boys to understand how to have positive relationships with women (and everyone else). 'These men do not need to be their biological dads,' writes Maggie Dent in *From Boys to Men*.[37] 'However, they do need to be good men, not abusive or toxic men, and men who have grown up to be mature, not adolescents in grown men's bodies.' They could be grandparents, coaches, family friends or neighbours who provide a model for how to be a good man.

Sex and porn

If you're still dealing with toilet training, tantrums or skinned knees, you may be tempted to skip this section and file sex and porn away into the 'I'll worry about that later' part of your parenting brain. We're sorry to tell you that the parents of our generation don't have that luxury. The avalanche of porn is not coming at some point in the future, it is already here.

It's hard to get exact figures about how old boys are when they start accessing porn. There are some reports of boys as young as five seeing porn for the first time,[38] with the vast majority of boys seeing it by age thirteen or younger.[39] The younger boys are when they first see porn, the more likely they are to grow into men who want power over women.[40]

This can lead to some warped views about relationships. For example, adolescent health nurse Chantal Maloney says some teen boys are genuinely surprised to discover that girls don't like being called 'bitch' or having men demand sex from them, because when boys see this in porn, the women seem to love it. 'Some videos are violent or are showing women giving four blow jobs to four different men, and the women are shown [to be] "loving" this,' Maloney says. 'Young men (particularly those who have not had much experience in relationships) then go on to believe that this is what you do . . . and [that] women enjoy it.' Maloney says it is not uncommon for boys in early adolescence to request oral sex that they don't even want from girls at parties. They are just role-playing what they've seen in porn and what they think is expected of teen boys. And, sadly, many of the girls oblige, even though they don't want to, because they are also role-playing what they believe is expected of teen girls.

The scary reality is that we cannot anticipate or prepare our boys for all the harmful porn they are going to see. While we should absolutely do what we can to limit boys' exposure to violent and degrading porn, unless you're living in a log cabin in the middle of nowhere with no wi-fi, your boy is going to access it or be exposed to it. This means that rather than giving boys a one-off 'sex and porn talk' in the vain hope of preparing them and minimising the damage, we need to open the 'sex and porn chat door'.

We need to open that door so wide that our boys *want* to talk to us about it. When they see porn, we want them to feel comfortable enough to tell us. When they hear things about sex that they don't understand or have questions about, we want to be their go-to source of information. And we want to get in first so they learn about sex and romantic relationships from us, and not from an unscrupulous industry monetising dominance, disrespect and the absence of body hair.

How to open the door and keep it open

Here's the thing about doors: they don't open on their own. And they don't stay open without us keeping them that way.

If you're like many parents of our generation, you'd probably rather stick a pencil in your eye than actively encourage your boy to have regular chats with you about sex and porn. This might especially be the case if you were raised in a family that approached sex with secrecy and shame, and where 'the talk' started and ended with 'don't get pregnant' or 'don't get her pregnant', or your preparation for puberty was a book that mysteriously appeared on your bed one day that nobody ever mentioned. But our boys need us to get over our discomfort and step up.

You make yourself the go-to person for information on sex and porn by taking the opportunity to provide this information regularly in a neutral and non-threatening way. You're essentially creating a habit when he's young in the hope that he'll keep speaking to you about these topics when he's older. Don't wait to have these conversations if and when your boy comes to you with questions – get on the front foot and create the opportunities.

Never fly off the handle or make your boy feel like he has done something wrong – even if he has sought out the porn himself. It is natural and normal for him to be curious, and if you want to keep the door open so you can guide and advise him about sex and porn, the last thing you want to do is punish or shame him for it. Several parents have told us about their little boys coming to them in a panic or a fit of tears 'confessing' that they'd accidentally seen porn on their iPads. They had learned that porn was very bad, so when they clicked on the wrong link and saw it, they assumed that *they* were also very bad and they freaked out. One little boy thought it meant he was going to jail. For every boy who 'confesses' to his mum or dad, there must be many more who are too scared to say anything, and who don't get the support they need from a trusted adult.

You can try to work these conversations into daily life, without even referring to porn. For example, if your boy is running around the house naked, tell him it's fine to be naked in your house but that it's not okay to be naked on the iPad. Let him know that if he ever sees naked people on the iPad he should come and tell you. Similarly, if he's playing with a camera around bath time, whether on your phone or with a toy one, tell him that nobody is allowed to take photos of him without his clothes on and that he's not allowed to take photos of anybody else without their clothes on either. Let him know that if somebody does want to take a naked photo of him, or if he sees photos of naked people on the internet, he should come and tell you.

Sexual health educator Amy Lang recommends telling your son explicitly that he will *never* get into trouble if he asks you or tells you about sex or porn.[41] Tell him that the only reason you want him to tell you when he sees it is so that you can talk to him about it, check that he's okay and make sure it doesn't happen again.

If, for whatever reason, you can't be your boy's go-to person for sex and porn chats, then find someone who can be, such as a grandparent, uncle or family friend. This person needs to be available and able to give accurate and healthy information that is based on your values. If this go-to person is going to be you, then read on and we'll tell you how to have these conversations and make them as effective and un-awkward (well, slightly less awkward) as possible.

The birds and the bees

Conversations about intimacy, relationships and porn should happen alongside discussions about bodies and sex. These can start very early. One of the simplest ways you can do this is to call body parts by their correct names. We can't expect our boys to have important conversations about their bodies and other people's bodies if we can't even bring ourselves to correctly name body parts. Ideally we should be able to say 'penis', 'testicles' and 'anus' the same way we are able to say 'head', 'arms' and 'legs'.

Similarly, when your boy has an erection, name it. Say something like, 'You're having an erection. Your penis goes stiff sometimes.' If he's really young, tell him that his penis needs to become erect for when he's grown up and he wants to make a baby. If he's older, tell him he needs an erect penis to be able to have certain types of sex because the erect penis goes in the vagina. You might be cringing right now. We're not going to pretend that any of this is easy for parents. But here's the thing: if we can't name body parts or talk about what they do and why, then our kids are going to pretty soon work out that these body parts – and what is done with them – are so taboo that they can't be openly discussed, and we will have ruined our chance of becoming their go-to source of information.

There is also a very practical safety reason for correctly naming body parts. Some sexual predators target children who do not know the correct names for genitals. They reason that these children are less likely to have been taught about body safety or to have open communication about this topic with a trusted adult, and are therefore easy targets.[42] And if these kids do ring alarm bells about abuse, their cries for help may not be heard if they can't clearly articulate what has happened to them.

If you menstruate, there is no need to ever hide this fact or your period products from your boy. We are doing our boys a grave disservice if we are keeping them ignorant about how the bodies of half the population work. Your boy is also going to be a better husband and father if he's not freaked out by women's natural bodily functions. Tell him simply that you bleed every month and that this is necessary for women to have babies.

The added bonus of starting to name body parts early is that you'll have more practice for when you need to tackle more confronting discussions when your boy is older. Sure, you may never be able to say 'the penis goes in the vagina' with the same calmness and matter-of-factness as 'the dirty clothes go in the washing machine', but if you start early you may get to a point where you're able to do this without breaking out in a cold sweat.

But isn't he too young?

Some parents have told us that they think children should be much older before having conversations about sex. But ask yourself: Why shouldn't we tell kids early about sex? If you are concerned that educating your boy about it will make him have sex earlier, then you can cross that off your list of things to worry about. This is a myth that has kept children ignorant – not innocent – for far too long. Decades of evidence shows that the more informed your boy is about sex, the older he's likely to be when he first does it. And the safer he's likely to be.[43] Amy Lang says, 'When your kiddos are as smart about the birds and the bees as they are about math or reading, they are more likely to wait as long as possible, have healthy relationships and be safer from abuse and assault.'[44] Empower your boy with knowledge about sex so he can make better choices.

The more comfortable we are about sex, the more likely it is that our kids are going to come to us for information, which is our end goal, isn't it? Even if you don't agree with everything we've just said, the biggest reason of all to talk about sex is that if you don't tell your kids about it early, someone else is going to beat you to it. And chances are they are not going to be nearly as accurate, and they may not have your boy's best interests at heart.

No matter how uncomfortable or freaked out or horrified you might be by something your boy tells you or shows you, it is important to remain calm, factual and welcoming.

'I've got no idea what's going on in his head'

Strong relationships are obviously important when it comes to a boy's peer group. But what about your boy's relationship with you? One of the biggest concerns that emerged from parents' feedback was about how to get boys to open up and communicate. Some parents spoke of the heartbreak of being shut out of their son's life, saying it was like living with a stranger. Other parents were concerned that their boy wouldn't confide in them, leaving them unable to help and guide him. Some were really frustrated with their boy's lack of communication. 'My daughter tells me exactly what's going on in her life,' one mother said. 'If something happens at school she'll tell me exactly what happened, what was said, how it was said and [give me] a blow by blow account . . . But my son tells me nothing. I've got no idea what's going on in his head.'

The parents whose boys are currently talking openly with them feared that it was just a matter of time until their boys shut them out. They'd heard the horror stories – that just like flicking a switch, their sweet little boy would cut them off, and the most they'd get out of him for the next decade would be grunts and requests for food.

If your end-of-day conversations with your son go something like the following, you're not alone.

'How was school?'

'Good.'

'What did you do?'

'Nothing.'

At a purely practical level, you might get more out of your son if you follow Maggie Dent's simple rule: snack before chat. Before you ask him how his day was, make sure his tummy is full and his blood sugar is up. You might even want to bring a sandwich to school pick-up to speed up the process.

Another quick fix for the 'How was your day?' conversational graveyard is getting the timing right. Early-years educational director Kate Hall says that when you pick your boy up from preschool or school, he's most likely exhausted. The last thing he probably wants to do is have to go over who he played with, what he ate and what the teacher said. Hall says your boy is far more likely to want to tell you about his day after he's had time to wind down.

Unfortunately, this may be right when you're trying to get him into bed. 'Parents will say, "Oh, but I'm trying to get them to sleep, I just want them to go to sleep so I can get dishes done and go to bed myself,"' says Hall. 'Well, that's how he felt when you drilled him at 3.30!' The answer, Hall suggests, is shifting his bedtime 10 minutes earlier so you can build in 10 minutes of chatting before you turn the lights out and rush off to do all the night-time cleaning up and admin, or just sit down with a cup of tea.

Your boy might be more willing to open up when he is by your side rather than right in front of you, such as when you're going for a walk or sitting in the car, because it can feel less confronting.

You can also try a soothing activity such as using playdough or Lego. For example, while your boy is building away, you can be his assistant and find all the pieces he needs. When he's calm and in the flow of things he will be more relaxed and potentially more likely to talk to you. And keep a lookout for signs that your boy wants to talk to you. 'If your son keeps hanging around, offers to help around the house out of the blue or keeps mentioning an issue in passing, however casually, find ways to draw him out,' suggests Tanith Carey.[45]

Make it a habit

One night a friend who had an uncommunicative boy decided to sit at the end of his bed at bedtime and see what would happen, instead of switching the light off and rushing out like she normally did. Within a few moments her son started talking, and talking and talking. The next night she did the same thing and got the same level of communication.

On the third night her son got in first. 'Are you going to do that thing where you sit on my bed for a chat again tonight?' he asked.

The lesson here is that once you find the right time and the right activity or conditions for your boy to feel comfortable talking to you, try to make a habit or a tradition of this. If you start when he's young and just keep doing it, it will more likely endure as he enters his teen years. You may even find that he's the one who is pushing you to maintain the routine.

Treat them and what they say as gold

When we were first-time parents, a maternal health nurse told us that you should smile whenever you see your baby. Mostly that's easy to do. But it applies especially when they're on the change table, staring up at you, watching you like a hawk. And, yes, this applies even when they've produced the world's stinkiest, stickiest poo. The maternal health nurse told us not to screw up our faces when our baby produced a prize-worthy poo. Your baby will see that, they told us, and think you're not happy to see them.

While the maternal health nurse was talking about babies, this is a lesson for life. As your kids get older, when their faces are dirty and their clothes are filthy and aren't on properly, don't let your first response be to screw up your face. Instead, let your face light up every time you see them because they are them and you love them.

That applies doubly when your child speaks. Kate Hall recommends approaching each conversation with the understanding that whatever they say to you is precious. 'They're sharing their most inner self with you,' says Hall. 'Honour that. Don't shoot them down.' You might get a monosyllabic grunt or a fully formed sentence. Whatever it is, resist the temptation to jump in with solutions, to minimise concerns, criticise or laugh. Your boy is still learning to express himself. His first or even his twenty-eighth attempt to express himself may not be quite right. If our responses to our boys' efforts to make themselves heard or understood cause them to feel ashamed or lead to a lecture or some sort of punishment, they will shut down and be reluctant to open up again. Boys are also more likely to want to talk if we really listen to what they say, and they feel heard, understood and supported. So, as hard as it is, resist the urge to pre-empt what your boy is saying or to rush in with a quick 'fix'.

This doesn't mean that we shouldn't intervene or correct them. Remember: your boy is still learning about the world and there will be times when he gets things wrong and needs your guidance, but go gently. If you want him to keep speaking openly with you, make yourself the coach or the trusted advisor rather than the judge and jury. And be really mindful about teasing him. Ribbing or making jokes that might seem trivial or fun to us can be genuinely upsetting to a boy. Children often don't understand sarcasm, nuance or subtleties. If he thinks you're not going to take him seriously or you're going to make fun of him, then he's not going to share his gold with you.

Fostering safe communication with your boy is an antidote to any shame he might be feeling. As we discussed in chapter two, shame is believing that you are fundamentally bad and unworthy of love. If your boy grows up with too much shame – with the belief that there is something deeply and incurably wrong with him – it will be almost impossible for him to like himself. The good news is that shame is like a gremlin: it's destroyed by light. If your boy feels safe enough to be honest and open with you about his mistakes, bad choices and insecurities, and you listen with empathy and understanding, and you support and guide him rather than punishing or ridiculing him, he can learn self-compassion and forgiveness. He will be able to like himself.

We cannot say this strongly enough: the old-school belief that shame makes people behave well is dead wrong. Shame is dangerous. It is far more likely to *cause* bad behaviour than cure it. And this can have devastating repercussions for a boy's whole life.

Clinical psychologist Dr Sue Johnson says that children who grow up without having deep and meaningful conversations in which they are able to open up about their feelings, fears, mistakes and needs will be unlikely to be able to do this when they are older, because they have never learned how it's done. She tells a story of a middle-aged man who sobbed the first time he opened up and shared his true feelings with his wife in a relationship counselling session.[46] 'I've been alone all my life, haven't I?' he said. That is a tragedy – and one you can spare your boy from.

Like most of us, boys are more inclined to do things if they make them feel good. So naturally they are more likely to want to open up to their parents if it is emotionally satisfying and safe to do so. Boys are no different from the rest of us. They are at their best when they feel secure and worthy – when they like themselves. The benefits of your son opening up to you and sharing his true feelings, fears and vulnerabilities go beyond enhancing his wellbeing and your connection in the present moment. These conversations will give him the template, the skills and the confidence to have intimate conversations throughout his life that will lead to more fulfilling relationships with friends, partners and, eventually, perhaps his own children.

Just tell me what to do!

One of the most damaging stereotypes for boys and men is that of the lone ranger – the stoic, self-sufficient man who goes through life without needing anyone. Boys, and the men they become, need strong relationships just as much as women do in order to live full, meaningful and healthy lives. And the time for your boy to learn the skills necessary to develop a foundation for strong relationships is now.

- Friendship skills don't always develop naturally. You may need to specifically teach your boy how to make a friend, choose good friends and be a good friend.
- The best way for your boy to stand up for himself is by using the right words, not a right hook. Help your boy to come up with and practise his clever comeback line (p. 179).
- Help your boy to practise articulating and defending his no-go zones, such as 'I don't like . . .' or 'I don't do . . .'
- Teach your boy that pranks and jokes are only funny if *everyone* is laughing. If he wouldn't be happy if something was done to him, he shouldn't do it to someone else.

- To get your boy to open up and talk to you, make sure he's not hungry or tired. Find a time when he is comfortable talking, and create a habit out of this. Treat whatever he tells you as gold.

7

A boy who likes himself is himself

A pussy at the park

Two of our friends became fathers a month apart. Their boys are now toddlers and they have been regularly taking their sons to the park together. Matthew's son, Ari, is one of those boys who can't sit still and who is utterly fearless. He'll fly down hills on his scooter; the steeper the better. He'll climb anything he can find and leap off it. When he crash-lands he gets back up and wants to do it all over again. George's son, Henry, meanwhile, prefers playing in the sandpit to leaping off swings, and scares quite easily.

Seeing the difference between the two boys, George tells Matthew that he's concerned Henry is growing up to be 'soft'. George says he gets frustrated and angry when Henry doesn't want to take part in the high-risk play that Ari gravitates to. When Henry falls over and cries, George tells him to get up and stop being a sook. Without a hint of irony or jest, George once said matter-of-factly, 'My son is such a pussy. I need to toughen him up.' This conversation, we should add, happened in 2022. It's not a throwback to the 1960s or 1970s.

The idea that there is a certain way of being a boy is what some researchers call 'the Man Box'. You can probably take a guess at the kinds of qualities associated with the Man Box, even if you've never heard the term before. They're the familiar qualities associated with masculinity: being tough, not showing any emotion or vulnerability, never asking for help, being the breadwinner, always being in control and controlling women, and using violence to solve problems. Research shows that, far from being a relic of past eras, the Man Box is alive and well in modern society. And, as we saw with sweet little Henry at the park, shaping boys to fit into the narrow confines of the Man Box begins at an alarmingly young age.

This chapter looks at the consequences of trying to fit boys into the Man Box. We'll show you that, like most boxes, the Man Box is as restrictive as it is boringly predictable. It is a way to squelch the life out of your boy, to take away his authenticity, his spark; and, in many cases, it turns him against his nature to create a certain kind of boyhood; a certain kind of male experience. Our aim is to convince you that far from being natural and normal, the qualities associated with the Man Box are manufactured and artificial. They are attempts to impose on boys – and the men they become – certain attitudes and ways of behaving that are anything but innate. And we'll show what the alternative might be, to enable your boy to escape the restrictions of the Man Box. This requires a different way of thinking about our roles as parents, one that involves moving away from the desire to sculpt boys to fit some pre-existing ideal and instead allowing our boys to flourish on their own terms and in their own direction. But before we get to that, let's see how forcing your boy to adhere to these types of masculine values is not just bad for society, but, more pressingly, a disaster for our boys.

Boxed in

If there is one thing the Harry Potter books taught us, it's that growing up in a confined space, such as a bedroom under the stairs, is anything but healthy. You may not have a boy wizard, but the research shows that the similarly restrictive Man Box is not good for boys or for men. Matt Tyler, executive director of The Men's Project at Jesuit Social Services, and his team have carried out extensive research on the Man Box in Australia. The results paint an alarming picture.

The research shows that boys who genuinely endorse the stereotype of the Man Box (rather than just going along with it when they feel they have to) are more likely to have poor mental health and to abuse drugs and alcohol, and are more than twice as likely to express suicidal thoughts (64 per cent of men in the top Man Box quintile reported suicidal thoughts in the two weeks prior to completing the survey). They are also more likely to perpetrate bullying (both online and in real life), and they are far more likely than those outside the Man Box to be victims of it. Half of the young men surveyed who subscribe to unhealthy masculine stereotypes have experienced physical bullying, compared to only 15 per cent of boys who are not inside the Man Box.[1]

Boys who have been forced inside the Man Box are also less likely to seek help when they need it, and are more likely to express their frustration in outbursts that lead to disciplinary action at school. Melissa Abu-Gazaleh, managing director of the Top Blokes Foundation, which aims to increase boys' engagement in school, told the *Sydney Morning Herald* that 'this then becomes a self-fulfilling prophecy where the male student then has lower aspirations to be better or achieve more'.[2]

Men who have been raised to believe in the Man Box stereotype are more likely to be involved in a car accident. More than a third of these men had been in a car accident in the year prior to completing the survey, compared to 11 per cent of men outside the Man Box.[3] With statistics like this, it's not surprising that boys being harmed or doing harm to others was one of the biggest fears parents shared with us.

If you're freaking out at these statistics, take a breath. These outcomes only apply to boys who *hold* or subscribe to the values of the Man Box. Tyler says that 'Many men don't personally endorse these Man Box ideas but they still perceive social pressures to perform it.' The difference between believing in these values and behaviours and sometimes feeling pressure to perform them is really important. It is also reason to hope, because, as parents, we can get in first to influence these values in our boys.

Can't we just let boys be boys and men be men?

There are those who say that masculinity was fine in the past and that people are just complicating everything. These people see the values associated with the Man Box as the natural and normal way to be a man, and attempts to complicate it as woke nonsense. Can't we just allow boys to be boys and men to be men?

Here's the thing: there is nothing natural or normal about the values and attitudes of the Man Box. If you doubt that, ask yourself: If it's so natural, why is so much effort put into creating and enforcing these attitudes and behaviours? Why do we as a society go to such lengths to police boys' behaviour? And why do parents such as George feel the need to harden up their sons and stop them from being 'pussies'? If being 'hard' was really inherent to being a boy or man, then George wouldn't need to be concerned about this. His young son would just 'harden up' as he grew up, irrespective of the environment around him.

The only reason that parents like George feel the need to intervene is that the Man Box is created. It's a decision people make – whether consciously or not – to create boys and men in a certain way. It may not feel like a choice, because most of us don't make this choice consciously or individually. We inherit these values from those around us and then we go along and do the same thing that was done to us.

Make no mistake, the values of the Man Box are everywhere in society, so there is no doubt your boy is going to be exposed to them and be told that 'real men' adhere to these unhealthy masculine stereotypes. 'Two thirds of the men we surveyed told us that since they were a boy, they've been told a "real man" acts this way,' says Matt Tyler. More than half of the young men surveyed said their parents had taught them that a 'real man' should act strong even if he feels nervous or scared.[4]

There will inevitably be people in your boy's life and in the playground who will try to police his behaviour and try to get him to go along with these stereotypical values. They'll call him a pussy or a wimp when he steps outside the Man Box, or tell him to harden up when he shows emotion or vulnerability. But – and this is a really big but – he has a choice over whether or not he believes in the values of the Man Box.

This is where you come in!

Stone parenting and seed parenting

The Man Box is an extreme example of what we call stone parenting. Stone parenting is the idea that our children come to us as unformed lumps of stone and that it is our job as parents to chisel away in order to sculpt them into successful adults. Stone parents spend years hacking away at their boys' weaknesses and at the personality traits and opinions that they consider undesirable. In the vast majority of cases, this is motivated by love. A parent has decided the best way for their child to be, and with the very best intentions, they see their role as bringing forth the masterpiece that they have conceived.

The opposite of stone parenting is seed parenting. Seed parents view their child as a precious and unique seed that has yet to fully bloom and become. They see their job as parents as providing the right environment and support structures to nurture the seed, but they trust their boy to grow and bloom in his own way and in his own time. They will provide a trellis and be a guide, but how their boy unfurls and the specific shape he grows into are up to him.

In practice, most of us are a mixture of stone and seed parents. But we may tend towards one style of parenting over the other. Or we may be stone parents in some contexts and seed parents in others. For example, we may be intent on sculpting the perfect athlete, but more laissez faire when it comes to artistic capability. Or we may want our boy to excel at maths and science, but leave him to his own devices when it comes to drama or the arts.

Put down your chisel and pick up your watering can

Seed parents have a much greater chance of bringing up a boy who likes himself. This is because, to like himself, a boy must be able to grow into the person that *he* chooses, not a version of himself that conforms to a restrictive model that has been chosen for him or laid down in advance by today's society, no matter how well-intentioned. 'The first step we know for self-confidence is the parent has to figure out who their child is, not what they want their child to become,' says educational psychologist Dr Michele Borba.[5] A boy who likes himself needs to know and value his authentic self, and to help him do this, so do we.

Sadly, your boy is going to face all sorts of pressures to contort himself into the Man Box. But, at the very least, you can make your home a safe haven where your boy is free to drop the pretence, be himself and express himself with authenticity. Protect him, while you can, from pressures that will chisel away at his natural self, from forces that want to push him into the Man Box. Give him the time, space and freedom to discover who he really is, the values he wants to hold, and the type of man he wants to grow into.

Seek out opportunities to teach your boy to think critically about the values of the Man Box. TV shows and movies are a great way to do this. For example, when you see media where men use violence to solve a problem, ask him if he's noticed that men do this in a lot in movies. Ask him if there might be other ways of solving problems. If the male protagonist spends his time saving girls or women, ask your boy if he thinks that's necessary. Does he think that the girl or woman might be able to save herself or solve her own problems?

Similarly, you can use sports to think about the idea of winning at all costs. What would happen if your boy (or his team) didn't win? Most of the time there can only be one winner, so get him to think about all the people who didn't win. Has something terrible happened to them as a result? Are their lives over because they didn't win? Most likely the answer is no. Losing might be disappointing, but life goes on.

Where possible, point out examples of men doing good. Ideally, these examples will demonstrate many different ways of being a man. These men could be activists, artists, businesspeople, politicians, teachers or athletes. They may exemplify alternative ways of being a man, or they may be examples of the very best values we associate with traditional masculinity. The aim here is not to erase all aspects of traditional masculinity. As we said in the introduction, there are many traditionally 'masculine' values that are worth not just keeping, but celebrating.

Our aim is not to show boys healthy masculinity, singular, but healthy masculinities, plural. There is no one-size-fits-all version of masculinity. 'The last thing we want to do is make another Man Box,' says Matt Tyler. 'This is not about saying that there is one way to be a man or a boy. It is about saying we want to break free of the constraints that we know exist as a result of the Man Box. And we want to promote as much flexibility as possible.'

We won't always be around to protect our boys from people who will be wielding chisels to shape them into the Man Box. We need to build our boys' foundation of authenticity so that they can withstand the pressures of the Man Box as much as possible. Refer back to the techniques in the power perspective chapter (chapter one) to help your boy learn to trust his own judgement rather than letting other people determine his worth. His peer group is important, so help him choose friends who are good for him, and get him to practise defending his no-go zones and go zones with you, so that when he is pressed to conform to the Man Box he will have the skills to stand up for himself or walk away (see chapter six).

These strategies might not sound like much in isolation. But as your boy's first teacher, you have the influence to shape him. It's the constant, consistent, slow, unremarkable everyday lessons that win out in building your boy's foundation of authenticity.

But what if your boy's authentic self makes him a target?

We were staying at a beach resort that sold long, multicoloured hair extensions called mermaid braids. Almost every little girl at the resort had the sparkling extensions braided into their hair.

And just one little boy.

Watching the boy bounce along joyfully swinging his purple and blue mermaid braids was both beautiful and surprising. It was wonderful to see parents who supported their boy to make choices outside the Man Box, but it got us thinking that out of all the hundreds of boys staying at the resort, there was only one who wanted – or was allowed – to have them. It was an illustration of just how early little boys learn to reject things that are considered feminine.

We later found out that the boy with the braids was Knox, the oldest son of social media superstars Sarah and Brad Kearns.[6] Through their DaDMuM social media platform they spend a lot of time challenging gender norms and writing about the challenges and joys of raising three boys to be their authentic selves.

In his early years Knox was blissfully ignorant of the 'rules' around what boys are supposed to like and do.

'Knox is just Knox, unapologetically himself, and people struggle with him a little bit because they do put kids in boxes,' says Sarah Kearns. 'He likes motocross and he likes mermaids and he likes birds and dinosaurs and pink and blue.'

But then it was time for Knox to go to school, and his parents started to worry about the backlash and bullying their boy would face if they continued to allow him to be his authentic self.

'It was something that my husband definitely struggled with,' says Sarah. 'He was initially saying, "Knox can have whatever he wants, he can do whatever he wants at home, but don't let him take it to school, because what's going to happen when the other kids see it?"'

It's not surprising that Sarah's husband, Brad, felt this way. He would know firsthand how cruel kids can be to boys who do not conform to the Man Box.

'But my instincts and my heart just said that it's more important for Knox to know that we support him 100 per cent in every choice he makes, and he has that safe space in us [where] he can always be himself,' says Sarah. 'It was more important for us to teach him not to hide who he is from the world, to be himself, and be confident in who he is.'

Instead of trying to change their son, Sarah and Brad turned their attention to giving him the skills to deal with the backlash that might come.

1. Explain that people see the world in different ways

'We told him there's lots of different opinions and some children have been raised with the idea that blue is for boys and pink is for girls,' says Sarah. 'That was a really difficult concept for him. He said, "I don't understand how a puppy dog pencil case could be a girl's one. Why do only girls get puppy dogs?"'

2. Role-play standing up for himself (see chapter six)

'We gave him little things to say, like if somebody says, "That's a girl's pencil case," he would be able to come back and say,

"I'm a boy and it's mine. And I like it," or "There's no such thing as girl colours and boy colours.'"

3. Build his power perspective (see chapter one)

'We say all the time, what other people say or think about you is none of your business. It's what you think of you that's important,' Sarah says.

Parents can chisel away at their boy's authentic self with the very best of intentions. There's no doubt that it's painful for a boy to not be fully accepted at school. But we would argue that it is infinitely more painful for him to feel like he's not accepted at home, by the people who are supposed to love him the most.

Help your boy find and grow his strengths

So many of the behaviours and traits associated with the Man Box are driven by fear and a sense of lack. They are attempts to make up for some kind of deficiency, whether real or perceived. For example, displaying physical strength in the hope of concealing weakness, exercising dominance to mask a lack of control, repressing emotions out of a fear of being unable to handle them, or lashing out in an attempt to hide vulnerability.

Enabling your boy to flourish into his authentic self requires you to find and amplify his strengths rather than trying in vain to cover and compensate for perceived lack. A strength is something that blooms from within your boy. It's natural and internal. He may need your support and encouragement to develop it, but the seed already lives within him.

It's important to distinguish a strength from a skill. A skill is something that a child can develop as a result of external pressure and sculpting. Think of the boy who excels at the violin as a result of his daily practice, but who hates every minute of it. Playing the violin does not give him joy or make his heart sing. He's not doing it for him, he's doing it to please his parents or for some other external motive. Strengths, on the other hand, are things your boy is naturally good at or shows potential in. But they are also things that energise him and that he chooses to do without prompting or nagging.[7]

Discover his strengths

If you are unsure what your boy's strengths are, watch him. Catch the moments of joy in your house. What activities is he naturally drawn to? What activities does he become so engrossed in that you have to drag him away from them at bedtime? What subject does he know so much about that he could go on and on for hours?

If he's old enough, ask him what he thinks his strengths are. What does he love doing? What activities make him feel good? What would he do more of if he could? Your job is then to listen and resist the urge to chip in with your opinion or stories about your experience.

Michele Borba say to make sure you are noticing the things he pulls you to do as opposed to what you're pushing him to do. 'To discover their strengths they want to know you care about what their unique experiences in the world are, not necessarily how you did things,' says Jenifer Fox, author of *Your Child's Strengths*.[8] 'Let them find their own paths; they may not want to play basketball just because you did. Sometimes kids forgo their own passions to please you.'

Try to resist the urge to compare your boy's strengths with any siblings', or with anyone else for that matter. When you compare, his strengths will become an external measuring stick for self-worth rather than an internal source of joy, motivation and competence.

Notice and comment on his strengths

Once you have identified your boy's strengths, remark on them when you see him use them. His strengths are fundamentally part of who he is, his authentic self. If you don't value and cherish his authentic self, how can he? For example, if your boy's strengths are his social skills and manners, you might say, 'That was very polite of you to thank Tom's mum for driving you home. You have such great manners.' If his strength is sports, you could say, 'You were such a great team player today.' Child and teen development specialist Dr Robyn Silverman recommends dropping your boy's strengths into conversations with casual comments such as, 'You're the kind of person who [mention his strength].' 'And then watch your boy get a little taller,' she says.[9]

When your boy is facing a challenge, you can empower him by encouraging him to call on one of his strengths.[10] For example, if your boy's strength is his persistence and tenacity, and he's struggling to complete a school project, you might say, 'Now is the time to call on your never-give-up attitude to help you finish your project.' If he knows he has the strength of tenacity, then he will have more faith in his ability – and therefore more motivation – to complete his schoolwork.

Develop his strengths

To further encourage the growth of your boy's strengths, seek out opportunities for him to use and develop them. This may mean stopping other activities and resisting the urge to spend precious hours trying to fix his weaknesses instead.

Grow his strengths by listening, learning and validating them. Our friend Meagan, for instance, has a boy who is obsessed with American football and who has the strength of researching and retaining minute details about players, games and history. Before her son exhibited this strength, Meagan had never watched a game of football in her life. She's now the person you'd want on your pub trivia team should there be any football questions. By taking an interest in her son's interest and strength, Meagan was essentially telling him daily that he matters and that he's worthy. In years to come she will be able to remind her boy of his exceptional strength in retaining and regurgitating information and how he can apply that same strength to other pursuits such as history exams or memorising mathematical equations.

Find role models who also exhibit or value your boy's strengths. For example, if your boy has the strength of fairness and good sportsmanship, then make sure you choose a team for him with a coach who also shares these values, rather than one who has a kill-or-be-killed attitude. If your boy is drawn to gardening and you can't even keep your grass alive, then see if there is a neighbour or friend he could garden with occasionally so he can develop his strength and see that it is valued by others.

Help! My boy doesn't seem to have any strengths!

Your boy does have strengths. We guarantee it.

But if you're having trouble thinking of his strengths, don't feel bad – blame what psychologists refer to as our 'negativity bias'. If you've not heard of the negativity bias, it's our tendency to pay more attention to and attach stronger emotions to negative information and stimuli than positive things.[11] If you've noticed that you tend to focus more on the low grades on your boy's report card rather than the high ones, that's the negativity bias at work. Similarly, if you find yourself focusing more on one negative remark from his teacher rather than all the positive ones, that's the negativity bias kicking in. Or, if you focus on the chores your boy didn't do, and fail to notice the ones he did do, that's the negativity bias again. This bias can apply to behaviour as well as to achievements or talents. As a general rule, parents are likely to notice and remark on the few times their children are rude or disrespectful and to overlook the many times they are polite and considerate.

On top of our brain's negativity bias, we have an education system that often expects little boys to sit still, stay quiet, concentrate and perform academic tasks that they may not yet be capable of doing. Add in the social pressure to create the 'perfect' child, and the constant measuring and comparing of children lest they 'fall behind' or fail to 'get a head start', and we end up with well-meaning parents reaching for their chisels in an attempt to 'fix' their boy's perceived flaws rather than recognising, celebrating and nurturing his good qualities.

If you're still not sure what your boy's strengths are, then have a look at the list of strengths in the appendix at the back of this book (p. 227). We bet you will find many things your boy is good at. And while you're there, have a look for your own strengths. Our parents' generation was even more likely to raise their kids with a corrective approach to our weaknesses rather than a promotional approach to our strengths. It's quite possible that you have not fully realised all the wonderful and unique strengths that you have either.

But won't he get a big head?

If you're worried that focusing on your boy's strengths might give him a big head or an over-inflated sense of his own competence, don't be. If your boy is going to grow up liking himself then it is essential that he knows he's good at things. Kids who have a solid foundation of self-worth don't need to boast and try to convince people about their achievements. They just take it for granted that they are good and valuable people.

Professor Lea Waters, the founding director of the Centre for Positive Psychology (now the Centre for Wellbeing Science) at the University of Melbourne, says it is a myth that the best way to develop our kids' optimism and resilience is to correct their weaknesses. 'We think that if we chisel off their weaknesses then they will feel good about themselves. But it doesn't work like this. What they understand is that "I am wrong and bad and need to be fixed,"' writes Professor Waters in *The Strength Switch*.[12]

This makes sense. After all, feeling good about yourself doesn't come from the promise that you might be good enough at some point in the future, after you've fixed this weakness or corrected this flaw. Kids don't live in the future. They live in the present. They need to know that they are good enough and are valued for who they are right now.

Unhealthy and limiting masculine stereotypes make matters even worse when it comes to focusing too much on chiselling off boys' weaknesses. Not only do we expect boys to be stoic and tough enough to handle being constantly called out and criticised for their weaknesses, old-school parenting dictates that they need this.

Boys who are lucky enough to be raised by parents who focus on their strengths are less likely to suffer from depression,[13] are more joyful and have better relationships. This includes their relationships with their parents![14] Just like us, our kids are going to feel a greater connection with, be more cooperative with and want to spend more time with someone who sees the good in them rather than someone who constantly points out their faults.

Strength reinforces strength

Focusing on strengths is self-reinforcing. If your boy feels valued for using his strength, he'll want to do it again, and the more he does it the better he will become at it,[15] which will propel him into a happier, healthier and more successful life.[16] Not only does this approach make for a happier home (for everybody!), it also helps boys do better at school. They cope better with issues like homework deadlines and problems with friends, and are

216

more resourceful and have higher levels of academic achievement, when they are conscious of their strengths and know that these strengths are valued.

This isn't about denying reality or ignoring your boy's weaknesses. It might sound counterintuitive, but according to Professor Waters, the best way to help your boy address his weaknesses is to spend most of your time noticing and developing his strengths. To illustrate this point, let's go back to Sam and Liam, who we've talked about in previous chapters. Sam is growing up with seed parents who focus on his strengths. Liam, however, has stone parents who love him dearly but who are parenting the way they were parented, and who consequently spend most of the time focusing on the parts of Liam they feel they need to 'fix'.

These two boys have very similar skills and capabilities. They have pretty much the same strengths and the same weaknesses. And one of the weaknesses they share is spelling. They both struggle with spelling. But their approaches to this weakness are totally different.

Sam has built his identity on all the things he's good at. He thinks, 'I'm a really creative person who can build anything. And I need some extra help with spelling.'

Liam, on the other hand, has built his identity on what he's not good at. He thinks, 'I'm terrible at spelling. Even when I try, I suck at it. I'm dumb.'

Do you see the difference? Both boys struggle with spelling – at the moment. But Sam's not crushed by it because this weakness doesn't define him. Liam, by contrast, has learned to measure his self-worth by what he can't do. And why wouldn't he think like this? In his mind, at least, that's what everyone's always talking about. Liam falling behind, Liam needing to catch up, Liam needing to try harder, Liam not being good enough.

And the sad thing is, even though these boys' capabilities are evenly matched right now, in a couple of years' time, if nothing changes, Sam will most likely surge ahead – not just with his strengths, but with improving on his weaknesses too. And Liam really will be left behind.

Why?

Because when Sam does his catch-up spelling lessons, he's not upset and fighting it. He doesn't take his struggle with spelling as proof that he's a failure. He doesn't define his self-worth by his spelling test results, so he isn't anxious and resistant and closed down. Spelling is just something he needs extra help with. And because he's been raised not to fear failure – as we covered in our chapter about mastery (chapter five) – he's not afraid of making mistakes. His parents have helped him develop his 'failing well' story, so he knows that – just like when he first started roller-blading and he couldn't even stand up – with time and practice, he will be able to do it. He's also learned to measure his success backwards, so that rather than looking ahead and comparing himself with what the kids in the top spelling group can do, he reminds himself that at the beginning of the year he couldn't even spell the days of the week, and now he's even getting some of the months right.

Liam's catch-up spelling sessions, on the other hand, end in tears and frustration because all poor Liam can think about is how he's failing at spelling and therefore failing at life. And for him every spelling session is just more proof of that.

Think about how you feel when people are overly critical and focus on your weaknesses, flaws or faults. Does this motivate you? Does it make you feel loved and valued and inspired? If you're like most people, the answer will be no. Of course we need to guide and correct our kids, but this can be done without con-stantly focusing on their faults and shredding them with criticism. Dr Robyn Silverman says that when you look at your child and you see their deficits first, they will think that they can do no right. 'Define him by his strengths – that is who he is – and consider his weaknesses [as] simply areas that you're working on,' she says.[17] Be the trellis, not the chisel. Your words have tremendous power.

Use them to help your son bloom instead of cutting him down. Parenting has a negativity bias as well. Everyone is so quick to point out what we are doing wrong as parents. And very often we are our own harshest critics. Focusing on your boy's strengths will help you see the wonderful little person you are nurturing and raising, and the great qualities he has that enrich him, you and the world. You will realise that despite any concerns you might have about not being a good-enough parent, you are actually doing a lot right.

Love and raise the boy you have, not the one you thought you were going to get

Valuing your son's strengths sounds obvious, but for many parents it is difficult in practice. This is especially the case if his strengths are wildly different from yours or from your preconceived notion of what your boy would be. We all had a vision of what our children were going to be like and what sort of parents we were going to be. Children are very good at shattering that fantasy! You might have wanted your boy to be athletic and sporty, but his strengths might be in computer programming or gaming. Maybe you wanted him to be academically inclined, but his strength is his physicality or working with his hands.

Recognising and cherishing your boy's strengths can be especially complicated if they are different from those society dictates boys and men should have. For example, society says boys need to be fearless and alpha, so if your boy is gentle and thoughtful it might be hard to see these qualities as strengths to nurture rather than as weaknesses to fix.

There is no gentle way to say this, so our apologies for being blunt: You need to raise the boy you have, not the one you thought you were going to get.

We may think we are helping our boys by motivating and pushing them to achieve certain things and be a certain way, but

instead we may be chiselling away at their innate sense of worthiness by creating what Professor Brené Brown calls 'if/when
prerequisites'.[18] Some examples that may apply to boys include:

I'll only be good enough when I make the football team.

My parents will love me more if I lose weight.

I'll be worthy if I get a good report card.

My parents will be proud of me if I hang out with the popular
kids.

Child and family mental health expert Claire Orange says that
for many parents, love for a child can be mixed with grief that the
child you always wanted isn't the one you got.

And guess what? That's okay. It's perfectly normal to feel grief
that the boy you have is different from the one you expected.
These feelings of grief do not make you a bad parent or a bad
person. What's important is how you express and deal with
that grief.

And we all must deal with any grief or disappointment if
we are going to be the parents our boys need us to be in order
to grow up liking themselves. Letting go of expectations our
children cannot meet – of the 'shoulds' that we always felt a boy
must be – is one of the greatest acts of bravery and love that a
parent can perform.

If your grief is so severe or complicated that you or your partner
cannot deal with it on your own, then you may wish to seek professional counselling. To live an authentic life, every child needs
to be loved and accepted for who they are, and we encourage every
parent to do whatever is necessary to achieve that.

We are not suggesting this is easy. It's not. We all carry our
own baggage about parenting and expectations for our children.
The more baggage you have been burdened with in your own life,
and the further your child is from the expectation you had, the
harder it is to overcome the grief. But it can be done. If your boy
is different from what your family or community expects him to
be, then he will need your unwavering acceptance even more. We

must be the counterforce to a world that seeks to tell our boys that they are wrong or not enough. And to succeed, we must push back with equal or greater force.

If things are less complicated, the answer is simpler – to shift your perspective and spend most of your time focusing on and nurturing your boy's strengths rather than correcting his weaknesses.

Don't let homophobia destroy his authentic self

We have heard stories of parents being furious at early-years educators for letting their boy dress up in princess dresses or play with dolls, as if close exposure to tulle or lace might infect their boy. Just to be clear: girl germs aren't real. We know of one dad who wouldn't let his son share a double swing with another boy because 'He's not into dudes'. (And no, we're not embellishing. Those were his actual words.) Similarly, we have received many anguished emails from parents who felt they had done something wrong because their son was gay, or they thought that he might be.

If your son blooms into a boy or man who is gay, then that is exactly who he is supposed to be. It can be very difficult for parents to come to terms with this, especially if they have grown up in homophobic homes or communities. In addition, many of the values and attitudes that keep boys and men in the Man Box are grounded in homophobia.

But the reality is that no amount of chiselling will change your boy's sexuality. This is not something that you have any control or influence over. What you do have a choice in is how you are going to react to it. You cannot pull your boy from the path he is travelling, so you have to decide if you will walk that path beside him and support him in navigating a world that at times will be cruel to him. Will you be there to pick him up, have his back and reassure him that he is inherently lovable and acceptable? Or will

221

you stay stuck in Man Box values and make your boy walk his path alone, without your help and support?

If you do not walk with him, you will be watching him slip further and further away from you. This will not only be heart-breaking for you, but will be devastating for your boy. It can be hard to be gay in a homophobic world, and your boy needs your love and acceptance more than ever.

The gift of unconditional love

The most courageous and loving thing we can do as parents is to see and value our boy for who he really is, not what society expects him to be. If you want your boy to grow up liking himself, then he must be supported to grow into the best version of the person he chooses to be. We cannot make this choice for our children, no matter how well-intentioned or sharp our chisels are. When your boy is free to be anything he wants to be, he will succeed because he's doing what comes naturally to him.

And this isn't just warm and fuzzy feel-good stuff (although it is that too!). Unconditional love is the basis for his future emotional wellbeing. Professor Brené Brown has interviewed thousands of people over many years, trying to work out the secret formula for emotional wellbeing. She has taken into account gender, age, education, socio-economics and life experiences, and found that there is only one difference between people who feel a deep sense of worthiness and belonging and those who struggle through life without it. 'Those who feel lovable, who love, and who experience belonging simply *believe they are worthy* of love and belonging,' she writes in *Daring Greatly*.[19]

How do you create the belief of worthiness in your boy? By always treating him as if he is worthy – as if his worthiness is as fixed and unequivocal as his name, his date of birth or his eye colour. It's just a fact. It's not about what he achieves, what he weighs, what he will own, what he will do for a living, how much he will earn or who his friends are. What we should be aiming for is to bring up our boys to believe they are good enough all the time – no matter what. And to believe this, they need to know that we believe it first.

This is what psychologists call unconditional positive regard, which means to consider someone worthy all the time, not just when they are pleasing us, winning or impressing us. Unconditional love is one of the deepest longings of every human being,[20] but only a rare few are lucky enough to grow up with it. Let your beautiful, wonderful, unique boy be one of them. When we realise that our children are not us, that they are their own unique person who has their own gifts and quirks and who will make their own victories and mistakes, we can give ourselves permission to put down our chisels and pick up our watering cans. We can learn to love and approve of our boys without prerequisites or conditions, even though we will not always approve of their choices.

Just tell me what to do!

The Man Box is a set of traditional 'masculine' values that society tries to impose on all boys to one degree or another. It tells them that they must never show weakness, emotion or vulnerability, never ask for help, and use violence to exert their dominance. Boys and men who are crammed inside the Man Box have poorer mental health and academic performance, are more likely to suffer from addiction and partake in reckless behaviour, and have less satisfying relationships. They also are denied the opportunity to grow into the men they choose to be.

- Make your home a safe haven in which your boy is free to step out of the Man Box so that he can be authentic, explore his identity and have the freedom to develop his own values rather than conforming to the rigid (and harmful) values prescribed to him by society.

- Put down your chisel and pick up your watering can so that you can bring up the wonderful, unique boy you have, rather than forcing him to be the child you thought you were going to get.
- Spend most of your time and effort discovering, valuing and developing your boy's strengths, rather than always trying to fix his weaknesses, so that he can define his self-worth and identity by the things he can do rather than by what he can't.
- When your boy walks into the room, smile and let your face light up with the love you have for him. If he is going to grow up believing that he is worthy and inherently lovable, he needs to see that you believe it too.

Conclusion

Congratulations on making it to the end of *Bringing Up Boys Who Like Themselves*! It takes courage to reflect on our own parenting and the social expectations we have grown up with about how boys should be and what we should expect from them. It takes even more courage to reject the values and limitations of traditional masculinity that are harmful to our boys.

But courage is contagious. Your courage to bring up your boy to like himself is a gift not just to him, but to those around you. Change has to start somewhere. Let it be in the kind and supportive smile you offer another parent who is sitting beside her boy, allowing him to feel his emotions, rather than shutting them down. Let it be in your enthusiasm and validation for the boy who chooses to wear fairy wings to preschool. Let it be in your gentle suggestion to a friend that allowing 'boys to be boys' hurts boys as well as girls. Let it be in the boy you are raising to go into the world as a man of character.

We have outlined many strategies in this book for raising your boy to like himself. All of them are backed by studies and have been implemented in real life, by busy and complicated families.

Even so, not all of these strategies will work for your boy and your family, so we encourage you to take what works for you and leave the rest. But if you are to take just one thing from our book, let it be this:

What your boy wants and needs more than anything is what we all want and need – to be seen, valued and accepted for exactly who we are in this moment. We don't want to have to win a race, ace a test, or transform our bodies to feel worthy. We want to be enough right now, exactly as we are. This is the greatest gift a parent can give to a child, and it costs us nothing. We all have it within our power to give this gift right now.

Appendix

It's not always easy to put your child's strengths into words. While we may be able to see these strengths in action, parents often struggle to name them. This can make it difficult to praise and nurture those strengths. Instead, we can revert to focusing on our child's weaknesses and shortcomings.

The following is a list of strengths that we have gathered and adapted from Strengths Profile,[1] Angela Duckworth,[2] Michele Borba[3] and the Values in Action Inventory of Strengths.[4] Take a look and identify the beautiful, unique combination of strengths that your boy possesses.

Character strengths

Adaptability

Admits mistakes

Alternative perspectives

Authenticity

Bounce-back

Bravery

Caution

Confidence

Conscientiousness

Courage

Curiosity

Detail orientation

Determination

Drive

Endurance

Follow-through

Gentleness

Good judgement

Gratitude

Honesty

Hope

Humanity

Humility

Humour

Moderation

Moral compass

Optimism

Persistence

Personal responsibility

Perspective

Pride

Prudence

Resilience

Self-awareness

Self-belief

Self-control

Sense of adventure

Sense of equality

Sense of fairness

Spirituality

Stickability

Time management

Trustworthiness

Wisdom

Work ethic

Zest for life

Social strengths

Ability to inspire and motivate others

Affectionateness

Compassion

Competitive spirit

Courteousness and politeness

Dependability

Desire to help

Emotional awareness

Empathy

Explaining ability

Forgiveness

Friendliness

Generosity

Inclusiveness

Kindness

Leadership

Listening skills

Love

Modesty

Persuasion

Sense of service

Sharing and turn-taking

Social connectivity

Social intelligence

Teamwork ability

Academic strengths

Extensive vocabulary
Love of learning
Planning and organisational
  ability
Problem-solving skills
Reading ability

Remembering ability
Sense of innovation
Strategic awareness
Technical skills
Thorough knowledge of a topic

Physical strengths

Acrobatic ability
Agility
Athletic ability
Balance and dexterity
Coordination
Dancing ability

Gracefulness
Physical endurance
Spatial awareness
Speed
Strength

Artistic strengths

Acting and role-playing skills
Appreciation of beauty
Artistic expression
Comedic skills and joke-telling
Creativity
Drawing and painting skills
Fine art skills

Musical ability
Photographic skills
Self-expression
Singing ability
Storytelling ability
Written expression and poetry

Additional strengths your boy has

-
-
-
-
-

-
-
-
-
-

Emotion Wheel

Naming is taming, so use this emotion wheel to help your boy identify and name what he is feeling. Encourage him to move from the centre of the wheel to the outer ring so that he is being specific about his feelings.

Acknowledgements

Thank you to the parents, carers and champions of boys who told us in so many ways that boys deserve to grow up liking themselves. You are absolutely right! Your boys are fortunate to have such loving and passionate advocates.

We are also deeply grateful to all the parents, carers, educators and other experts who had the courage and generosity to share their stories and wisdom in this book so that we all can benefit.

We are extremely fortunate to have friends and family who are our support crew, trusted advisers and reality checkers. Thank you: Helen Di Natale, Sonja Ebbles, Kate Edwards, Michael Edwards, Nathan Edwards, Cecelia Felderhoff, Zana Glavanic, Kate Hall, Ellis James, Rebecca Lowth, Michelle Mitchell, Anna Muir, Alyson O'Shannessy, Frank Scanlon, Valerie Scanlon, Meg Sweeney and Wendy Tuohy.

Thank you to our formidable agents, Selwa Anthony and Linda Anthony, for your endless support and invaluable advice.

We are delighted and honoured to continue to work with Penguin Random House. Thank you to our publisher, Sophie Ambrose. We could not ask for a better champion. Thank you to our editor, Melissa Lane, and our proofreader, Cressida McDermott, for your many excellent suggestions and guidance. Thanks also to our publicist, Bella Arnott-Hoare, for your enthusiasm, strategy and insight, and our marketing expert, Rebekah Chereshky, for your attention to detail and support.

And to our darling Violet and Ivy, we are so lucky to be your parents.

Notes

Introduction

1 Seavey, Carol A., Phyllis A. Katz, Sue Rosenberg Zalk, 'Baby X: The effect of gender labels on adult responses to infants', *Sex Roles*, vol. 1, June 1975, pp. 103–9.

2 Giese, Rachel, *Boys: What it means to become a man*, Seal Press, New York, 2018.

3 'Australia's children', Australian Institute of Health and Welfare, updated 25 February 2022.

4 'Data and statistics', Lifeline, n.d.

5 'Key performance measures for schooling in Australia', Australian Curriculum, Assessment and Reporting Authority (ACARA), n.d.; acara.edu.au/reporting/national-report-on-schooling-in-australia/national-report-on-schooling-in-australia-data-portal/key-performance-measures-for-schooling-in-australia#view1

6 'Australian boys' and girls' enjoyment of reading', Australian Council for Educational Research (ACER), 6 May 2021.

7 Mol, Suzanne E., Jelle Jolles, 'Reading enjoyment amongst non-leisure readers can affect achievement in secondary school', *Frontiers in Psychology*, vol. 5, October 2014.

8 Paton, Graeme, 'Reading for pleasure "boosts pupils' results in maths"', *Telegraph*, 11 September 2013.

9 Venning, Laura, 'Why is reading for pleasure important?', The Reading Agency, n.d.

10 Willard, Jennifer, Amy Buddie, 'Enhancing empathy and reading for pleasure in psychology of gender', *Psychology of Women Quarterly*, vol. 43, issue 3, 2019, pp. 398–403.

11 Baker, Jordan, 'Boys falling far behind girls in HSC and at university', *Sydney Morning Herald*, 14 June 2022.

12 Ibid.

13 Graham, Linda J., Callula Killingly, Kristin R. Laurens, Naomi Sweller, 'Suspensions and expulsions could set our most vulnerable kids on a path to school drop-out, drug use and crime', The Conversation, 15 September 2021.

14 'Eating disorders in males', National Eating Disorders Collaboration, updated November 2021; nedc.com.au/assets/Fact-Sheets/NEDC-Fact-Sheet-Eating-Disorders-in-Males.pdf

15 '360,000 Australian men living with an eating disorder', The Butterfly Foundation, 11 June 2019.

16 'Body dysmorphic disorder (BDD)', Better Health Channel, n.d.

17 Mitchell, Heidi, 'Men's body-image issues got worse during the pandemic – even if many didn't realize it', *Wall Street Journal*, 14 August 2022.

18 Lewis, Tanya, 'How men's brains are wired differently than women's', *Scientific American*, 2 December 2013.

19 Connor, Steve, 'The hardwired difference between male and female brains could explain why men are "better at map reading"', *Independent*, 3 December 2013.

20 Ibid.

21 Hurlbert, Anya C., Yazhu Ling, 'Biological components of sex differences in color preference', *Current Biology*, vol. 17, no. 16, August 2007, pp. R623–5, cited in Rippon, Gina, *The Gendered Brain: The new neuroscience that shatters the myth of the female brain*, Vintage, London, 2020.

22 Cited in Paoletti, Jo B., *Pink and Blue: Telling the boys from the girls in America*, Indiana University Press, Indiana, 2012.

23 Fine, Cordelia, 'New insights into gendered brain wiring, or a perfect case study in neurosexism?', The Conversation, 4 December 2013.

24 Rippon, Gina, *The Gendered Brain: The new neuroscience that shatters the myth of the female brain*, Vintage, London, 2020.

25 Ibid.

26 Ibid.

27 Ibid.

28 Johnson, Katharine, Melinda Caskey, Katherine Rand, Richard Tucker, Betty Vohr, 'Gender differences in adult-infant communication in the first months of life', *Pediatrics*, vol. 134, issue 6, December 2014, pp. e1603–e1610.

29 Doyle, Kathryn, 'Parent-infant communication differs by gender shortly after birth', Reuters, 5 November 2014.

30 Mascaro, Jennifer S., Patrick D. Hackett, Kelly E. Rentscher, Matthias R. Mehl, James K. Rilling, 'Child gender influences paternal behavior, language, and brain function', *Behavioral Neuroscience*, vol. 131, no. 3, 2017, pp. 262–73.

31 Ibid.

32 O'Neal, Elizabeth E., Jodie M. Plumert, Carole Peterson, 'Parent–child injury prevention conversations following a trip to the emergency department', *Journal of Pediatric Psychology*, vol. 41, issue 2, March 2016, pp. 256–64.

33 Ibid.

34 Reiner, Andrew, 'Talking to boys the way we talk to girls', *New York Times*, 15 June 2017.

35 Abdelmoneim, Javid, *No More Boys and Girls: Can our kids go gender free?*, BBC, Outline Productions, 2017.

36 Abdelmoneim, Javid, *No More Boys and Girls: Can our kids go gender free?*, episode 1.1, BBC, Outline Productions, 2017.

37 Rippon, *The Gendered Brain*.

38 Ibid.

Chapter One: A boy who likes himself has a power perspective

1 Kohn, Alfie, *The Myth of the Spoiled Child: Coddled kids, helicopter parents and other phony crises*, Beacon Press, Boston, 2018.

2 Ibid.

3 Clear, James, email newsletter, 13 October 2022; jamesclear.com/3-2-1/october-13-2022

4 Seligman, Martin, with Karen Reivich, Lisa Jaycox and Jane Gillham, *The Optimistic Child*, Random House Australia, North Sydney, 2011.

5 Strickland, Bonnie R., 'Internal versus external locus of control: An early history', *Perceived Control: Theory, research, and practice in the first 50 years*, John W. Reich and Frank J. Infurna (eds.), Oxford University Press, Oxford, 2016.

6 Seligman, Martin, *Flourish*, William Heinemann, Sydney, 2011.

7 Gale, Catharine R., G. David Batty, Ian J. Deary, 'Locus of control at age 10 years and health outcomes and behaviors at age 30 years: The 1970 British cohort study', *Psychosomatic Medicine*, vol. 70, no. 4, 2008, pp. 397–403.

8 Tindle, Hilary A. et al, 'Optimism, cynical hostility, and incident coronary heart disease and mortality in the Women's Health Initiative', *Circulation*, vol. 118, 2009, pp. 1145–6.

9 Seligman, *Flourish*.

10 Seligman, with Reivich, Jaycox and Gillham, *The Optimistic Child*.

11 Borba, Michele, *Thrivers: The surprising reasons why some kids struggle and others shine*, Putnam, New York, 2022.

12 Adapted from Rotter, J. B., 'Generalized expectancies for internal versus external control of reinforcement', *Psychological Monographs*, vol. 80, no. 1, 1966, pp. 1–28.

13 Borba, *Thrivers*.

14 Twenge, Jean M., Liqing Zhang, Charles Im, 'It's beyond my control: A cross-temporal meta-analysis of increasing externality in locus of control, 1960–2002', *Personality and Social Psychology Review*, vol. 8, issue 3, 2004, pp. 308–19.

15 Duckworth, Angela, *Grit: The power of passion and perseverance*, Random House, London, 2016.

16 Seligman, with Reivich, Jaycox and Gillham, *The Optimistic Child*.

17 Gershon, Livia, 'The self-help mantra that got better and better', *JSTOR Daily*, 13 August 2020.

18 Coué, Émile, *Self Mastery Through Conscious Autosuggestion*, Malkan Publishing Co., New York, 1922.

19 Brown, Derren, 'Derren Brown makes high wire walker to fall – trick or treat', YouTube, 15 June 2012; youtube.com/watch?v=kTO94wJXQoc

20 'Most skips on a tightrope in one minute', Guinness World Records, n.d.

21 Coué, *Self Mastery Through Conscious Autosuggestion*.

22 Cohn, Patrick, 'Sports visualization: The secret weapon of athletes', Peak Performance Sports, n.d.

23 Guarino, Joseph, 'Prepping for public speaking with creative visualization', Institute of Public Speaking, n.d.

24 Slimani, Maamer, David Tod, Helmi Chaabene, Bianca Miarka, Karim Chamari, 'Effects of mental imagery on muscular strength in healthy and patient participants: A systematic review', *Journal of Sports Science and Medicine*, vol. 15, issue 3, September 2016.

25 Reivich, Karen, Andrew Shatté, *The Resilience Factor: 7 keys to finding your inner strength and overcoming life's hurdles*, Three Rivers, New York, 2003.

26 Seligman, with Reivich, Jaycox and Gillham, *The Optimistic Child*.

Chapter Two: A boy who likes himself has strength of character

1 Sennett, Richard, *The Corrosion of Character: The personal consequences of work in the new capitalism*, W. W. Norton, New York, 1999.

2 Sullivan, Anna, 'Schools' tough approach to bad behaviour isn't working – and may escalate problems', The Conversation, 27 May 2016.

3 Tsabary, Shefali, *Out of Control: Why disciplining your child doesn't work . . . and what will*, Namaste Publishing, Vancouver, 2014.

4 Ibid.

5 Meier, Madeline H., Wendy S. Slutske, Andrew C. Heath, Nicholas G. Martin, 'The role of harsh discipline in explaining sex differences in conduct disorder: A study of opposite-sex twin pairs', *Journal of Abnormal Child Psychology*, vol. 37, no. 5, July 2009, pp. 653–64.

6 Siegel, Daniel J., Tina Payne Bryson, *No-drama Discipline: The whole-brain way to calm the chaos and nurture your child's developing mind*, Bantam, New York, 2014.

7   Tsabary, *Out of Control*.

8   Siegel and Bryson, *No-drama Discipline*.

9   Brown, Brené. *Daring Greatly: How the courage to be vulnerable transforms the way we live, love, parent, and lead*, Portfolio Penguin, London, 2013.

10   Ibid.

11   Dent, Maggie, *Mothering Our Boys: A guide for mums of sons*, Pennington Publications, California, 2018.

12   Siegel and Bryson, *No-drama Discipline*.

13   Schumann, Karina, Michael Ross, 'Why women apologize more than men: Gender differences in thresholds for perceiving offensive behavior', *Psychological Science*, vol. 21, no. 11, 2010, pp. 1649–55.

14   Dent, *Mothering Our Boys*.

15   Carey, Tanith, *The Friendship Maze: How to help your child navigate their way to positive and happier friendships*, Octopus Publishing Group, London, 2019.

16   Dent, *Mothering Our Boys*.

17   'If he can see it, will he be it? Representations of masculinity in boys' television', Geena Davis Institute on Gender in Media, 2020; seejane.org/wp-content/uploads/if-he-can-see-it-will-he-be-it-representations-of-masculinity-in-boys-tv.pdf

18   Brackett, Marc, 'Dr. Marc Brackett and Brené on "Permission to Feel"', *Unlocking Us with Brené Brown*, 14 April 2020.

19   Ibid.

20   Ibid.

21   Brackett, Marc, Bringing Up Boys Summit, Happy Families, 2022.

22   Brown, Brené, *Brené Brown: Atlas of the Heart*, HBO Max, 2022.

23   Bringing Up Boys Summit, Happy Families, 2022.

24   Tsabary, Shefali, Parenting Mastery 2023 Online Summit, 20–23 February 2023.

25   Bringing Up Boys Summit, Happy Families, 2022.

26   Brackett, Marc, Bringing Up Boys Summit, Happy Families, 2022.

27   Ibid.

28   Johnson, Sue, '#529: Iconic therapist Dr. Sue Johnson – how to improve sex and crack the code of love', *The Tim Ferriss Show*, 26 August 2021.

29   Layous, Kristin, Katherine Nelson, Eva Oberle, Sonja Lyubomirsky, Kimberly A. Schonert-Reichl, 'Kindness counts: Promoting well-being and peer acceptance through prosocial behavior', *PLOS ONE*, vol. 7, no. 12, December 2012, p. e51380.

30   Garner, Pamela W., 'Prediction of prosocial and emotional competence from maternal behavior in African American preschoolers', *Cultural Diversity & Ethnic Minority Psychology*, vol. 12, no. 2, April 2006, pp. 179–98.

31 Jones, Damon E., Mark Greenberg, Max Crowley, 'Early social-emotional functioning and public health: The relationship between kindergarten social competence and future wellness', *American Journal of Public Health*, vol. 105, no. 11, November 2015, pp. 2283–90.

Chapter Three: A boy who likes himself has body confidence

1 Manual [@menofmanual], 'Today marks the first day of Mental Health Awareness Week . . .', Instagram, 13 May 2019; instagram.com/p/BxZT3I-lJKG/

2 McLean, Siân A., Eleanor H. Wertheim, Susan J. Paxton, 'Preferences for being muscular and thin in 6-year-old boys', *Body Image*, vol. 26, 2018, pp. 98–102.

3 Grogan, Sarah. *Body Image: Understanding body dissatisfaction in men, women and children*, Taylor & Francis Group, London, 2021.

4 Edwards, Kasey, 'Destructive body shame has crossed the gender divide', *Sydney Morning Herald*, 20 May 2019.

5 Grogan, *Body Image*.

6 Ibid.

7 Ibid.

8 Baghurst, Timothy, S. Griffiths, Stuart B. Murray, 'Boys and girls prefer hyper-muscular male action figures over normally-muscular action figures: Evidence that children have internalized the muscular male body ideal', *North American Journal of Psychology*, vol. 20, no. 1, March 2018, pp. 159–70.

9 Ibid.

10 Ibid.

11 'Eating disorders in males', National Eating Disorders Collaboration, updated November 2021; nedc.com.au/assets/Fact-Sheets/NEDC-Fact-Sheet-Eating-Disorders-in-Males.pdf

12 Gorrell, Sasha, Stuart B. Murray, 'Eating disorders in males', *Child and Adolescent Psychiatric Clinics of North America*, vol. 28, no. 4, October 2019, pp. 641–51.

13 Griffiths, Scott, Phillipa Hay, Deborah Mitchison, Jonathan M. Mond, Siân A. McLean, Bryan Rodgers, Robin Massey, Susan J. Paxton, 'Sex differences in the relationships between body dissatisfaction, quality of life and psychological distress', *Australian and New Zealand Journal of Public Health*, vol. 40, no. 6, December 2016, pp. 518–22.

14 Murray, Stuart B., Jason M. Nagata, Scott Griffiths, Jerel P. Calzo, Tiffany A. Brown, Deborah Mitchison, Aaron J. Blashill, Jonathan M. Mond, 'The enigma of male eating disorders: A critical review and synthesis', *Clinical Psychology Review*, vol. 57, November 2017, pp. 1–11.

15 'Who is affected?', National Eating Disorders Collaboration, n.d.

16 Dahill, Lucy, Deborah Mitchison, Natalie M. V. Morrison, Stephen Touyz, Kay Bussey, Nora Trompeter, Alexandra Lonergan, Phillipa Hay, 'Prevalence of parental comments on weight/shape/eating amongst sons and daughters in an adolescent sample', *Nutrients*, vol. 13, no. 1, January 2021, p. 158.

17 Ibid.

18 Ibid.

19 Gillison, Fiona B., Ava B. Lorenc, Ester F. C. Sleddens, Stefanie L. Williams, Lou Atkinson, 'Can it be harmful for parents to talk to their child about their weight? A meta-analysis', *Preventive Medicine*, vol. 93, December 2016, pp. 135–46.

20 Berge, Jerica M., Richard F. MacLehose, Katie A. Loth, Marla E. Eisenberg, Jayne A. Fulkerson, Dianne Neumark-Sztainer, 'Parent-adolescent conversations about eating, physical activity and weight: Prevalence across sociodemographic characteristics and associations with adolescent weight and weight-related behaviors', *Journal of Behavioral Medicine*, vol. 38, no. 1, February 2015, pp. 122–35.

21 Smith, James [@jamessmithpt], 'Swimmers Body Illusion . . .', TikTok, 30 June 2022; tiktok.com/@jamessmithpt/video/7114995091336383749

22 Ibid.

23 Satter, Ellyn, 'Concerned about your child's eating habits? Ellyn Satter has answers', *Respectful Parenting: Janet Lansbury Unruffled*, 27 April 2022.

24 Ibid.

25 Ibid.

26 Satter, Ellyn, 'Raise a healthy child who is a joy to feed: Follow the Satter Division of Responsibility in Feeding', Ellyn Satter Institute, n.d.

27 Satter, Ellyn, 'Concerned about your child's eating habits? Ellyn Satter has answers', *Respectful Parenting: Janet Lansbury Unruffled*, 27 April 2022.

28 Ibid.

Chapter Four: A boy who likes himself has balance

1 Warren, Diana, Galina Daraganova, Meredith O'Connor, '8. Preschool and children's readiness for school', Growing Up in Australia, October 2018.

2 'The real truth about transitioning into pre-primary in Western Australia', Maggie Dent, 18 January 2021.

3 Xie, Sha, Hui Li, 'Does tiger parenting work in contemporary China? Exploring the relationships between parenting profiles and preschoolers' school readiness in a Chinese context', *Early Child Development and Care*, vol. 188, issue 12, 2018, pp. 1826–42.

4 Moore, Lela, 'How too much parental pressure can affect kids' mental health', Psych Central, 19 May 2022.

5 Ibid.

6   Borba, Michele, *Thrivers: The surprising reasons why some kids struggle and others shine*, Putnam, New York, 2022.

7   Ibid.

8   Tsabary, Shefali, *Out of Control: Why disciplining your child doesn't work . . . and what will*, Namaste Publishing, Vancouver, 2014.

9   Ibid.

10 Voyager Tennis, 'How to raise a champion – with Ash Barty's dad Rob Barty', YouTube, 6 July 2020; youtube.com/watch?v=dWHZL6aRBuE

11 Dweck, Carol S., *Mindset: The new psychology of success*, Ballantine Books, New York, 2016.

12 Duckworth, Angela, 'Angela Duckworth: How to cultivate your character strengths', *Finding Mastery: Conversations with Michael Gervais*, 23 February 2022.

13 Kohn, Alfie, *No Contest: The case against competition*, Houghton Mifflin, Boston, 1992.

14 Ibid.

15 Duckworth, Angela, *Grit: The power of passion and perseverance*, Random House, London, 2016.

16 Colliver, Yeshe, Linda J. Harrison, Judith E. Brown, Peter Humburg, 'Free play predicts self-regulation years later: Longitudinal evidence from a large Australian sample of toddlers and preschoolers', *Early Childhood Research Quarterly*, vol. 59, 2022, pp. 148–61.

17 Ibid.

18 Borba, *Thrivers*.

19 Ibid.

20 Duckworth, *Grit*.

21 Borba, Michele, 'Ep 83: 7 character strengths to raise "Thrivers" Dr. Michele Borba', *Raising Good Humans*, 26 February 2021.

22 Werner, E. E., 'Vulnerable but invincible: High-risk children from birth to adulthood', *European Child & Adolescent Psychiatry*, vol. 5, supplement 1, 1996, pp. 47–51.

23 Borba, Michele, 'Ep 83: 7 character strengths to raise "Thrivers" Dr. Michele Borba', *Raising Good Humans*, 26 February 2021.

24 Ibid.

25 Ibid.

26 Tsabary, Shefali, *The Conscious Parent: Transforming ourselves, empowering our children*, Namaste Publishing, Vancouver, 2010.

27 Houghton, Stephen, David Lawrence, Simon C. Hunter, Michael Rosenberg, Corinne Zadow, Lisa Wood, Trevor Shilton, 'Reciprocal relationships between trajectories of depressive symptoms and screen media use during adolescence', *Journal of Youth and Adolescence*, vol. 47, 2018, pp. 2453–67.

28   'Guidelines on physical activity, sedentary behaviour and sleep for children under 5 years of age', World Health Organization, 2019; apps. who.int/iris/bitstream/handle/10665/311664/9789241550536-eng.pdf

29   Orben, Amy, Andrew K. Przybylski, 'The association between adolescent well-being and digital technology use', *Nature Human Behaviour*, vol. 3, 2019, pp. 173–82.

30   Ibid.

31   'The health impacts of screen time – a guide for clinicians and parents', Royal College of Paediatrics and Child Health, January 2019.

32   'Growing up in a connected world', United Nations Children's Fund (UNICEF), 2019; unicef-irc.org/publications/pdf/GKO%20Summary%20 Report.pdf

33   Ibid.

34   Ibid.

35   Pace, Thomas, 'I almost lost my sons to "Fortnite"', *Chicago Tribune*, 18 April 2018.

36   'Fortnite is like cocaine, destroyed our child's life, claim parents', *Times of India*, 8 October 2019.

37   North, Anna, 'When novels were bad for you', *New York Times*, 14 September 2014.

38   'State of play – youth and online gaming in Australia', Office of the eSafety Commissioner, 5 March 2018; esafety.gov.au/sites/default/files/2019-07/ Youth-and-online-gaming-report-2018.pdf

39   'Internet gaming', American Psychiatric Association, reviewed January 2023.

40   'Gaming disorder', World Health Organization, n.d.

41   Johannes, Niklas, Matti Vuorre, Andrew K. Przybylski, 'Video game play is positively correlated with well-being', *Royal Society Open Science*, vol. 8, no. 2, February 2021, p. 202049.

42   Wood, Richard T. A., 'Problems with the concept of video game "addiction": Some case study examples', *International Journal of Mental Health and Addiction*, vol. 6, no. 2, April 2008, pp. 169–78.

43   'Child rights and online gaming: Opportunities & challenges for children and the industry', United Nations Children's Fund (UNICEF), August 2019; unicef-irc.org/files/upload/documents/UNICEF_CRBDigitalWorld SeriesOnline_Gaming.pdf

44   Livingstone, Sonia, Kruakae Pothong, 'Imaginative play in digital environments: Designing social and creative opportunities for identity formation', *Information, Communication & Society*, vol. 25, issue 4, 2022, pp. 485–501.

45   Gray, Peter, Parenting Mastery 2023 Online Summit, Shefali Tsabary, 20–23 February 2023.

46   Ibid.

47 Livingstone, Sonia, Kruakae Pothong, 'Imaginative play in digital environments: Designing social and creative opportunities for identity formation', *Information, Communication & Society*, vol. 25, issue 4, 2022, pp. 485–501.

48 'Inquiry into the approaches to homework in Victorian schools', Parliament of Victoria – Education and Training Committee, August 2014; parliament.vic.gov.au/images/stories/committees/etc/Homework_Inquiry/Homework_Inquiry_final_report.pdf

49 Horsley, Mike, Richard Walker, *Reforming Homework: Practices, learning and policy*, Palgrave Macmillan, South Yarra, 2013.

50 Cho, Miree, Jon Quach, Peter Anderson, Fiona Mensah, Melissa Wake, Gehan Roberts, 'Poor sleep and lower working memory in grade 1 children: Cross-sectional, population-based study', *Academic Pediatrics*, vol. 15, no. 1, 2015, pp. 111–16.

51 'Sleep needs across the lifespan', Sleep Health Foundation, updated February 2015; sleephealthfoundation.org.au/files/pdfs/Sleep-Needs-Across-Lifespan.pdf

52 Borba, *Thrivers*.

Chapter Five: A boy who likes himself has mastery and independence

1 Seligman, Martin, with Karen Reivich, Lisa Jaycox and Jane Gillham, *The Optimistic Child*, Random House Australia, North Sydney, 2011.

2 Seligman, Martin, *Flourish*, William Heinemann, Sydney, 2011.

3 Borba, Michele, *Thrivers: The surprising reasons why some kids struggle and others shine*, Putnam, New York, 2022.

4 Bandura, Albert, *Self-efficacy: The exercise of control*, W. H. Freeman and Company, New York, 1997.

5 Seligman, with Reivich, Jaycox and Gillham, *The Optimistic Child*.

6 Ibid.

7 Hendry, Erica R., '7 epic fails brought to you by the genius mind of Thomas Edison', *Smithsonian Magazine*, 20 November 2013.

8 'I've missed more than 9,000 shots in my career . . .', Forbes Quotes, n.d.; forbes.com/quotes/11194/

9 Seligman, with Reivich, Jaycox and Gillham, *The Optimistic Child*.

10 Bandura, *Self-efficacy*.

11 Seligman, Martin, *Learned Optimism: How to change your mind and your life*, William Heinemann, Sydney, 2011.

12 Bandura, *Self-efficacy*.

13 Ibid.

14 Brown, Brené, *Daring Greatly: How the courage to be vulnerable transforms the way we live, love, parent, and lead*, Portfolio Penguin, London, 2013.

15 Ibid.

16 Ibid.

17 Snyder, C. R., *The Psychology of Hope: You can get there from here*, Free Press, New York, 2003.

18 Dent, Maggie, *Mothering Our Boys: A guide for mums of sons*, Pennington Publications, California, 2018.

19 Janis-Norton, Noël, *Calmer, Easier, Happier Boys: The revolutionary programme that transforms family life*, Hodder & Stoughton, London, 2016.

20 Dent, *Mothering Our Boys*.

21 Seligman, with Reivich, Jaycox and Gillham, *The Optimistic Child*.

Chapter Six: A boy who likes himself has strong relationships

1 Bringing Up Boys Summit, Happy Families, 2022.

2 Carey, Tanith, *The Friendship Maze: How to help your child navigate their way to positive and happier friendships*, Octopus Publishing Group, London, 2019.

3 Way, Niobe, Carol Gilligan, Pedro Noguera and Alisha Ali (eds.), *The Crisis of Connection: Roots, consequences, and solutions*, New York University Press, New York, 2018.

4 'Friendship for men in middle-age? Here's what you told us about how to find it', ABC News, 6 May 2016.

5 Cox, Daniel A., 'Men's social circles are shrinking', The Survey Center on American Life, 29 June 2021.

6 Pearson, Catherine, 'Why is it so hard for men to make close friends?', *New York Times*, 28 November 2022 (updated 19 December 2022).

7 Abdullah, Maryam, 'Why friendships are important for boys' health', *Greater Good*, 18 September 2018.

8 'Media release: Depression, suicidality and loneliness: Mental health and Australian men', Ten to Men: The Australian Longitudinal Study on Male Health (TTM), Australian Institute of Family Studies, 16 September 2020; aifs.gov.au/sites/default/files/mediarelease-ttm_insights-mental_health_0. pdf

9 Way, Niobe, *Deep secrets: Boys' friendships and the crisis of connection*, Harvard University Press, Cambridge, 2011.

10 McKelley, Ryan A., 'Unmasking masculinity: Helping boys become connected men', 21 August 2018; uww.edu/documents/orsp/NITT18/ Ryan%20McKelley%20Unmasking%20Masculinity%20Presentation.pdf

11 Simpson, Jeffry A., W. Andrew Collins, SiSi Tran, Katherine C. Haydon, 'Attachment and the experience and expression of emotions in romantic relationships: A developmental perspective', *Journal of Personality and Social Psychology*, vol. 92, no. 2, February 2007, pp. 355–67.

12 Monke, Audrey, '10 friendship skills every kid needs', Sunshine Parenting, n.d.

13 Carey, *The Friendship Maze*.

14 Monke, Audrey, '10 friendship skills every kid needs', Sunshine Parenting, n.d.

15 Carey, *The Friendship Maze*.

16 Bringing Up Boys Summit, Happy Families, 2022.

17 Louick, Rebecca, '5 key steps for raising assertive kids', Big Life Journal, n.d.

18 Ibid.

19 Bringing Up Boys Summit, Happy Families, 2022.

20 Ibid.

21 Healy, Karyn, 'Fighting back may stop some children from being bullied', The Conversation, 16 November 2015.

22 Whitson, Signe, *8 Keys to End Bullying: Strategies for parents & schools*, Norton Professional Books, New York, 2014.

23 Healy, Karyn, 'Fighting back may stop some children from being bullied', The Conversation, 16 November 2015.

24 Walker, Sonja, 'How to beat bullying: 10 clever comeback lines for kids', Kids First, n.d.

25 Whitson, *8 Keys to End Bullying*.

26 'Definition of bullying', National Centre Against Bullying, n.d.

27 Brown, Brené, *Brené Brown: Atlas of the Heart*, HBO Max, 2022.

28 'Alleged Brisbane beer bottle sexual assault "not rape, just a Jackass-type prank blown out of proportion", lawyer says', ABC News, 26 October 2015.

29 'Three men found guilty of raping teenager with bottle on Australia Day', *Brisbane Times*, 28 July 2017.

30 The Associated Press, 'Girls start believing men are smarter than women as early as 6 years old', *Fortune*, 28 January 2017.

31 Tilley, Cristen, 'Book week: Analysis of bestsellers suggests kids' bookshelves are on a lean', ABC News, 22 August 2018.

32 Ferguson, Donna, 'Must monsters always be male? Huge gender bias revealed in children's books', *Guardian*, 21 January 2018.

33 Devlin, Peter, '"This is Grammar, boys – that means nothing under a seven": Students at exclusive private school rate formal dates in degrading "Tinder boot camp" video', *Daily Mail*, 6 August 2016.

34 Aubrey, Sophie, 'The boys who started the "Slut of the Year" got expelled. And that's exactly what they deserved', Mamamia, 21 July 2016.

35 'St Kevin's College students rating, sexualising female staff', *Herald Sun*, 3 May 2022.

36 'Wesley College students reported for misogynistic March 4 Justice comments', ABC News, 17 March 2021.

37 Dent, Maggie, *From Boys to Men: Guiding our teen boys to grow into happy, healthy men*, Pan Macmillan Australia, Sydney, 2020.

38 'Age of first exposure to pornography shapes men's attitudes toward women', American Psychological Association, 3 August 2017.

39 Parliament of Australia, House of Representatives Standing Committee on Social Policy and Legal Affairs, '3. Age verification for online pornography', *Inquiry into age verification for online wagering and online pornography*, 5 March 2020; aph.gov.au/Parliamentary_Business/Committees/House/Social_Policy_and_Legal_Affairs/Onlineageverification/Report/section?id=committees%2freportrep%2f024436%2f72615#footnote6target

40 'Age of first exposure to pornography shapes men's attitudes toward women', American Psychological Association, 3 August 2017.

41 Lang, Amy, Tracy Gillett, Raised Good Online Summit, 23 September 2022.

42 Elliot, Michele, Kevin Browne, Jennifer Kilcoyne, 'Child sexual abuse prevention: What offenders tell us', *Child Abuse & Neglect*, vol. 19, no. 5, 1995, pp. 579–94.

43 'International technical guidance on sexuality education: An evidence-informed approach' (revised edition), United Nations Educational, Scientific and Cultural Organization (UNESCO), 2018; unaids.org/sites/default/files/media_asset/ITGSE_en.pdf

44 Lang, Amy, Tracy Gillett, Raised Good Online Summit, 23 September 2022.

45 Carey, *The Friendship Maze*.

46 Johnson, Sue, '#529: Iconic therapist Dr. Sue Johnson – how to improve sex and crack the code of love', *The Tim Ferriss Show*, 26 August 2021.

Chapter Seven: A boy who likes himself is himself

1 The Men's Project, Michael Flood, 'The Man Box: A study on being a young man in Australia', Jesuit Social Services, 2018; cdn.jss.org.au/wp-content/uploads/2022/08/28111318/The-Man-Box-A-study-on-being-a-young-man-in-Australia-1.pdf

2 Baker, Jordan, 'Boys falling far behind girls in HSC and at university', *Sydney Morning Herald*, 14 June 2022.

3 The Men's Project, Michael Flood, 'The Man Box: A study on being a young man in Australia', Jesuit Social Services, 2018; cdn.jss.org.au/wp-content/uploads/2022/08/28111318/The-Man-Box-A-study-on-being-a-young-man-in-Australia-1.pdf

4 Ibid.

5 Borba, Michele, 'Ep 83: 7 character strengths to raise "Thrivers" Dr. Michele Borba', *Raising Good Humans*, 26 February 2021.

6 DaDMuM, 'Every day at the resort he watched as the little girls came back with their hair braided . . .', Facebook, 28 December 2021; facebook.com/dadmumofficial/posts/pfbid0mLEqxT6Z9ZDFM52PnYMAxR19XTouP7XtvU9VgSdWaAuh5T984SPHo6pmUQ2UncW9l

7   Waters, Lea, *The Strength Switch: How the new science of strength-based parenting can help your child and teen to flourish*, Ebury Australia, Sydney, 2017.

8   Fox, Jenifer, '10 tips for discovering your child's strengths', HuffPost, updated 6 December 2017.

9   Silverman, Robyn, 'TPP 061: Dr. Robyn Silverman talks about nurturing character strengths in our kids', *TILT Parenting: Raising differently wired kids*, 13 June 2017.

10   Waters, *The Strength Switch*.

11   Vaish, Amrisha, Tobias Grossmann, Amanda Woodward, 'Not all emotions are created equal: The negativity bias in social-emotional development', *Psychological Bulletin*, vol. 134, no. 3, May 2008, pp. 383–403.

12   Waters, *The Strength Switch*.

13   Gander, Fabian, René T. Proyer, Willibald Ruch, Tobias Wyss, 'Strength-based positive interventions: Further evidence for their potential in enhancing well-being and alleviating depression', *Journal of Happiness Studies*, vol. 14, no. 4, August 2013, pp. 1241–59.

14   Waters, *The Strength Switch*.

15   Silverman, Robyn, 'TPP 061: Dr. Robyn Silverman talks about nurturing character strengths in our kids', *TILT Parenting: Raising differently wired kids*, 13 June 2017.

16   Borba, Michele, 'Ep 83: 7 character strengths to raise "Thrivers" Dr. Michele Borba', *Raising Good Humans*, 26 February 2021.

17   Silverman, Robyn, 'TPP 061: Dr. Robyn Silverman talks about nurturing character strengths in our kids', *TILT Parenting: Raising differently wired kids*, 13 June 2017.

18   Brown, Brené, *Daring Greatly: How the courage to be vulnerable transforms the way we live, love, parent, and lead*, Portfolio Penguin, London, 2013.

19   Ibid.

20   Fromm, Erich, *The Art of Loving*, Harper & Brothers, New York, 1956.

Appendix

1   strengthsprofile.com

2   Duckworth, Angela, *Grit: The power of passion and perseverance*, Random House UK, London, 2016.

3   Borba, Michele, *Thrivers: The surprising reasons why some kids struggle and others shine*, Putnam, New York, 2022.

4   'Find your 24 character strengths', VIA Institute, n.d.

Want to know more about bringing up your
boy to like himself? Scan the QR code or go to
www.boyswholikethemselves.com/more